Principles of Leisure Counseling

by
Larry C. Loesch
and
Paul T. Wheeler

Copyright ©1982
EDUCATIONAL MEDIA CORPORATION ®
P.O. Box 21311
Minneapolis, Minnesota 55421

Library of Congress Catalog Card No. 81-82902

ISBN 0-932796-10-9

Current Printing of this Edition (last digit):

5 4 3 2 1

No part of this book may be reproduced or used in any form without the expressed permission of the publisher in writing. Manufactured in the United States of America.

Production editor—

Don L. Sorenson

Graphic design—

Earl Sorenson

To our fathers
WILLIAM O. LOESCH
and
WALTER H. CARLYLE

We would also like to express our sincere appreciation to Barbara Loesch for her invaluable contributions to the development of this book.

Table of Contents

Preface iv

Chapter I: An Introduction to Leisure 1
- Factors Influencing Leisure 8
- The Importance of Leisure 16
- The Leisure Problem 22
- The Need for Leisure Counseling 25
- Discussion Questions 26
- Study Activities 26

Chapter II: Leisure in Perspective 27
- Toward Defining Leisure 28
- A Goal-based Leisure Definition 36
- Dynamics of Leisure Activities 38
- Functions of Leisure 43
- Some Potential Benefits of Leisure 48
- Some Potential Liabilities of Leisure 52
- Discussion Questions 54
- Study Activities 56

Chapter III: Leisure Counseling 57
- Leisure Mental Health 58
- Goals of Leisure Counseling 61
- Purposes of Leisure Counseling 64
- Leisure Counseling Defined 65
- Leisure Counseling and Counseling Orientations 72
- Discussion Questions 84
- Study Activities 84

Chapter IV: A Leisure Counseling Model 85
- Needed: New Leisure Counseling Models 89
- The Triangulation Leisure Counseling Model ... 92
- The Affective Dimensions 96
- The Behavioral Dimensions 100
- The Cognitive Dimensions 103
- Goals of the TLC Model 108
- Discussion Questions 110
- Study Activities 110

Chapter V: Assessment in Leisure Counseling — 111

- Assessment of Leisure Attitudes — 113
- Assessment of Leisure Values — 117
- Assessment of (Leisure) Psychological States — 119
- Assessment of Leisure Behaviors — 123
- Assessment of Leisure Satisfaction — 124
- Assessment of Leisure Interests — 127
- State of the Art — 133
- Guidelines for Assessment in Leisure Counseling — 134
- Discussion Questions — 136
- Study Activities — 136

Chapter VI: Individual Leisure Counseling — 137

- Stage I: Joining — 139
- Stage II: Exploration — 146
- Stage III: Action — 169
- Stage IV: Termination — 174
- Discussion Questions — 177
- Study Activities — 178

Chapter VII: Group Leisure Counseling — 179

- Perspectives on Group Leisure Counseling — 180
- Guidelines for Group Leisure Counseling — 183
- Stage I: Joining — 187
- Stage II: Exploration — 190
- Stage III: Action — 199
- Stage IV: Termination — 201
- Discussion Questions — 203
- Study Activities — 204

Chapter VIII: Developmental Leisure Counseling — 205

- A Perspective on Developmental Leisure Counseling — 206
- Process Guidelines for Developmental Leisure Counseling — 208
- TLC Developmental Leisure Counseling — 212
- Stage I: Joining — 213
- Stage II: Exploration — 214
- Stage III: Action — 228
- Stage IV: Termination — 230

Implementation 231
Discussion Questions 233
Study Activities 234

Chapter IX: The Fine Points of Leisure Counseling — 235

Coping with Negative Attitudes 236
Differentiating Counseling from Therapy 238
Using Audio-Visual Materials 238
Volunteerism 240
Humor 241
Sexism 241
Racism 242
Ageism 242
Confrontation 243
Co-lead Groups 244
Homework 245
Comprehensiveness 246
Evaluations 248
Discussion Questions 249
Study Activities 250

Chapter X: The Complete Leisure Counselor — 251

Professional Preparation for Leisure Counselors 252
Professional Development for Leisure Counselors 255
Professional Functions of Leisure Counselors 260
Evaluation of Leisure Counseling 266
Discussion Questions 270
Study Activities 270

Bibliography — 271

Preface

"Leisure counseling? What in the world is leisure counseling? Who needs it? Leisure is the fun part of life—people don't need counselors to help them figure out how to have fun. Must be another gimmick. Is someone trying to sell yet another counseling kit?"

These are a few of the questions and thoughts that ran through our minds (and mouths) several years ago when we were first exposed to the idea of leisure counseling. We were skeptical to say the least. But we began to think about it, and then we thought about it some more. After awhile it began to make a lot of sense to us. Maybe leisure wasn't so simple—or so easy—after all.

Our initial musing brought into focus some rather commonplace examples of both the complexities and perplexities of leisure. For example, we were both able to identify fairly extensive lists of our own leisure activities. The entries were diverse and varied along a number of dimensions: some represented considerable time investments while others did not; some were very phsycially active while others were sedentary; some were costly while most were relatively inexpensive; and so forth. Could there possibly be a thread running through each list? *Should* there be a thread through each list? Were we really as satisfied with our leisure activities as we could be?

These personal reflections prompted us to look further into professional areas. The first topic that came to mind was career counseling. We are both advocates of effective career counseling. However, we reject the often exposed notion that career counseling is a panacea for the ills of the world. In other words, we reject the idea that a job can *completely* fulfill all of a person's needs. Certainly work is important, and its conduct should be meaningful and satisfying. But just as certainly no person derives complete life satisfaction solely from work. There are always other sources of life satisfaction. One of those other sources often is, or should be, leisure.

We then turned to other topics of interest. For example, a common complaint of couples in marriage or family counseling is that they "never do anything together anymore." There is also a significant number of people who need help with stress reduction. Drug and alcohol abuse are also often integrally linked to general unhappiness in life. And what about adolescents and children who so often complain of being bored, and so turn to less than socially desirable behaviors? Leisure, and in turn leisure counseling, could be a part of these situations and others like them.

From these beginnings we began more concentrated studies and behaviors in the realm of leisure counseling. These activities have been meaningful, exciting, and helpful to us in our various profesional activities. More importantly, we came to believe that such activities could indeed be helpful to many professional counselors. This book has been developed from within this perspective.

We have tried to provide basic, though comprehensive, information and concepts for leisure counseling. We realize that some of the ideas presented will not be totally unfamiliar centsto professional counselors. In fact, many of the techniques and strategies suggested have been tested in other contexts. However, since leisure counseling is for many a new professional endeavor, we believe that the applications of the ideas presented here will be new for most professionals.

We wish you satisfaction in your own leisure and in that of your clients.

L.C.L.
P.T.W.

Larry C. Loesch, Ph.D., is a professor in the Department of Counselor Education at the University of Florida in Gainesville, Florida.

Paul T. Wheeler, Ph.D., is a counslor in private practice in Gainesville, Florida.

Chapter I

An Introduction to Leisure

Leisure, at least in its most rudimentary forms, is as old as the history of the human race. People have always had some discretionary time, done some things simply because they wanted to, and acknowledged the need to digress from subsistence activity.

Leisure is an accepted part of life; it's there, always has been, always will be. Yet surprisingly, it is only within the last several decades that the social sciences have begun to investigate leisure and its functions in the human life cycle.

The chains of habit are too weak to be felt until they are too strong to be broken.

Samuel Johnson

The understanding of leisure is far from complete, but the information accumulated thus far suggests some interesting tentative conclusions. Central among these is that leisure in general, and the psychology of leisure in particular, are extremely complex phenomena.

Interest in leisure is rapidly increasing among laypersons as well as professionals. For laypersons this interest is best exemplified by leisure enticements in the various mass media. For professionals it is evident from the rapidly accumulating professional literature on leisure. The complexity of leisure and this increasing interest have in turn lead to concern about the *quality* of leisure among people in a modern society.

Social scientists have responded to this concern from a number of perspectives. Sociologists, for example, have begun extensive investigations of leisure patterns and trends. Psychologists have begun investigating the psychological dynamics of leisure and formulating the theoretical foundations for the psychology of leisure. Recreation specialists have responded by incorporating sociological and psychological research findings and theories into activity planning and programming. Finally, a much more recent response has come from counselors who have begun to develop techniques to help people improve their leisure.

Since leisure counseling (i.e. facilitating the improvement of leisure) is such a recent endeavor among counseling professionals, substantive guidelines for leisure counseling are scarce. This book is therefore presented in the hope of providing fundamental information. The suggestions and techniques provided will be used most effectively by professional counselors. The term professional counselor is used here to mean someone who has specialized training and experience in the theory and practice of counseling. The term therefore encompasses a wide variety of persons in the helping professions such as school, college, community agency or rehabilitation counselors, counseling or clinical psychologists, or social workers.

Some Assumptions

There are certain assumptions underlying this book that influence its direction and approach. These assumptions are presented here to facilitate understanding and interpretation of subsequent discussions.

> When people are free to do as they please, they usually imitate each other.
>
> *Eric Hoffer*

The first and most important assumption is that leisure is a universal phenomenon among the human species. Allusion to this assumption was made in the very first paragraph of this book. However, it merits repeating. Everyone, no matter what age, sex, race, social status, or other characteristic or situation has at least some leisure. The primary implication of this assumption is that everyone may be in need of, or benefit from, leisure counseling.

Maybe you're thinking that infants don't have or need leisure? Try taking a rattle away from a baby who is happily playing with it. As for "leisure counseling" with infants, consider that child psychologists strongly recommend environmental and tactile stimulation for infants (e.g. toys, mobiles, etc.) to facilitate their psychosocial developments.

The universality of leisure is closely related to another basic assumption; namely, that there is a general complacency about leisure. People don't think very much about their leisure, except perhaps when it's not what they would like it to be. Rare are those individuals who have consciously evaluated their leisure and what it does or doesn't do for them. For most people, leisure counseling is looking at themselves in terms of a "new" dimension, and it takes some time for them to get used to it.

Most of the time I don't have much fun. The rest of the time I don't have any fun at all.

Woody Allen

A third basic assumption is that people form leisure habits and patterns primarily through chance and circumstance. Leisure habit formation is primarily reactive rather than proactive (Iso-Ahola, 1980a). People select leisure that is economically appropriate, the current "fad," or whatever. Often leisure pursuits are "chosen" on the basis of influence from peers, family, and other associates. Leisure counseling is therefore an attempt to counteract a haphazard approach to leisure selection.

Many people are dissatisfied, or at least not fully satisfied, with their leisure. This assumption is grounded in part on the research on leisure satisfaction among various types of persons. General disfaction is also obvious from other indicators.

Consider for example the tremendous economic investments made in leisure resources each year. Witness also the run to get into the latest fads. Golfers become tennis players, then joggers and now rollerskaters!

Clearly there is "searching" going on as people try to find the most satisfying leisure. The implication for leisure counselors is that people are indeed willing to devote time, energy, and perhaps even money to finding leisure satisfaction. This willingness and motivation can be used to facilitate the leisure counseling process.

Another related assumption is that leisure is important to people. Why else would they engage in so many searching behaviors? Unfortunately, while these behaviors represent manifestations of personal importance, few people fully comprehend the nature of this importance. Thus another primary goal of leisure counseling is to help people understand how and why their leisure is important to them.

A sixth assumption is that people need help in selecting appropriate leisure. This assumption is derived from consideration of the first five assumptions. To the extent they are true, it follows that people generally have not been successful in indentifying and utilizing the most beneficial forms of leisure for their individual needs and circumstances. Obviously this assumption provides the fundamental rationale for leisure counseling; if people were successful with their own efforts, their individual needs and circumstances. Obviously this

The final assumption underlying this book is that leisure counseling can help people find more appropriate, effective, and satisfying leisure. Unfortunately, the evidence to validate this assumption is still incomplete. However, the rapidly increasing numbers of people soliciting leisure counseling and the correspondingly increasing numbers of professionals providing leisure counseling services strongly support this assumption. Still, only the accumulation of empirical evidence over time will allow for definitive evaluation of the assumption. In the interim, this assumption is accepted as true since it reflects the intended goal for users of this book.

An Abbreviated History of Leisure

The understanding of leisure in a modern society is in part facilitated through consideration of the history of leisure. This history also has implications for leisure counseling in a modern society. More detailed descriptions of the history of leisure may be found in de Grazia (1962), Iso-Ahola (1980a), Kaplan (1960), Miller and Robinson (1963), Neulinger (1974), Pieper (1963), Taylor (1967), and Woody (1957). What follows here are some of the highlights that relate more directly to leisure counseling.

Leisure was a part of the prehistoric lifestyle as a trip to a natural history museum would readily verify. Most of the objects viewed would of course be tools, weapons and clothing which prehistoric peoples needed and used to survive. But among them would also be various objects with no discernible relationships to survival.

For example, objects have been found which have been determined to be crude "games" or the results of primitive "crafts" activities. Cave drawings have been found which depict people (apparently) "dancing." Of course the creation of cave drawings also was not entirely essential to the survival of prehistoric peoples. These then are the simple beginnings of leisure.

As the human species evolved and progressed, leisure came to be held in high regard. People had to invest so much time and energy in working to survive that "not working" became the ideal. For example, the ancient Greeks considered leisure to be "a concern to which both labor, as well as the daily toil of life, were subordinate" (Neulinger, 1971, p.4).

Aristotle presented the Greek outlook succinctly: The end of labor is to gain leisure. For Aristotle, leisure had intrinsic value; it was to be enjoyed simply for its own sake.

Similar philosophy and perspective on leisure were present in ancient Rome. The emperor Marcus Tullius Cicero is credited with stating:

> If the soul has food for study and learning, nothing is more delightful than an old age of leisure... Leisure consists in all those virtuous activities by which a man grows morally, intellectually, and spiritually. It is that which makes life worth living.

Cicero could afford to be philosophical! However, while most Romans also held leisure in high esteem, they took a much more pragmatic view of it. For them, leisure was simply nonactivity (Neulinger, 1974).

All paid employments absorb and degrade the mind.

Aristotle

The *Bible* also provides numerous references to leisure. An event in the Garden of Eden is among the more famous. After all, Eve didn't offer the apple to Adam because she thought he was hungry. No sacrilege is intended; for a modern day discussion of whether sex is leisure, see *The Leisure Information Newsletter, 6* (2), 1979. The Book of Genesis also provides the basis for a colloquial way of advising someone to partake of leisure, "Even the Almighty rested one day out of the week."

The Aristotelian emphasis on the intrinsic value of leisure continued through the Middle Ages. However, the early Christians somewhat realigned the perspective by suggesting that the highest or best form of leisure was contemplation (de Grazia, 1962). In turn, contemplation was seen as the way to obtain religious truth. Finding religious truth was salvation. Thus leisure was the pursuit of salvation which in turn was of paramount importance. Everything else, including work and other essential activity, was secondary (Woody, 1957).

After the Middle Ages, leisure began to lose its ideological primacy. This change is attributable to two factors: (1) rapid advances being made in the physical and biological sciences, and (2) the rise of craftsman ship (de Grazia, 1962). The scientific advances improved both the quality and duration of life and therefore altered the normative lifestyle. The major alteration was the opportunity for greater work productivity, which in turn lead to more lifestyle improvement, and so the cycle continued.

The rise of craftsmanship had a subtle yet even more profound effect. Craftsmanship activities resulted in *concrete* products which could be seen and admired. A sense of pride in one's work became the norm because the results were open to public inspection. This change was significant because it stood in direct opposition to the *abstract* process of contemplation.

These changes signaled the advent of the Protestant (Work) Ethic where work become the "ulimate" human activity. People were "identified" by themselves and others in terms of what they "did for a living" (Miller and Robinson, 1963). Even the so-called Industrial Revolution did not alter the emphasis placed on work. In fact, the "competition" between man and machine may have been further entrenched by the Protestant (Work) Ethic as people sought to prove they could make better products than machines could. Leisure was thus relegated to a place of relative unimportance in the human condition (Taylor, 1967).

To be able to fill leisure intelligently is the last product of civilization.

Arnold Toynbee

The Protestant (Work) Ethic remains as a dominant societal standard today. Moreover, leisure has moved from a place of unimportance to a point where it is often used with a negative connotation. Do you feel a touch of guilt, or at least defensiveness, when someone suggests you are leading a "life of leisure?" How do you feel when you have a day off or a vacation from work and someone comments, "It must be nice not to have to work for a living?"

Lessons from History

This brief history suggests several major implications for the understanding of leisure and for leisure counseling. One of these is that attitudes about leisure can be changed; the history of leisure is testimony for its susceptibility to change. However, it is just as obvious that such changes are not easily accomplished. At a societal level, leisure attitude changes may have to be accompanied or caused by other significant changes. At a personal level, leisure attitude change may result in conflict with a societal norm, thereby making the change process more difficult. Since attitude change is often a necessary part of the leisure counseling process, leisure counselors should remember that such change is possible but not easy to bring about.

> If hard work is the key to success, most people would rather pick the lock.
>
> Claude McDonald

Another important implication is that leisure, and all its associated attitudes, are subjectively interpreted. Each person individually decides what leisure is and what attitudes to have about it. Certainly there are general trends and commonalities which may be identified among groups of people. But just as certainly there are no guarantees that any particular individual can be characterized exactly by societal norms. Leisure counseling must therefore be approached as a highly personalized activity.

The final implication of importance here is that leisure behaviors, interpretations, and attitudes are integrally related with and influenced by a wide variety of other life factors. Even though leisure may be pursued or enjoyed for its own intrinsic value, the form an individual's leisure takes must necessarily reflect a complex set of factors. It is essential therefore that leisure counselors carefully consider the contextual nature of leisure.

Factors Influencing Leisure

The contextual nature of leisure raises a logical question; namely, what factors influence leisure? A simple yet valid response would be (literally) *everything*. The following are examples of *major* factors influencing leisure.

Changes in Work

Perhaps the most significant factor affecting leisure is rapid changes in the world of work. The most important among these changes is the continuing rapid advancement of technology. This is truly the Age of Automation. Technological automation has had two major implications for the world of work. First, many, many jobs are becoming easier, both physcially and psychologically. Therefore, people expend less "energy" in their work activities and in turn have more available to expend on nonwork (leisure) pursuits.

A second implication is that many jobs are simply being eliminated. This of course results in many people having to find new and different types of work. Changes in work situations are directly associated with changes in other aspects of life, including leisure.

Another change related to technology is the decline of craftsmanship. How many objects in today's living are "handmade?" The number of people who even have the *opportunity* to take personal pride in their work products or activities is rapidly decreasing. It seems reasonable to assume that most people like to have some activities which result in personal pride. Consequently, as work opportunities of this nature become fewer, people turn more to other possible sources. The alternative most often selected is leisure.

> My father taught me to work, but not to love it. I never did like to work and I don't deny it. I'd rather read, tell stories, crack jokes, talk, laugh—anything but work.
>
> *Abraham Lincoln*

Changes in the amount of time people actually spend working also influence leisure. The *Employment and Training Report of the President* (1978) offers some interesting information in this regard. For example, the average number of work hours per week continues to decline and this trend is expected to continue indefinitely. In addition, there has been a rapid increase in the percentage of persons selecting early retirement (i.e. before age 65). Two major reasons are cited for this second trend:

> For older men, more and better pensions programs, increased social security coverage and benefit levels, and the greater availability of disability insurance have been cited as explontions for earlier retirement.... Among younger men, longer school attendance and increased alternatives to work, including homemaking and leisure (partly because of increasing female participation), are undoubtedly contributing factors. (p. 24)

Shorter work weeks and early retirement obviously provide more time for leisure pursuits. The desirability of this situation is emphasized by a related conclusion from the report:

> Of the total number of persons aged 16 and over who were outside the labor force in 1977 (59 million), more than 90 percent did not want jobs. Most of the nonparticipants were women keeping house. The remainder were retirees, students, persons who were ill or disabled, and persons engaged in other nonwork activities, including leisure. (p. 25)

Flexittime (i.e. variable work hours by employee choice) is yet another factor influencing leisure. The desirability of flexittime scheduling for workers is already a strongly supported phenomenon and this support shows signs of increasing (Renwick et al, 1978). The reason most often cited for the desirability of flexittime is that it allows for greater flexibility in leisure scheduling (Renwick *et al,* 1978). Thus leisure is even given preeminence over some other reasons such as more time for families or just having more control over work situations.

A final change in the world of work that relates to leisure is what appears to be the beginnings of the decline of the work ethic. Numerous professionals have questioned the validity of the Protestant (Work) Ethic as the primary motivational force in a modern society. More importantly, they have also advocated that it probably should not be (e.g. Hoyt, 1977; Severinsen, 1979; Super, 1976). Perhaps the pendulum is swinging back toward the Aristotelian philosophy of leisure? If it is, attitudes about leisure are likely to become considerably more positive in the not too distant future.

Changes in Society

Changes in the nature of the people in our society also influence leisure. Although the birthrate has been "leveling off" in recent years, the total population continues to increase. As the population increases there is a corresponding change in leisure, particularly in regard to leisure opportunities provided.

For example, consider the rapid increase in the number of recreational parks, campgrounds and similar facilities during the last decade. Consider also the increasing billions of dollars spent each year in the development and maintenance of parks and recreational areas. These increases are not optional; they are literally demanded and necessitated by ever increasing numbers of people who want to use them.

A related population change is the increase in the average life span. Longer life expectancies, resulting primarily from improved medical services, are the norm. As society "grows older," there are corresponding changes in "average" values and attitudes. In general, the trend seems to be toward more positive attitudes about leisure.

> The only reason I ever played golf in the first place was so that I could afford to hunt and fish.
>
> Sam Snead

Changes in Economics

Leisure is also highly susceptible to economic influences. Leisure is big business; billions of dollars are spent annually on it and for it. Accordingly, factors that affect the economy in general also affect leisure. At present, two factors seem to be having the most influence on leisure. First, the "energy crisis" obviously affects leisure centered travel. Once a major leisure activity (particularly for families), leisure travel is rapidly decreasing. Consequently, alternatives to travel as leisure are being utilized much more frequently.

Second, inflation is also rapidly changing the nature of leisure. As people strive to hold down personal or familial expenses, they are turning more and more to less expensive types of leisure. Again, alternatives to what had been considered normal or traditional leisure pursuits are being utilized more frequently. The significant implication here is that current economic factors are resulting in changes in the manifestations of leisure. Whether these changes are positive or negative remains to be seen, but the changes are a certainty.

A more subtle economic influence on leisure is consumerism. Gunter and Moore (1975) have described what they term "consumptive leisure"—the *vicarious consumption* of an activity as opposed to actual participation in the activity. Spectatorship and television watching are perhaps the most common examples of consumptive leisure. The economic intent is to induce as many persons as possible to experience vicariously the leisure activity. The effectiveness of these efforts is unquestionable; consumptive leisure is easily the most common form in our society.

Changes in Institutions

The size of government is increasing. More than fifty percent of the labor force either works for a municipal, state or the national government, or in a business subsidized by government. This is but one way government influences people's lives. It also obviously influences them in many other ways. Indeed, government philosophies, activities, and policies affect all aspects of life, including leisure. Some of the influences on leisure are fairly evident.

> Education is the carpentry of the mind. It is an edifice of information and logic. An educator once said, "Raising a child is very much like building a skyscraper. If the first few stories are out of line, no one will notice. But when the building is 18 or 20 stories high, everyone will see that it tilts."
>
> *Jim Bishop*

For example, when highway speed limits were reduced to 55 mph, travel plans had to be adjusted accordingly. Other influences are more indirect. For example, the decision to move all legal holidays to Mondays did not alter the total number of work days off during the year, but it did alter the combinations of those days. Leisure plans were modified accordingly (again, travel plans being an obvious example).

Changes and "current trends" in educational systems and philosophies also affect leisure. The majority of people with children in schools expect schools to provide recreational and leisure activities for their children. Similar attitudes are held by children themselves (Gholson, 1979). However, sometimes educational movements and priorities (such as the so-called "back to basics" movement) are seemingly in direct contradiction with such expectations.

If the schools are supposed to focus on basic learning skills, all other activities become secondary and, in some cases, almost superfluous. Perhaps this is why some professionals suggest that schools have been ineffectual in providing students with leisure skills. Travers et al (1978) state this position succinctly, "The schools have done little to prepare individuals to face leisure" (p. 125). If schools don't prepare children for leisure, then they must obtain that preparation elsewhere. Whatever that "elsewhere" is will have a lot to say about future leisure trends and attitudes.

Changes in People

The most significant changes influencing leisure are those occurring within the people in our society. In combination with, or perhaps as a result of, the changes previously discussed, these personal changes are indeed significant.

Some of the most often discussed changes are those in children. The most frequently cited behavior is television watching. Orthner (1975a) cites figures projecting that children born in 1974 will have watched more than 22,000 hours of television by the time they reach eighteen years of age. By comparision, these same children will have had less than 11,000 hours of classroom instruction.

I find television very educating. Every time someone turns it on I go into another room and read a book.

Groucho Marx

Television watching is but one type of leisure activity, yet it is apparently the primary (perhaps only?) one for children. The importance here is that children thus develop very limited perspectives on leisure. Today's children will define tomorrow's leisure. Unless something intervenes, it is not difficult to speculate what the nature of that leisure will be.

Another segment of the population experiencing change is youth. Kenniston (1971) suggests that even the connotation of the term youth (as an age referent) is changing, "We are witnessing today the emergence on a mass scale of a previously unrecognized style of life, a stage that intervenes between adolescence and adulthood" (p.7).

Berger (1971) calls this age period "almost endless adolescence" and suggests that it occurs roughly between the ages of 17 and 30. He goes on to suggest that "youth" in this context is characterized by disengagement from societal obligations, postponement of adulthood, prolonged preparation for living through (unnecessarily) extended education, prolonged dependence on parents, and increased amounts of ineffectively used leisure time.

Gunter and Moore (1975) and Bosserman and Gagon (1972) add that this is a period of unforced choice, allowable volunteerism, prolonged irresponsibility and emotional drifting. The unfortunate implication is that there is an increasing trend for young persons to use leisure as an "escape" from normal life responsibilities.

Also among the more evident personal changes are those for women. The most important of these relative to leisure is the number of women entering the labor force. Some women go to work because they want to and therefore voluntarily change the nature of their leisure. The rest enter the labor force because they have to, usually for economic reasons, and are therefore forced to change their leisure.

> Few people at the beginning of the nineteenth century needed an adman to tell them what they wanted.
>
> *John Kenneth Galbraith*

Additional changes in women's leisure are associated with changing women's sex roles. With the advent of the reduction of sex role stereotyping (though it is by no means yet complete), women are being freed to engage in leisure pursuits which have traditionally been unavailable to them. The important point is that regardless of the reasons, women's leisure is changing, and rather dramatically at that. Since women comprise more than 50% of the population, these changes are likely to be strong determiners of the nature of leisure in the future.

Personal changes among men are also influencing leisure. In some ways these changes parallel those for women. For example, more men are now participating in leisure activities which traditionally were "restricted" to women. In addition, as more women enter the labor force, there are some changes in work patterns among men. In some dual-career families, men experience less "pressure" to be the "family provider." Their work attitudes are adjusted accordingly, and this often includes placing greater value on leisure.

Other changes are seemingly unique to men. These include their reactions to changing women's roles as well as to reductions in stereotypes about men. While the implications of these reactions for men's leisure are as yet unclear, it seems reasonable that the changes in men's leisure also will be extensive and dramatic.

Changes in Families

The final types of changes to be considered are those in the family. Most of the changes previously discussed at least indirectly also affect families and family leisure. However, the family plays a unique role in leisure development. Parental activities and attitudes are particularly important. As Brightbill and Mobley (1977) suggest:

> The role of parents in preparing children for leisure is large . . It implies exposing children to the best of leisure pursuits, stimulating and rewarding good leisure habits as a wise parent does in helping to develop good eating, sleeping, and work habits. (p. 109)

Leisure also serves an important function in family development, particularly in terms of family cohesion (Carisse, 1975; Gunter and Moore, 1975). The adage that "the family that plays together stays together" is well supported in the professional literature on families. Unfortunately, there is an apparent trend in families today to relinquish their leisure functions (Orthner, 1975a). This trend has significant implications for leisure since people must therefore find or develop leisure from other situations. Again, at present the nature of these other situations is as yet unknown.

The Importance of Leisure

Given that leisure is susceptible to so many different influences, it is legitimate to question the importance of leisure. A simplistic perspective would be that leisure is a very personal experience and that each person individually determines its importance. Unfortunately, such a perspective provides little useful information for leisure counselors. Therefore, it seems more appropriate to examine the ways leisure fits into people's lives because these different ways have implications for the nature and directions of leisure counseling.

Several authors have provided general models of leisure across the life span. The one which probably reflects leisure as most people see it is the "linear life plan," as described by Best and Stern (1976). They suggest that life consists of three stages, with a primary focus in each stage. Their first stage focuses on education and lasts from birth through the end of formal education (usually high school or college). The second stage, work, covers most of adult life. Retirement (roughly interpreted as synonomous with leisure) is the third stage. It covers the remaining life period after termination of work.

This model is grounded in the Protestant (Work) Ethic since work is the focal point. That is, education is viewed as the preparation for work, while retirement (leisure) is the "reward" for having worked. Both education and leisure are thus of secondary importance from this perspective. In fairness, it should be noted that Best and Stern themselves do not deemphasize or denigrate education or leisure; they simply describe what appears to be the current perspective.

A more recent model has been proposed by Bolles (1978) in his book *The Three Boxes of Life.* He rejects the linear life plan and suggests that there are three major components to life at any point in time. These are identified as learning, work and play (leisure). Bolles suggests that these components are subjectively defined; work for one person may be play (leisure) for another, and so on. Unfortunately, the impression is given that these three components are compartmentalized in life.

Accordingly, Loesch (1980) developed the "life flow" model which contains essentially the same factors (learning, work and leisure), but which emphasizes the interrelatedness of the factors. The life flow model is "fluid" to the extend that the distinctions between factors are flexible, transitory, and often subtle. For example, what starts out as leisure may easily transpose into work "before the person knows it."

These three models are presented graphically in Figure 1. Since the Best and Stern model is (apparently) such a popular conceptualization, it is the one that leisure counselors are most likely to encounter from their clients. On the other hand, either the Bolles or Loesch models may be the ones that leisure counselors want to work toward with their clients. In any event, each of these models emphasizes the importance of leisure since they all incorporate it into the life perspective.

Figure 1

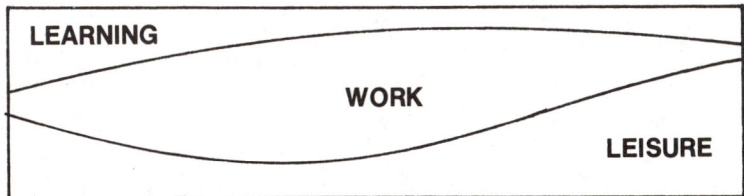

Play is the primary leisure activity of children. The importance of play in a child's development has been emphasized by many (e.g. Bruner, Jolly, and Sylva, 1976). This importance is usually focused on two essential developmental processes. The first is that play (leisure) is the child's primary form of learning. Through play children not only gain essential life information but also learn how to learn. Thus play (leisure) is the primary way that children learn life coping skills. The second process inherent in children's play (leisure) is socialization. It is primarily through play that children develop interpersonal skills.

Some authors (cf. Bruner, Jolly, and Sylva, 1976; Butler, Gotts, and Quisenberry, 1978) have made distinctions among different types of children's play. Following the lead of the models discussed previously, they write of "educational" play, "work" play, and "play (leisure)" play. Such distinctions seem unnecessary. No matter what it is called, children's play (leisure) is essential to their eventual effective development.

In every real man a child is hidden that wants to play.

Freidrich Nietzsche

Leisure also serves a primary function in transitions among developmental life stages as the opportunity for "safe" trial-and-error. Since leisure is flexible by virtue of its personal definition, and therefore can be easily rejected or maintained, people are freed to "experiment" with various learning and socialization activites without fear of irreversible repercussions in their lives. Leisure is thus extremely important because it provides such safe opportunities.

Leisure is also important in another regard relative to developmental life stages. The process of moving from one developmental stage to another is often difficult because of the psychological pressures and problems involved. Leisure may facilitate the transition process by offering the opportunity for psychological "escape" during the transition period. This type of leisure involves reliance on established, satisfying leisure. People may rely on the stability of their leisure during the difficulties of their stage transitions.

It's the most unhappy people who fear change the most.

Mignon McLaughlin

Leisure and Mental Health

The learning and socialization processes in developmental stages and the transitions through those stages may be summarized as the involvement of the self. The effective and successful evolvement of the self is of course one common definition of mental health. Thus linkage is made that leisure facilitates the development of mental health.

The significant relationship between leisure and mental health is also evident from other perspectivies. For example, the opportunity for self expression is also essential for mental health. Historically, opportunities for self expression were expected from the world of work. However, some authors (e. g. Allen, 1980; Kaplan, 1975; Neulinger, 1974) point out that such opportunities are becoming increasingly restricted in the work world. Leisure, as the alternative, is increasingly becoming the situation where people find such opportunities (Etzioni, 1978).

America is the country where you buy a lifetime supply of aspirin for one dollar, and use it up in two weeks.

John Barrymore

Mental health may also be considered from any of a number of personality theory perspectives. One of the most commonly espoused personality theories is Henry Murray's *needs* theory. In essence, this theory purports that people have various needs which must be fulfilled in order for them to be mentally healthy. Needs are related to behaviors in that people engage in specific behaviors either in the attempt to fulfill needs or because needs are being met as a result of the behaviors.

A number of authors (e.g. Tinsley and Kass, 1978; Neulinger, 1978) have emphasized that leisure provides an excellent method of need gratification. Further, they suggest that the flexibility inherent in leisure allows for concurrent gratification of various different needs. Leisure is therefore important because it facilitates mental health through need fulfillment.

The final aspect of mental health and leisure to be considered here is the aspect of self satisfaction. As pointed out earlier, opportunities to achieve self satisfaction in the world of work are rapidly decreasing in number. Assuming that the need for feelings of self satisfaction have not decreased, these feelings must be obtained from other sources. Leisure is the logical place to obtain those feelings (Klieber, 1972).

Moreover, the personal nature of leisure allows those feelings to be as intense as the person wishes them to be. Unlike work, people have a choice over the amount of personal (psychological) investment they make in leisure. The rewards (e.g. self satisfaction) they receive in return are proportionate to the investment. Leisure therefore is important not only because it allows for self satisfaction in the absolute sense, but also because it allows for varying degrees of self satisfaction. Effective mental health necessitates such flexibility.

All work and no play makes Jack a dull boy — and Jill a wealthy widow.

Evan Esar

There are two common life areas where the importance of leisure is accepted as obvious. The first of these is stress, which has been called the primary characteristic of a modern society (Toffler, 1970). Stress is evident everywhere; in work, in interpersonal relationships, and sometimes even in "leisure." Responses to stress are similarly evident. Increasing mental illness, rising divorce rates, and increasing job change frequencies are but a few examples. However, the major response has been medical. People consume billions of tranquilizers each year in the attempt to reduce or avoid stress. More recently, however, effective leisure is becoming an accepted alternative method for stress reduction (see *U.S. News and World Report,* 1977).

It would be nice to be able to suggest that leisure is being used for stress reduction because of its intrinsic value. Unfortunately, people seem to be turning to leisure by default. They seem to be reacting to the potential negative effects, both physiological and psychological, of the number of pills they take (*U.S. News and World Report,* 1977). But regardless of the reason, there is an apparent trend toward leisure as a primary method of stress reduction. It seems that people are finally heeding the age old advice to "take some time off and do something good for yourself."

Being bored is an insult to oneself.

Jules Renard

A related phenomenon is boredom. It is related in that boredom may result in its own unique type of stress. While stress usually results from too much or too intense activity, boredom is characterized by lack of activity (Keen, 1977). Boredom seems particularly prominent among children and youth. It has been cited (see Loesch, 1981) as a major reason for many of the so-called negative behaviors among children and youth such as delinquency, vandalism, drug abuse and other asocial behaviors. Participation in leisure is a logical way to counteract boredom. While this response to boredom is obviously not yet wide spread, leisure's importance is no less diminished.

Boredom is a vital problem for the moralist since half the sins of mankind are caused for fear of it.

Bertrand Russell

These then are a few of the major aspects of the importance of leisure. This importance has lead to developments in the scientific study of leisure. These studies have in turn discovered some surprising and interesting results.

The Leisure Problem

Neulinger (1974) cites the publication of Veblen's *The Theory of the Leisure Class* in 1899 as the beginning of modern day social science interest in leisure. Unfortunately, although Veblen provided a comprehensive perspective and offered some stimulating ideas, his lead was not followed for several decades. Sporadic studies on leisure only began to appear in the professional literature in the 1930s. Following the theoretical precedent set by Veblen, these studies were almost exclusively sociological investigations of leisure behavior, time, and activity patterns (Neulinger, 1974).

This sparcity continued until the late 1950s. It was about this time that sociologists began to increase their interest in leisure, and the professional literature shows a corresponding increase in leisure based entries. These writings were, however, still almost totally sociological. Max Kaplan is the person most commonly associated with this emergent sociological interest in leisure. In fact, he and his associates have provided most of the significant theoretical and research information on the sociology of leisure.

The law of Norway calls for everybody there to have at least four weeks of vacation a year. But the Norwegian medicoes say that may not be enough, particularly for the older folk. Five weeks are prescribed for those over age 40, six weeks for those over 50, and seven weeks for those over 60. Please note, that's merely the medical recommendation, not yet legislated.

L. M. Boyd

The study of leisure from psychological perspectives apparently began in the early 1960s. However, the professional literature entries were relatively infrequent until the early part of the 1970s. Even then, most of the writings and studies pertinent to the psychology of leisure appeared in publications outside the psychological disciplines.

It has only been within the last half dozen years that leisure has been "legitimized" as a topic for psychological investigation and discussion. The name most frequently associated with this movement is John Neulinger. His book, *The Psychology of*

Leisure (1974), is by far the most often cited, and it seems destined to become a "classic" for its role in stimulating interest in the psychology of leisure.

The purpose of this lead in has been to emphasize the extremely short history of the scientific study of leisure. The amount of significant and substantive information about leisure that has been accumulated is small in comparison to many other social science topics. However, even in light of these circumstances, one "fact" has already been established and it shows no signs of being refuted. That fact is that leisure is a problem for many, many people.

Stated in the simplest possible terms, leisure is a problem because there is so much of it available. The most obvious dimension of this problem is time; many people are experiencing an inability to cope effectively with increased amounts of leisure time (McKechnie, 1974). Neulinger (1974) identifies three major aspects of the leisure time problem.

The first is feelings of threat due to the lack of inner (i.e. psychological) resources for making effective leisure decisions. Faced with increased amounts of leisure time, people need to make decisions about how to spend it. Unfortunately, there are no guidelines, even in the form of social traditions, for making such decisions. The result is that people are frustrated when confronted with leisure (time) decisions. As these episodes of frustration become more frequent, people become afraid of, or threatened by, even more leisure time and the corresponding inability to deal with it.

People who are considered workaholics may really just be having fun. The only thing that distinguishes work from pleasure is which activity you prefer doing.

Susan Ellis

A second aspect is the feelings associated with the view of leisure as "nonproductive" activity. The prominence of the Protestant (Work) Ethic reinforces the idea that expended effort should "produce" something (usually tangible). Since leisure is typically viewed as "nonproductive," people feel guilty and ashamed about the amount of time they spend being "nonproductive". These feelings increase in direct proportion to increases in leisure time.

The final aspect is the feeling of lack of self development and self fulfillment during leisure time. Again, the Protestant (Work) Ethic reinforces the idea that the place to improve or enhance oneself is in one's work. As work time decreases, so do opportunities for self fulfillment. The result is feelings of stagnation and uselessness. People often feel they have lost some of the meanings in their lives when they lose some of their work.

The second major dimension of the leisure problem is the number of available activities. At first glance this wouldn't seem to be a problem. However, the situation raises many of the same psychological quandaries that excessive leisure time does. For example, the number of potential choices available necessitates that decisions be made. But again, most people don't have guidelines for effective decision-making in regard to leisure activity selection.

Excessive leisure options also may introduce frustration. Approach-approach conflicts abound. On the other hand, there are also many approach-avoidance conflicts. Consider the person who wants to enter a new leisure pursuit but who lacks the fiscal resources to do so. Or how about the individual who wants to participate in some leisure activity but finds that an interpersonal conflict results?

The problem of leisure is also a problem of people's dissatisfaction with themselves, compounded by their inabilities to cope with situations. As Caslver (cited in Orthner, 1975a) states:

> . . . Now when so many have leisure, they have become detached from themselves, not merely from earth. From all the widened horizons of our greater world a thousand voices call us to come near, to understand, to enjoy, but our ears are not trained to hear them. The leisure is ours but not the skill to use it. So leisure becomes a void, and from the ensuing restlessness men take refuge in delusive excitations or fictitious visions, returning to their earth no more. (pp. 54-55)

The Need for Leisure Counseling

If past history is a valid indicator, it is unlikely that left to their own devices people will solve their own leisure problems. Certainly they will do something, and so the time will while away. But the quality will not be there. It will take guided effort to make leisure as fully meaningful and satisfying as it could be. Counselors can provide such guidance.

> Experience proves that most time is wasted, not in hours, but in minutes. A bucket with a small hole in the bottom gets just as empty as a bucket that is deliberately kicked over.
>
> *Paul Meyer*

Leisure counseling is the professional response to the leisure problem. Leisure counseling has evolved almost simultaneously with the psychology of leisure. It shares the same problems and the same potentials. It derives its developmental impetus from the desire to make the psychology of leisure an applied science. Thus the psychology of leisure and leisure counseling are integrally related, yet each has its own unique characteristics (McDowell, 1977b; Overs, 1975).

Leisure counseling provides an exciting new frontier for professional counselors, and it may even be the last frontier of the profession. Almost every other aspect of the human condition has been addressed by the counseling profession, with topics ranging from abortion to zealousness. The methods similarly have ranged from assertiveness training to zen. Yet through all that leisure has surprisingly been neglected.

It is indeed regretful that leisure has had to become a "problem" before it received professional attention. However, the need for leisure counseling is evident and the profession is responding. Alleviation of the leisure problem would be a meritorious accomplishment in its own right. However, if leisure counseling is combined with other counseling efforts, the potential benefits for the people counselors serve are enormous.

Discussion Questions

1. In what way is leisure emphasized in the mass media (e.g. newspapers, radio, television)? What do you think are the major intentions of these emphases? What are your personal reactions to these emphases?
2. Think for a little while about your own leisure. What were the major circumstances that guided or influenced your leisure toward what it is now? What people influenced your leisure most significantly, and how?
3. What do you think were the major (i.e. most popular) leisure activities during each of the last four decades? What circumstances do you think influenced leisure the most during each of those decades?
4. What examples can you cite of how changing men's and women's sex roles are reflected in leisure today?
5. How does leisure contribute to your personal mental health? What does your leisure do for you? What do you wish your leisure could do for you?
6. Is the "leisure problem" increasing or decreasing in severity among people in our society, and why?

Study Activities

1. Look through a current, local newspaper and make a list of the leisure activities that are emphasized in it. How many different ones did you find? Which ones receive the greatest emphasis?
2. Talk to a person who is at least twenty years older than you and ask that person to respond to discussion question number three above. How similar are the responses to yours?
3. Ask each of any three of your friends to respond to discussion question number two above. What similarities and difference are there among the factors influencing their leisure and those influencing yours?

Chapter II

Leisure in Perspective

Thoughout the first chapter leisure was discussed extensively but never specifically defined. This omission was intentional. It serves to emphasize that people can, and very often do, discuss leisure on the basis of *assumed* mutual understanding and interpretation of the term. In actuality, however, leisure may be defined in any of several ways, depending on an individual's personal preference.

It follows that if mutual interpretation of the word leisure is *assumed* in the leisure counseling process, then that process may be seriously undermined if in fact the counselor and the client are interpreting leisure differently. Consequently, it is important for leisure counselors to be aware of the possible definitions of leisure. Relatedly, it is also important to identify the definition of leisure which will underlie the remainder of this book.

All animals except man know that the ultimate of life is to enjoy it.

Samuel Butler

Toward Defining Leisure

Leisure definitions may be divided into five major categories: time, activity, work related, psychological, and models. It should be noted, however, that these categories merely reflect the focal points of the definitions. The distinctions between categories are tentative at best because there is often overlap or compounding among the categories. Moreover, most authors present definitions of leisure that simultaneously incorporate several dynamics.

The beginning of wisdom is the definition of terms.

Socrates

Time Based Definitions

The majority of time based leisure definitions are esentially *residual* in nature. That is, leisure is time left over after the time spent on something else. Very often the "something else" is existence or subsistence activity. Authors such as Clawson (1964), Weiss (1964), and Brightbill (1960) all define leisure in this way.

Perhaps the strongest advocacy for this type of definition is that offered by Brightbill and Mobley (1977, p. 5), ". . . Leisure is best identified with time—time beyond that required, organically, for existence and subsistence. . . ." Such definitions are of course very general since they simply dichotomize all of a person's time.

More recently, some authors who use time based leisure definitions have attempted to partition a person's total time into multiple categories, with leisure being just one of them. Exemplary in this regard is Bolles (1978) who writes of work time, nonwork time (e.g. going to and from work), personal care time, sleep time, house and family care time, and leisure time. However, even when multiple time categories are used, leisure is still usually viewed as residual time (cf. Bolles, 1978, p. 374).

Other time based leisure definitions do not incorporate the concept of residuality, but simply view leisure time as antithical to some other type of time. Parker (1971) offered a simple dichotomous example: All time is divided into work time and nonwork (leisure) time. He described work as "sold" time and leisure as "unsold" time. Finally, Winters and Hansen (1976) attempted to lessen the distinctions between various types of time by conceptualizing a continuum with work time and nonwork (leisure) time as the poles.

Time based definitions of leisure have both advantages and disadvantages for leisure counselors. On the positive side, many laypersons espouse what is essentially a time based definition of leisure. It is not at all unusual to hear laypersons speak of "leisure time" as if the two words were inseparable. Therefore, leisure counselors may be safe, at least initially, in using a time based definition with laypersons.

A man who dares to waste one hour of time has not discovered the value of life.

Charles Darwin

In addition, many social scientists (particularly social psychologists and sociologists) have found favor with time based leisure definitions because time is easily quantifiable. This quantification capability facilitates research on leisure and therefore appeals to professionals interested in more rigorous studies of leisure.

The disadvantages of time based leisure definitions arise from the incompassing natures of such definitions. For example, is a simple time dichotomy such as work and nonwork sufficient for effective understanding of leisure? If multiple time categories are used, how many should there be and what factors should be considered in distinguishing among them? In general, time based leisure definitions have some value, but that value is really very limited because of the lack of specificity.

Activity Based Definitions

Activity based definitions of leisure are the least common type. However, they provide a unique perspective on leisure because of the interpretive possibilities they allow. Dumazedier (1967) provided a representative example of this type by suggesting that leisure is any activity engaged in by choice. Bull (1972) said almost the same thing be describing leisure as "discretionary" activity. And finally, Parker (1971) presented a schema which categorizes activities from constraint (i.e. obligatory) to freedom (i.e. nonobligatory) on a continuum.

> The more you do, the more you are.
>
> *Angie Papadakis*

The obvious commonality among these activity based leisure definitions is the aspect of personal choice. In other words, an activity is leisure (and vice versa) if a person chooses to define it as such. This perspective allows activities which would typically be defined as "work" to be "leisure," if that's the way individuals view them. This may be the basis of the so-called "workaholic" syndrome. An individual who doesn't differentiate between work and leisure activities may be identified as a "workaholic" by others because they don't agree with the individual's lack of differentiation.

> Tell me what you are busy about, and I will tell you what you are.
>
> *Goethe*

Activity based definitions of leisure also have advantages and disadvantages. The major advantages are that an individual literally may define any activity as leisure. An advantage for social scientists is that activities are behavioral, and therefore observable and quantifiable manifestations of leisure. The disadvantages are essentially the same. Who should, or can, define an activity as leisure? Are subjective definitions of an activity appropriate, particularly when they conflict with other people's interpretations? In general, activity based leisure definitions are valuable to leisure counselors to the extent that they emphasize (subjective) personal choice, which is a typical counseling goal. However, that same subjectivity may introduce new problems, particularly those associated with value based decision making.

Work Related Definitions

Work related leisure definitions have been popular among professional counselors because they fit well with current emphases on vocational (career) development, education, and counseling. These definitions are akin to time based leisure definitions in that they are also typically residual. That is, the focus is on work and leisure is something secondary or supplemental to work.

Two of the more commonly cited work related leisure definitions were provided by Wilensky (1960). In the first, he described the situation of an individual who holds a job that is not meaningful to the individual in ways that it should be. He then described *compensatory leisure as* that which helped the individual "compensate" for the lack of meaningfulness in work through participation in "meaningful" leisure activities. An example of this situation might be the person who values physical fitness but who has a relatively sedentary job and therefore plays raquetball as a leisure activity.

The second type described by Wilensky is the situation where the individual has a job which is meaningful. The individual would then engage in *spillover leisure w*hich is designed to allow the individual to continue to find meaningfulness in leisure activities. An example of this might be a computer programmer who enjoys the "mental gymnastics" of the job and who continues this enjoyment through playing chess as a leisure activity.

On the surface, the compensatory and spillover leisure definitions seem to make a lot of sense. In addition, they would seem to be definitions that laypersons would readily accept and understand. However, Burdge (1969) raised insightful criticisms of these definitions. He noted that the compensatory definition implies that an individual should engage in leisure activities directly opposite those in the individual's work. Burdge points out that this opposition (of activities) may not always be feasible or desirable. He raised the question of what happens when the leisure activities (that are opposites of the work activities) also are not meaningful to the individual.

In regard to the spillover definition, he suggested that this may simply be "force of habit" and not really a situation of free choice. Again, the issue of the desirability of such a situation also may be raised. Burdge's comments on the compensatory and spillover leisure definitions emphasize a critical point for leisure counselors. Even though a particular definition may seem appropriate from a common sense point of view, it may in fact not be appropriate upon closer scrutiny.

> If a man has important work, and enough leisure and income to enable him to do it properly, he is in possession of as much happiness as is good for any of the children of Adam.
>
> R. H. Tawney

Another perspective on work and leisure has been presented by Godbey and Parker (1976). They saw three broad approaches to the work-leisure relationship. The first follows the Protestant (Work) Ethic in that work is the "serious business" of life. Leisure is a subsidiary part of life, or is nonexistent. The second follows the Aristotelian tradition where leisure is the main aspect of life and work is merely a means to that end. In the third, leisure and work are integrated as parts of the whole, each having the ability to enrich the other. Three patterns are evident: priority of work, priority of leisure, and equal priority of work and leisure.

The work-leisure relationship possibilities of Godbey and Parker are not really "definitions" in the usual sense of the term since neither work nor leisure is explicitly defined. However, implicit in the three relationships are that both work and leisure are highly subjective experiences, and that they therefore can only be defined by a given individual.

The importance of their discussion for leisure counselors is that they emphasize leisure and work as the two major aspects of life. Again, this is a perspective held by many laypersons. It should be noted, however, that there is one major limitation to all work-related definitions of leisure; namely, that they are difficult to apply to persons who don't work.

Psychological Definitions

Psychological definitions of leisure center on the subjective nature of the human experience. Most often these types of leisure definitions reflect an attitude adopted by the individual. For example, de Grazia (1962) wrote of leisure being something uniquely personal, a state of the mind and/or the quality of a feeling about an activity. Similarly, Pieper (1963) wrote of leisure as a mental and spiritual attitude separable from any or all external factors. Besag (1975) took a simplistic approach and described leisure as "something with intrinsic value" which is pursued for joy.

The most comprehensive psychological defintion of leisure is that provided by Neulinger (1974):

> Leisure is a state of mind; it is a way of being, of being at peace with oneself and what one is doing. (p. xv)

Neulinger (1974) goes on to clarify this definition by emphasizing personal freedom in leisure:

> Leisure has one and only one essential criterion, and that is the condition of perceived freedom. Any activity carried out freely, without constraint or compulsion, may be considered to be leisure. To *leisure* implies being engaged in an activity as a free agent and of one's own choice. (pp. 15-16)

While this definition catches the essential characteristics of leisure, it does not allow for variations in the quality of the leisure experience. Two additional points must be made. One is the understanding that *perceived freedom* is not an all-or-nothing affair; there is always the question of degree, and, in this sense, leisure implies an ideal state at the extreme end of the continuum of *perceived freedom*.

The second point is that there are at least two additional dimensions that may be useful in distinguishing among different types of leisure. These dimensions are the *motivation* for the activity (*intrinsic to extrinsic*) and the goal of the activity (*instrumental to final*).

Leisure counselors should find favor with Neulinger's leisure definition since it incorporates the often espoused counseling goals of personal choice and personal happiness. However, it should be remembered that apparently very few laypersons accept this type of leisure definition (Neulinger, 1967).

Models of Leisure

Models of leisure is a phrase used here to encompass leisure definitions (or explanations) that incorporate multiple dynamics and factors simultaneously. In general, these models attempt to interrelate many of the "singular" definitions of leisure described previously.

Some models of leisure attempt to identify the essential characteristics of the leisure experience. Typical of this type is a list provided by Sutherland (1957). He offered six characteristics of enjoyable leisure: integrity of purpose, objectivity, opportunity to change goals, egalitarian social relationships, skills use and development, and (personal) growth.

> There's so much spectating going on that a lot of us never get around to living. Life is always walking up to us and saying, "Come on in, the living's fine." And what do we do? Back off and take its picture.
>
> *Russell Baker*

A similar but more comprehensive list is presented by Kaplan (1960), who lists the following "essential elements" of leisure: an anthithesis to work, an expectation of pleasure, minimal social obligation, perceived freedom, value appropriateness, a range of personal importance, and playfulness. These offerings are indeed comprehensive, yet that comprehensiveness may also be too unwieldly for practical purposes in leisure counseling.

Other models of leisure attempt to present a "fluid" perspective on leisure. For example, Murphy (1975) presented a "dynamic conceptualization of leisure" which is diagrammed as a series of concentric rings on a continuum base of "constraint/obligation" to "spontaneity/self-determination". The rings from the inside to outside are "concepts of time," "concepts of work," and "concepts of leisure." The point of this model is that time, work and leisure are integrally related. This integration is conceptualized by allowing the individual to determine the respective sizes of the rings and therefore their interrelationships.

Shepard (1974) presented a model of leisure which incorporates socio-psychological dynamics, in particular self esteem and alienation. In this model, individuals who fail to obtain self esteem in their work will attempt to obtain it through their leisure. Similarly, individuals who feel alienation in their work will attempt to alleviate these feelings through their leisure. This model is highly flexible in that these situations may be either short-term (e.g. on a particular day) or continuing. This reasoning is similar to Wilensky's (1960) "compensatory" definition of leisure, but focuses on psychological dynamics as opposed to activities.

The last model of leisure to be discussed here is that presented by Kelly (1972). He suggested that the two basic aspects of leisure are *discretion* and *work-relation*. Discretion may be dichotomized into *chosen* and *determined*. Work-relation may be dichotomized into *independent* and *dependent*. A four cell model results.

Kelly (1972) identified these four cells as *pure* leisure (chosen-independent); *coordinated* leisure (determined-independent); *complementary* leisure (chosen-dependent): and *non* leisure (work?) (determined-dependent). The flexibility of this model is in terms of the respective cell sizes for any given individual. The cell size determiners may be either the amount of time invested, or the number (frequency) of activities appropriate for each cell, or both, for a given individual.

Models of leisure would seem beneficial for leisure counselors in that they emphasize both the large numbers of factors affecting leisure and the complex interrelationships among them. However, these same characteristics would also seem to limit their usefulness with laypersons. That is, their comprehensive natures may be more than the average layperson wants to contend with in the leisure counseling process.

These then are examples of the major ways in which leisure has been defined or conceived. They range from the very simple to the relatively complex. All have both advantages and disadvantages for both leisure counselors and laypersons. Most importantly, the diversity of these examples points out the difficulty in defining leisure and the need for leisure counselors to consider *very carefully* any leisure definition they may choose to adopt.

A Goal-based Leisure Definition

It would be easy to suggest that leisure counselors should simply adopt whatever definition they may like. Moreover, a legitimate case could probably be built for this suggestion in light of the widely varying philosophies and orientations among leisure counselors. However, such flexibility might make interpretations of at least parts of the remainder of this book difficult. Accordingly, it is appropriate to provide a leisure definition which at least provides a general direction for this book.

The definition to be used here is: Leisure is any activity an individual knowingly (i.e. consciously) chooses to define as leisure. There are several aspects of this definition which merit attention. The first is that this definition represents a goal or an end point, something to be achieved. It is a psychological perspective that people should adopt if leisure counseling has been effective. As a goal it implies direction. However, it does not imply a starting place nor does it necessarily imply the most appropriate means to the goal. These decisions are left to the leisure counselor and the client.

A key word in this definition is *knowingly*. In order for a person to define an activity as leisure the person must be consciously aware that a decision to do so has been, or is being, made. This rules out leisure "by default" or habit. Such activities may eventually be defined as leisure by the individual, but conscious consideration of them must first occur. This conscious awareness is essential to the leisure counseling process. If it is not present, then leisure "counseling" would be nothing more than a haphazard sequence of events.

Inherent in this definition also is an emphasis on personal choice. Leisure *is* a subjective experience; no one can define exactly for another person what that person's leisure should be. Leisure counseling can, and should, help a person achieve a personal interpretation of leisure. It cannot, and should not, *give* the person an interpretation to use.

This definition also focuses on leisure as *activity;* leisure is *doing* something, even if that something is "doing nothing" in the colloquial sense. This facet of the definition is important for leisure counselors who are supposed to be human *behavior* specialists. Leisure behavior is a manifestation of a person's definition of leisure. To help a person clarify psychological perspectives on leisure without relating those perspectives to behaviors is to limit greatly the potential effectiveness of leisure counseling.

This definition also purposely ignores several factors which have been related to leisure by others. Most notably, there is no reference to work. Certainly the psychological aspects of work and leisure *may* be interrelated. However, just as certainly these sets of dynamics may be considered independently. The omission of the work referent allows the leisure counselor, and more importantly the client, the opportunity to decide whether the interrelationships are significant enough to be considered within a particular leisure counseling relationship. In essence, a definition of leisure without a work referent affords greater flexibility in leisure counseling.

Time is also not mentioned in the definition given. Time all too often becomes a criterion for the meaningfulness or importance of an activity. Obviously there are people who engage in activites for only very short periods of time, yet find those activities extremely meaningful and rewarding. Conversely, there are others who invest significant amounts of time in activities that hold little or no meaning for them. Using "time invested" as a criterion for leisure meaningfulness is therefore inappropriate for a great many people.

This definition is thus a synthesis derived from the other leisure definition examples cited. To be sure, it has its limitations. It certainly doesn't reflect the perspectives of leisure held by most laypersons. It also doesn't provide a specific prescription for how leisure counseling should be conducted. And it won't find great favor with leisure counseling researchers who have to operationalize it for their studies. However, in spite of these limitations, it does provide a goal for leisure counselors and clients. That in itself is sufficient justification for its careful consideration. As Laurence Peter says, "If you don't know where you're going, you'll probably wind up someplace else."

Dynamics of Leisure Activities

Adoption of a definition is a fundamental starting place in beginning to understand the nature of leisure. However, a definition is just a beginning because by necessity it must be general. Accordingly, other information must be used to enhance further the understanding of leisure.

For example, it is helpful to look at leisure activities in terms of their various (potential) dynamics. A convenient way to do this is to elaborate on some possible bipolar dimensions of leisure activities.

Individual vs. Group. One important dynamic of a leisure activity is how many people must be involved in it. At one end of the continuum are those activities which are basically singular in nature. Some examples of this type are certain craft activities, art (painting), jogging, and so on.

At the other end of the continuum are those activities which must have involvement by more than one person. The most common examples of this type are team sports (it's hard to play football by oneself). This underlying continuum (dynamic) is interpreted from the participant's perspective. Just because more than one person is participating in an activity at a given point in time doesn't make it a group activity. For example, it is not uncommon to see groups of people jogging together, but jogging is still an individual activity. Group leisure activities *necessitate* cooperation and interrelationships among participants; individual leisure activities don't.

Intellectual vs. Nonintellectual. The basic dynamic underlying this continuum is the relative amount of cognitive functioning necessary to conduct the activity. There is no way to exemplify the extremes of this continuum without "insulting" someone! Be that as it may, *in general,* an activity like chess might be considered toward the intellectual end whereas an activity like chopping wood might be considered toward the nonintellectual end. The key to interpreting this dynamic is determining whether a prospective leisure activity participant considers the activity to be intellectual, nonintellectual, or somewhere in between.

Competitive vs. Noncompetitive. This dynamic centers on the degree of competition involved in a particular activity. Sports and games are usually the types of activities considered to be competitive. On the other hand, many individual activities, such as sewing or needlepoint, are often considered to be noncompetitive.

However, again, caution should be exercised in making generalizations. Some individual activities can be highly competitive, such as painting something to be entered into an art contest. Conversely, some noncompetitive games for children have recently been introduced.

Active vs. Passive. The underlying dynamic for this continuum is psychological involvement (i.e. concentration). Active leisure activities in this regard are those which necessitate that the participant pay close attention. Reading and pottery-making are good examples.

> When I have nothing to do for an hour, and I don't want to do anything, I neither read nor watch television. I sit back in a chair and let my mind relax. I do what I call idling. It's as if the motorcar's running but you haven't got it in gear. You have to allow a certain amount of time in which you are doing nothing in order to have things occur to you, to let your mind think.
>
> *Mortimer J. Adler*

By contrast, passive leisure activities are those that necessitate much less attention. Being a spectator at a sporting event or listening to Muzak in an office building might be good examples. As with the other dynamics, it is difficult to make generalizations. Television watching, for example, might be active or passive depending of the individual's degree of "absorption" in what's being telecast.

Physical vs. Nonphysical. The obvious dynamic underlying this continuum is the amount of physical activity necessitated for participation in a particular leisure activity. Most sports would fall toward the physical end of this continuum.

Conversely, sedentary activities such as reading or meditation would generally fall toward the nonphysical end. It should be remembered, however, that some activities, such as camping, may be both physical and nonphysical depending on which time segment in the activity is considered.

> There's nothing to match curling up with a good book when there's a repair job to be done around the house.
>
> Joe Ryan

Short-term vs. Continuing. The schedule a person uses for various leisure activities is another important dynamic. Short-term activities may be interpreted as those engaged in for relatively restricted time periods and only infrequently. A yearly skiing trip vacation would be an example of this type.

On the other hand, continuing leisure activities are those engaged in on a regular and relatively frequent basis. Just about any leisure activity could be an example of this type as long as it is relatively "ongoing" for the person. One common example might be weekly attendance at civic club meetings.

> Success is being able to hire someone to mow the lawn while you play golf for exercise.
>
> Bits & Pieces

Vocation Congruent vs. Vocation Incongruent. This dynamic is derived from the compensatory leisure definition described earlier. However, the term vocation is broadly interpreted here to include any of a variety of life activities, including both work in the traditional sense and work in the nontraditional sense (e.g. non paid housekeeping).

Examples of these types of leisure activities may only be presented in reference to whatever the person defines as work. One such example might be that if a person's "work" is maintaining a household, then a vocationally congruent leisure activity might be doing volunteer work at a hospital and a vocationally incongruent leisure activity might be searching for buried objects with a metal detector.

Self oriented vs. Other oriented. Whether a leisure activity serves ultimately to benefit oneself and/or others is another dynamic which should be considered in understanding leisure. Implicit in this dynamic is the assumption that any leisure activity will benefit the participating person in some way. The question then becomes to what extent others will benefit.

At the self oriented end of the continuum are those activities which are highly personal in nature. Some examples might be meditation, optional educational experiences, or physical fitness exercises. Volunteer activities such as those at hospitals and other human service organizations best exemplify the other oriented end of the continuum.

> If people really liked to work, we'd still be plowing the land with sticks and transporting goods on our backs.
>
> *William Feathers*

Person centered vs. Product centered. This dynamic establishes a continuum focusing on the outcome or result of a leisure activity. If leisure activities are used to facilitate social interaction for the participant, they would fall toward the person centered end of the continuum. Parties and club activities are common examples of this type.

On the other hand, leisure activities which yield tangible products would fall at the other end of the continuum. Crafts and collecting activities are common examples of this type.

> I asked a friend who had just returned from a long walk in the woods what she had observed. "Nothing in particular," she replied. How was that possible, I asked myself. I, who cannot hear or see, find hundreds of things to interest me through mere touch. I feel the delicate symmetry of a leaf. I pass my hands lovingly about the rough shaggy bark of a pine. Occasionally, if I am very fortunate, I place my hand gently on a small tree and feel the happy quiver of a bird in full song.
>
> *Helen Keller*

High Risk vs. Low Risk. The amount of perceived personal danger is the basis of this dynamic continuum. This perceived danger might be psychological, physical, or both. Leisure activities such as mountain climbing and gambling would generally be considered high risk activities. Conversely, walking or gardening would generally be considered as low risk activities.

The key word in this dynamic is obviously "perceived." What might seem dangerous to one individual may by "quite natural" to another. Literally millions of people invest in the stock market each year. However, many more people don't because it's "too risky."

Expensive vs. Inexpensive. This dynamic focuses on the financial aspects of leisure activities. Money matters are always personal and whether an activity is expensive or inexpensive is always a subjective decision. Accordingly, generalities about representative examples are at best made tentatively, except for the most blatant circumstances.

For example, collecting mint condition antique Rolls Royces would probably be expensive whereas walking would probably be inexpensive. However, if walking is your favorite leisure activity but you only want to do it on the French Riviera, chances are you're going to have an expensive leisure activity.

Essential vs. Optional. This dynamic is also derived from the perceived freedom aspect of leisure. It may seem to be a contradiction in terms to speak of "essential leisure." However, consider the situation where physicians tell patients with ulcers that they must do some things that will help them (i.e. the patients) relax. Leisure would therefore be considered essential.

> Statistics indicate that, as a result of overwork, modern executives are dropping like flies on the nation's golf courses.
>
> *Ira Wallach*

Another example might be the "sedentary" executive who feels it essential to exercise in order to maintain good health. Of course all other leisure activities (i.e. those not perceived as essential) would fall toward the optional end of the continuum.

The essence of this dynamic is that "personal choice" is a matter of degrees; it is not an absolute.

These twelve dynamics are some of the major ones applicable to leisure activities. Others are possible since almost any dynamic applicable to leisure activities can be considered in light of a bipolar continuum. Leisure dynamics are not discrete; they occur in degrees of applicability.

A second, more important point is that any leisure dynamic is valid only from the participant's perspective. No one, not a friend, nor a relative, nor even a leisure counselor can determine for a person how that person should view a particular leisure activity dynamic. Consequently, it is important for leisure counselors to strive to understand fully how their clients' view these leisure activity dynamics for any and all of their leisure activities.

Functions of Leisure

Consideration of the dynamics of leisure activities is one way leisure counselors and their clients can gain a better understanding of clients' leisure. A related and equally important way is consideration of the potential functions of leisure in people's lives. Discussion and evaluations of these potential functions enables people to understand how leisure does, and more importantly could, fit into the rest of their lives.

Witt and Bishop (1970) suggested that a synthesis of the literature and research on leisure would yield four major functions of leisure in people's lives. These include catharsis, relaxation, compensation and task generalization.

Catharsis is the psychological process of releasing pent-up emotions. Leisure activities are *cathartic* therefore when individuals engage in such activities for the purpose of purging themselves of certain emotions. Very often, but not always, cathartic leisure activities are physical in nature. Consequently, a physical "calm" usually accompanies the psychological "calm" if the leisure activity has achieved its cathartic goal.

Leisure in Perspective 43

> I used to watch people leaving a Marx Brothers film, their cheeks stained from tears of laughter. Then they would say, "Wasn't that silly?" If they had been equally churned up by a Garbo movie, they wouldn't say that. They'd think they had been purged—you know, catharsis. But with comedy, people do not trust their reactions. The trouble is people do not have the courage of their laughter.
>
> S. J. Perelman

Leisure activities engaged in for the purpose of catharsis are usually intended to purge so-called *negative* emotions. In fact, it is common to hear of people who "do something" to get rid of their anxieties, frustrations, angers, and so on. However, cathartic leisure activities may also serve to reduce "positive emotion overloads." Consider the person who "celebrates" a vocational promotion, salary increase, or other positive event by going out to dinner, inviting friends to a party, and so forth. Thus leisure activities as catharis help individuals maintain emotional equilibrium.

Catharsis

Closely related to, but not synonomous with, catharsis is the relaxation function of leisure. This of course is how people most often think of leisure; as a means of relaxing. There are two aspects of the relaxation function of leisure activities. The first is *restoration*. This means that the individual participates in a leisure activity in order to restore, regain, or regenerate energy—particularly mental energy.

The time to realx is when you don't have time for it.

Samuel Butler

Restoration relaxation leisure activity usually occurs after an individual has had intensive involvement in some activity that was psychologically and/or physically tiring.

Relaxation

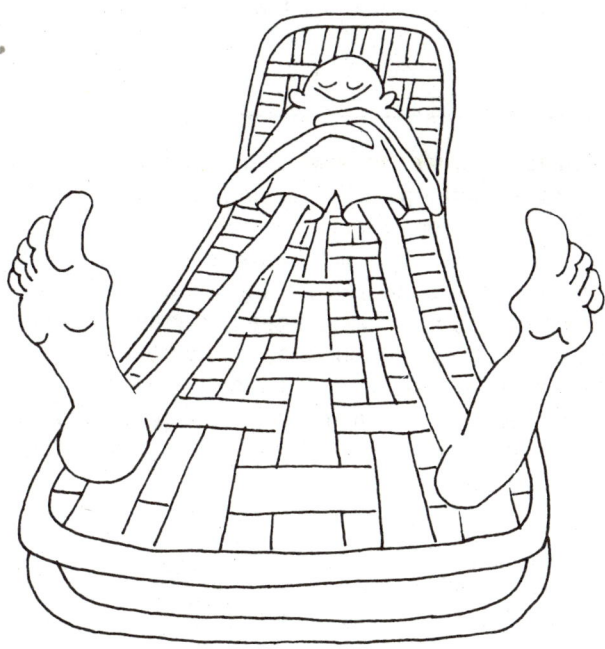

> To do nothing is in every man's power.
>
> *Samuel Johnson*

The second type is *diversion*. This means that the individual participates in a leisure acitivity in order to "escape" (i.e. be diverted) from some other activity. Diversion relaxation leisure activity usually occurs in the midst of another ongoing activity (e.g. work). This other activity may or may not be psychologically or physically fatiguing. However, it is almost always intense because of its ongoing nature.

Leisure activity as diversion in such situations offers change, but not necessarily an improvement, in psychological or physical functioning. As with catharsis, relaxation leisure activity helps an individual maintain psychological equilibrium. However, it may also help the individual maintain physical equilibrium.

> Not a shred of evidence exists in favor of the idea that life is serious.
>
> *Brendan Gill*

Leisure activity is *compensatory* when it helps an individual "make up" for something that is lacking or deficient in the individual's life. In this sense, leisure activity provides the mechanism for attaining goals whose achievement is either not possible or only partially successful through other activities. Thus when people are unable to meet a need or attain a goal on the job, with their families or friends, or in any other part of their lives, they may attempt to compensate for the void through their leisure activities. Leisure activities in this regard serve to help people have alternative methods of achieving goals, fulfilling needs, or actualizing desires.

Compensation

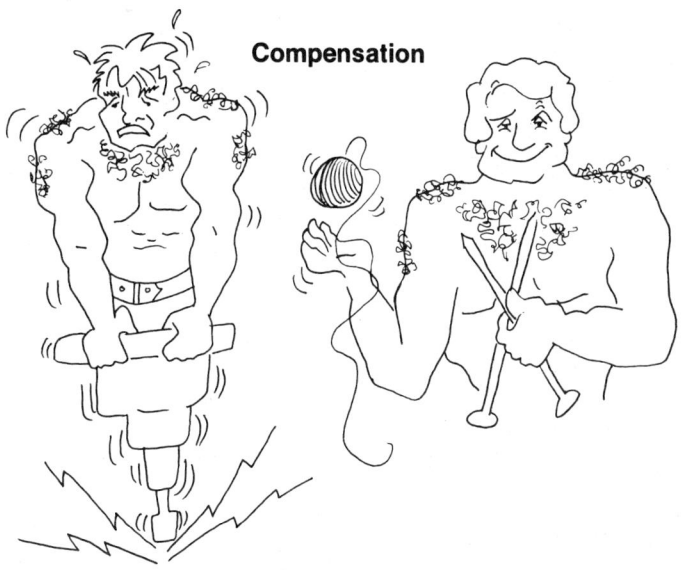

Task generalization may be defined as the tendency for a stimulus to which a particular response has been learned to evoke similar responses in various situations. A leisure activity can be this type of response. In general, leisure activity *task generalization* is the tendency to choose leisure activities that are similar to other life activities. Often leisure activities are task generalizations of work activities.

Task Generalization

Leisure in Perspective

However, leisure activities may also be task generalizations of other activities such as family or interpersonal activities, or life subsistence activities. Leisure activity task generalization is usually considered to be the opposite of leisure activity compensation. The former serves to continue (i.e. generalize) activities which help to achieve goals whereas the latter serves to establish alternative activities to achieve life goals.

These four major leisure activity functions provide a general framework for understanding how leisure activities might fit into other life functions. It would be erroneous, however, to assume that these leisure activity functions are independent of each other, or of other life functions activities.

Obviously, any leisure activity might fulfill several functions simultaneously. Thus while consideration of these functions can help leisure counseling clients better understand their leisure activities, caution should be exercised so that clients do not get the impression that a leisure activity can only fulfill one function.

Some Potential Benefits of Leisure

A legitimate question for leisure counseling clients to ask is, "What can my leisure activities do for me?" If leisure counselors don't have a ready answer, they probably also won't have their clients very long.

> Happiness is liking what you do as well as doing what you like.
>
> Laurence J. Peter

Happiness

The major benefit that people may achieve through leisure activities is some degree of *happiness*. This is what most people expect from their leisure and the professional literature overwhelmingly supports this expectation. The difficulty is that happiness is different things to different people. Charles Schulz made a lot of people smile when Snoopy issued the now famous phrase, "Happiness is a warm puppy." However, there are a lot of people who don't like puppies, warm or otherwise. In addition, each individual has many different types of happiness. There is happiness in the home, happiness at work, happiness in families, and so on. These differentiations necessitate the qualifier *some degree* of happiness.

Certainly no individual or set of leisure activities can provide a person *total* happiness, just as no one job can, nor one friendship can, nor any other limited and independent situation can. It is probably more appropriate therefore to say that leisure activities should lead to leisure happiness. If that happiness generalizes to other situations, fine; but to expect it to do so necessarily is unrealistic.

Creative Expression

A second commonly espoused potential benefit of leisure activity is the opportunity for *creative expression*. And in fact most leisure activities do allow for personal creativity. But again, creativity must be subjectively defined; what's creative for one person is not necessarily creative for another. In addition, some leisure activities (representing millions of participants) are almost totally devoid of creative potential. Ever heard of "creative" television watching? The point is that the opportunity for creativity through leisure activities is but one type of potential benefit; not a universal given.

Creativeness often consists of merely turning up what is already there. Did you know that right and left shoes were thought up only a little more than a century ago?

Bernice Fitz-Gibbon

Self Development

Self development (also called self improvement) is another commonly inferred potential benefit of participation in leisure activities. This is indeed a difficult one to nail down. No one seems to know for sure what self development is. However, a lot of people suggest that leisure activities facilitate it. In general (because that's the only way it can be discussed), it appears that self development is a highly subjective process whereby an individual becomes a "better" person.

A better person is usually interpreted to mean an individual who has greater self awareness, more effective interpersonal skills, greater sensitivity, more insight, and so on. Greater and more are relative to wherever the person began, which is difficult if not impossible to specify. In any event, leisure activities seem to offer strong potential for personal (psychological) development or improvement.

Self Fulfillment

A closely related potential benefit is the opportunity for self fulfillment through participation in leisure activities. This term is as nebulous as the previous one. The general implication is that people need to gain fulfillment from activities in their lives. Leisure activities have the potential to provide at least part of that fulfillment.

It should be noted that self development and self fulfillment are not necessarily interdependent. People who perceive themselves as fulfilled will not perceive themselves as needing self development. Consequently their leisure would be "maintenance" oriented as opposed to self improvement oriented.

Self Definition

A fifth potential benefit is the opportunity for self definition through leisure activity participation. This situation is analogous to the more common one where people find identity through their work. Some people achieve a sense of identity, either personal or social, through their leisure activities. This is particularly true of people who have unique leisure activities or who are exceptionally competent in their leisure activities.

> Every man has three characters—that which he exhibits, that which he is, and that which he thinks he has.
>
> *Alphonse Karr*

There are also those who have neither unique leisure activities nor exceptional skills, but who invest significant amounts of time in their leisure activities. This leisure activity "devotion" permits yet another type of self identification. Thus leisure activities have strong potential benefits for self identification through any of several different approaches.

Recognition

Recognition is a potential leisure activity benefit which is related to, but also distinguishable from, self identification. Self identification is a very personal phenomenon. Recognition, on the other hand, is a social phenomenon. A person who achieves self definition through leisure activity participation may or may not also receive (social) recognition for that participation. Conversely, a person who receives recognition for leisure activity particiption may or may not perceive self identification through that participation. Many people seek recognition through their leisure activities because they find it difficult or impossible to obtain it through their other (e.g. work) activities. To the extent that people want (social) recognition, leisure activities often provide an excellent means for them to obtain it.

Autonomy

Another potential benefit of participation in leisure activities is the opportunity for personal autonomy (i.e. psychological independence). People often use their leisure activities to "get away from it all." Through their leisure activities they are able to achieve a degree of solitude, a sense of strong personal control over situations, and a perception of behavioral freedom that may not be present in other aspects of their lives. Autonomy in this sense does not necessarily mean being physically alone. Rather, it means having a feeling of independence, regardless of the number of people involved in the activity.

Need Gratification

The potential for need gratification through leisure activity participation is perhaps the benefit most often alluded to in the professional literature (cf. Neulinger, 1974; Tinsley, Barrett, and Kass, 1978). People have a large variety of psychological needs which have to be fulfilled in order for them to be well adjusted and self satisfied. Some of these have been identified in terms of potential benefits previously discussed (e.g. autonomy, self development, recognition, etc.).

Others would include such things as needs for change, affliation, order, nurturance, achievement and deference. Obviously, different people experience these needs to differing degrees. However, the important point is that leisure activities potentially can be selected so as to fulfill any type of need or combination of needs.

Experimentation

The last benefit to be discussed here, and the one with perhaps the greatest potential from a counseling perspective, is the opportunity for life experimentation through leisure activity participation. Leisure activity participation is subjective and therefore highly flexible in terms of psychological and other types of involvements.

Leisure activities may be entered into safely; there need not be any serious repercussions if participation is continued or if it is terminated. This safety provides a psychological environment well suited to personal experimentation. People often can "be someone" or do some things in their leisure activities that are not possible in other spheres of their lives. Certainly there is a degree of psychological risk involved in any human behavior. However, this risk seems to be minimal within the context of leisure activity participation.

Some Potential Liabilities of Leisure

While leisure activities are generally accepted as positive human endeavors, particularly because of the potential benefits, they are not without their liabilities (Kaplan, 1960, 1975). The most significant ones for leisure counselors to be concerned about are those which are psychological in nature.

One of the most common psychological liabilities is for people to "get hooked on" a leisure activity to the extent that all other life activities are distant seconds in (perceived) importance. Glasser (1976) called this phenomenon "positive addiction," the tendency to become a "pleasure junkie." In essence, people in this situation are so involved in a leisure activity that everything else is either ignored or minimally attended to. Obviously this circumstance reflects an unhealthy psychological situation. Leisure activities are supposed to be enjoyed—but enjoyed within a reasonable perspective.

Another potential psychological leisure activity liability is an increase in, or creation of, stress. This idea may seem contradictory to some of the basic conceptualizations of leisure; most people engage in leisure activities with the expectation of reducing stress. However, if leisure activities are allowed to become disproportionately important in people's lives, stress may result. A common example would be stress resulting from drastically altered interpersonal relationships because of leisure activity time consumption.

For a more subtle example, consider individuals whose bodies are no longer able to achieve the physical fitness or coordination of some time when they were younger. If they continue to strive to achieve "what once was," a significant amount of stress may result. The most unfortunate part of this example is that it tends to be cyclical. When these same individuals begin to be aware of their stress, they often turn to their leisure activity to reduce it, and so the cycle begins again.

A variety of other factors are also potential leisure activity liabilities. For example, economic considerations are involved in the vast majority of leisure activities, either through monies directly invested in the activities or through monies not earned because of time spent in the activities. Familial liabilities may also occur if leisure activity participation disrupts family relationships and patterns. Finally, to a much less common extent, political, social, educational, and even legal liabilities may be inherent in participation in some types of leisure activities.

Having started with some potential definitions of leisure, this discussion has since wound its way through an additional definition of leisure and some leisure activity dynamics, functions, benefits, and liabilities. This path has been followed for two reasons. First, it has provided some information for leisure counselors to use in the actual practice of leisure counseling. Second, it has again emphasized the complexity of leisure and the corresponding need for leisure counselors to be well prepared for their professional endeavors. Together, these factors set the stage for a more thorough discussion of the leisure counseling process.

Discussion Questions

1. For each of the statements below, identify which type of leisure definition is implied. What are the advantages and disadvantages of each of these definitions for use in the leisure counseling context?

    A. Leisure is those activities engaged in to compensate for needs not met through vocational activities.

    B. Leisure is the time left over after vocational and life sustaining activities have been completed.

    C. Leisure and vocational activities are unrelated; each type has personal merit independent of the other.

    D. Leisure is those activities which fulfill a person's non-vocational social needs (which may include a lack of social relationships).

    E. Leisure is a state of the mind; an attitude.

    F. Leisure is those activities which allow the person to continue to fulfill needs that are in part met through vocational activities.

    G. Leisure is those activities which are not vocational or life sustaining.

2. Construct a diagram reflecting Kelly's model of leisure. Can you identify one activity for each of the four cells from your own life?

3. Leisure was defined here as any activity the individual knowingly chooses to define as leisure. What are the implications for leisure counseling if the word *time* is substituted for the word *activity* in the definition?
4. Twelve leisure activity dynamics were described in this chapter. Can you name two others that might be appropriate? Can you give examples of leisure activities that would represent the poles of the continua?
5. Identify one of your favorite leisure activities. What are your personal benefits and liabilities from your participation in that activity?
6. Suppose that as a result of leisure counseling a person engages in a leisure activity that creates a liability for the person that wasn't present before leisure counseling. Has an ethical standard of the counseling profession been violated?

Study Activities

1. Ask any ten people to define (briefly) leisure. Which type of definition is most frequently given? Which is least frequently given?
2. Visit individually five people while they are engaged in a leisure activity. Ask them *why* they are doing the activity. What are the similarities and differences among the various responses you receive?
3. Arrange for informal interviews with the managers of three stores that sell leisure activity items (e.g. athletic stores, toy stores, crafts shops, etc.). Ask each manager if they do any "leisure counseling" and if so, how? Ask them also which are the most popular and least popular items they sell, and why? What are the similarities and differences among the responses you received?

Chapter III

Leisure Counseling

The counseling profession is a plethora of enigmas. Impressive, isn't it? What it means is that there are a great many things in the counseling profession which are not very well understood. This lack of understanding is in part attributable to the casual use, or misuse, of language in the profession.

> Where there is no guidance, a people falls; but in an abundance of counselors there is safety.
>
> *Proverbs 11:14*

The first sentence is an extreme example. Unfortunately, such extremity is not really necessary to emphasize the point. For example, terms such as "mental health" and "counseling" are frequently bantered about in professional circles, but in actuality there is very little agreement about what they mean.

It was mentioned in the discussion of leisure definitions in the preceding chapter that the assumption of mutual understanding of a term may lead to problems between leisure counselors and their clients. Similarly, the casual use of important terms can lead to misunderstandings among professionals.

> By virtue of being born to humanity, every human being has a right to the development and fulfillment of his potentialities as a human being.
>
> *Ashley Montagu*

As with leisure definitions, there generally are no right or wrong interpretations of some of the more complex terms used in leisure counseling. Rather, there are simply interpretations preferred by various professionals based on their personal perspectives. Understanding these preferences is essential to understanding the ideas advocated by those professionals.

Leisure Mental Health

The fundamental goal of the counseling profession is to provide services which enable people to achieve mental health. This is indeed a noble goal. Unfortunately, the term "mental health" probably defies adequate definition. For an exercise in futility, try looking up mental health in a dictionary. Most dictionaries don't even list the term. Among those that do, the "definitions" provided are so vague as to be functionally useless. Obviously it is not a term which is easily conceptualized.

In response to the obvious inadequacy of simplistic definitions of mental health, psychologists have provided rather complicated explanations of what the term is supposed to mean. For example, in 1973 the major portion of an entire issue of *The Counseling Psychologist* (volume 4, number 2) was devoted to "The Healthy Personality." The eminent psychologist Robert W. White presented an exposition on the healthy personality, which was then followed by reactions to White's paper by 16 other prominent psychologists.

Most of the reactors congratulated White on his significant effort and then took the opportunity to critize all or part of the points he made. In doing so they of course offered their own biases on the nature of the healthy personality. This is just one illustrative example that even among some of the finest minds in the psychological professions, there is little or no agreement about the nature of mental health.

It is interesting to note that the use of the term "mental health" is a relatively recent trend in the counseling and psychological professions. Historically, professionals wrote and spoke much more commonly of "mental illness." Things were seemingly easier then. Being mentally ill meant not being mentally healthy.... Counselors and psychologists concentrated on the various forms of mental illness since they were often easier to identify and characterize than was mental health. Consequently, not much concern was given to worrying about a definition of mental health. The trouble surfaced when a very logical question was raised. To "cure" a person of an illness means to return that person to "health." But what was the (mental) "health" the person was being returned to?

Substantial credence was given to the problems of using the concept(s) of mental illness as the focal points of the counseling and psychology professions by Thomas Szaz in his book, *The Myth of Mental Illness*. In it he elucidated the dangers for society inherent in using inadequate definitions of mental illness, and in doing so also pointed out the limitations in attempting to define mental health.

In most mental illnesses the capacity to relax is as much impaired as the integrity of a bone destroyed by fracture.

Abraham Meyerson

The conclusion that must be drawn, regardless of whether the attempt is made to define mental health directly, or to approach it as not being mentally ill, is that mental health means different things to different people. Its definition is thus a very personal phenomenon. More importantly, it is unlikely that mental health can be defined explicitly enough so that (at least theoretical) agreement may be achieved among all professionals.

A Conception of Mental Health

Because of problems in attempting to find a precise definition, a holistic approach to the definition of mental health seems most appropriate. The word holistic means that a variety of factors, and more importantly their interrelationships, must be considered. Mental health, as used here, will therefore mean simultaneous, effective emotional and behavioral adjustment in both personal and social contexts.

People who are mentally healthy perceive themselves to be so. This seems obvious, and again emphasizes the subjective nature of mental health. However, a personal perception of mental health is a necessary but not sufficient condition. The "mental institutions" of this country are filled with people who don't think they are doing things out of the ordinary, but they are deemed mentally ill by society. Consequently, the social context of mental health necessitates that either a significant number of other people or a number of significant people must also perceive an individual as mentally healthy.

A person's mental health must be reflected in both emotions and behaviors. Some people don't feel that they are mentally healthy yet they behave as if they were. Conversely, some people feel mentally healthy but behave as if they weren't. Either of these situations belies true mental health. For true mental health to exist, there must be congruence between emotions and behaviors and between personal and social contexts. However, not all the vagaries are now clarified. What is "effective adjustment" for one person may not be effective adjustment for another person or other people. Similarly, "social context" may mean different things to different people. In the final analysis, it is difficult to reduce the subjectivity in any consideration of mental health.

All happiness depends on a leisurely breakfast.

John Gunther

The broad concept of mental health may be more specifically applied to leisure. The focal point of importance here is (holistic) "leisure mental health." This focusing is accomplished by defining leisure mental health as emotional and behavioral leisure activity adjustment in both personal and social contexts. The clarifications and limitations of the general concept of mental health may be similarly applied to the concept of leisure mental health.

Goals of Leisure Counseling

The goals of leisure counseling may be derived directly from the definition of leisure mental health. The overall goal of leisure counseling is of course to bring about leisure mental health. This general goal is most easily interpreted in terms of more specific goals relating to each of the components of leisure mental health.

The Personal Context

Leisure counseling is most often concerned with helping an *individual* achieve effective and satisfying leisure. Two possible exceptions are familial or marital leisure counseling. However, even in these cases there is a heavy emphasis on finding leisure which is effective for each person involved. In addition, even though group leisure counseling techniques may be used, the emphasis is still on helping each individual in the group find the personally most effective leisure. Consequently, a primary goal of leisure counseling is personally effective leisure.

No man is a failure who is enjoying life.

William Feather

In keeping with the other perspectives espoused previously, the achievement of personally effective leisure must be evaluated from the client's perspective. That is, the client is the person who makes the determination of whether or not this goal has been achieved. Therefore, an essential condition for leisure mental health is that people must *feel* (or believe) that their leisure is effective.

The Social Context

One of the basic laws of physics is that for any action there is an equal and opposite reaction. While the situation for human actions is not as clearly defined, the underlying principle holds true. Individuals rarely exist in isolation. Accordingly, any activity by one person is usually accompanied by a response (reaction) from one or more other people. Leisure is no exception to this principle. When a person engages in a leisure activity, other people respond to that activity. This then constitutes the social context of leisure.

The (social context) reactions to a person's leisure activity quite obviously may range from very negative to very positive. Just as obviously, persons may have widely varying degrees of concern about what other people think of their leisure activities. However, it is likely that each person has one or more other people whose opinions are considered important.

It is these "significant other" people who are the primary social context for the person. These people are important because the individual deems them (and their opinions) to be important. These people therefore have the "power" to influence a person's leisure. Consequently, a second goal of leisure counseling is leisure effectiveness in (primary) social contexts.

Some clarification seems appropriate here. Leisure being effective in the social context does not necessarily mean that other people agree with a person's leisure, want to share in it, understand it, or anything like that. What it does mean is that these people realize that the leisure activity is important and meaningful for the person and are willing to accept it on that basis. In other words, leisure is effective in the social context when people willingly accept a person's leisure activity, regardless of their own opinions about the activity.

The Emotional Context

Most of the literature and research in the counseling profession is concerned with human emotions. The same is generally true for leisure counseling. Thus, positive emotions (feelings) about leisure is another important (perhaps the ultimate) goal of leisure counseling. People should, in the final analysis, feel good, happy, excited, enthused, contented, cheerful, fortunate and any of a variety of other positive feelings about their leisure activities. Further, if leisure counseling has been *truly* effective, they should also experience many of these same feelings about themselves even when they are not engaging in their leisure activities.

The Behavioral Conext

Human emotions are related to human behaviors. No one knows for sure whether emotions dictate behaviors, or vice versa, or even if such a causal interpretation is possible. But the integral association between behaviors and emotions is undeniable. Accordingly, another goal of leisure counseling is behavioral appropriateness. Consideration of this goal necessitates that leisure counselors help clients carefully explore and evaluate their leisure behaviors. More importantly, leisure counselors must help clients clearly understand the relationships between their emotions and their behaviors relative to their leisure activities.

The Linguistic Context

In the preceding discussions of the goals of leisure counseling, words like effective and appropriate have been used rather casually. However, they are important words to consider for several reasons. First, they are highly personal and subjective. Again, it is the client who ultimately defines effective and appropriate.

Second, although these words are technically meant to be interpreted as "absolutes," they are more commonly interpreted as varying in degree. That is, in a technical sense (e.g. grammatically) something is either effective or ineffective, or appropriate or inappropriate. However, counselors and clients commonly speak of things as being "more" or "less" effective, or more or less appropriate. This tendency has conceptual and practical advantages.

A goal of leisure counseling is the achievement of the *most* effective and *most* appropriate leisure activities. For example, at some point in the leisure counseling process, clients may conclude that they have found effective and appropriate leisure activities. If, however, the leisure counselor believes that the client may find even "more" appropriate leisure activities, the leisure counselor would probably want to explore further possibilities with the client.

The Totality Context

Finally, the last goal of leisure counseling is the simultaneous achievement of all the other goals. Another way of saying this is that leisure counseling is a process where several goals must always be kept in mind. This is not to suggest that achievement of the various leisure counseling goals may not be sequential.

Leisure Counseling

In fact, quite the opposite is usually true. However, full achievement of the leisure mental health goals necessitates that at some point in time all of the leisure counseling goals must have been (simultaneously) achieved.

Purposes of Leisure Counseling

The general purpose of leisure counseling is to facilitate client achievement of the goals of leisure counseling. The goals are the ends; leisure counseling is a means to those ends. As was the case in considering the major leisure counseling goals, the general purposes of leisure counseling may also be considered from several, more restricted, perspectives.

Satisfaction

One seemingly obvious, and commonly espoused, purpose of leisure counseling is to help people achieve leisure activity satisfaction. Leisure satisfaction could be (and probably is) a "goal." However, it is included here because satisfaction with leisure activities should be progressive throughout the leisure counseling process. This increase in satisfaction probably is erratic. For example, even if people stop doing their typical leisure activities for a while, they may be "more satisfied" simply because of the change. Likewise, people might become "more satisfied" with their leisure activities simply as a result of thinking about them in different ways.

Regardless of the reason, however, there are usually intermediate levels of leisure satisfaction during the process before "complete" leisure activity satisfaction is achieved. Thus leisure counseling should facilitate movement through various stages of leisure activity satisfaction.

Adjustment

A concept closely related to, but not synonymous with, leisure activity satisfaction is leisure activity adjustment. The vast majority of people have more than one leisure activity. Typically they are more satisfied with some of their leisure activities than they are with others. Leisure activity adjustment means having a combination of leisure activities where each is as satisfactory as possible for a person. As with satisfaction, leisure activity adjustment proceeds in erratic stages over the course of leisure counseling, often times for the same reasons. Leisure counseling therefore should also facilitate movement through these stages of adjustment.

Remediation

Another common purpose of leisure counseling is remediation. To remediate means to correct (remedy) faulty or bad situations, and leisure counseling is often solicited in this context. That is, people seek leisure counseling because they want to "correct" their faulty (dissatisfied, misadjusted, unhappy, ineffective, etc.) leisure activity situations.

Prevention

Developmental counseling is the name given to counseling activities intended to prevent future problems or difficulties. Since leisure counseling may be conducted from this perspective, it is appropriate to use the term developmental leisure counseling. The purpose of developmental leisure counseling is to enable people to avoid problems with their leisure activities in the future by "intervening" in the present.

This intervention usually includes helping people develop skills such as information seeking, decision-making, and self evaluation skills relative to leisure activities. Another way of stating this is that the purpose of developmental leisure counseling is to help people become leisure self sufficient.

The goals and purposes of leisure counseling help to clarify the nature of leisure but they do not specifically define it. Rather, they provide a broad framework from which a large number of leisure counseling definitions are possible.

Leisure Counseling Defined

Definitions of leisure counseling are not nearly as numerous nor as varied as definitions of leisure. At first glance this would seem to be a desirable situation. It implies that there is probably consensus about leisure counseling and thus matters are greatly simplified. Unfortunately, such is not the case.

In fact, the lack of numerous and substantive definitions of leisure counseling seems to reflect a lack of professional effort and concern about definitions. Apparently, many people are content to practice "leisure counseling" with no need for a clear definition of what they are doing.

In fairness, it should be acknowledged that there are a considerable number of formidable problems which must be overcome in defining leisure counseling. For example, definitions of leisure counseling probably should, at least at a theoretical level, reflect a definition of leisure.

Given the numerous available definitions of leisure, the development of a leisure counseling definition which emcompasses all those definitions is of course difficult at best, and perhaps ultimately impossible. However, should difficulty be a legitimate criterion among professionals for avoiding the attempt? Further, is it unreasonable to expect that a definition of leisure counseling would *at least* reflect its author's preferred definition of leisure?

Problems with Definitions

Another problem in defining leisure counseling stems from the confusion surrounding the terms "leisure counseling," "avocational counseling," and "leisure education" (Neulinger, 1977, 1978). Some authors are "purists" and consistently use one term, even though some of the processes they describe might more appropriately be considered in the context of another term (cf. Brightbill and Mobley, 1977; Overs, Taylor, and Adkins, 1977).

Other authors seem to use the terms almost interchangeably and apparently vary the usage only in terms of the potential readership. Unfortunately, still others spend so much time trying to differentiate between these terms that the important points of their discussions are lost in the process! Squabbling among professionals about the fine distinctions among these terms is unnecessary. What is important is the usefulness of the definition provided. Innumerable professional counselors have noted the appropriateness of the use of "educational" techniques in the "counseling" process, and vice versa. A sound leisure counseling definition should allow for both possibilities.

Neulinger (1977) indentifies a third and very subtle factor influencing the nature of leisure counseling in general, and its definition in particular. This factor is the problem of "territoriality" among professionals. That is, even though leisure counseling is a relatively new professional endeavor, it has already become closely linked with three different professional areas: education, counseling, and psychotherapy (Neulinger, 1977).

Each of these three areas has "laid claim" to leisure counseling. Consequently, definitions provided by professionals in these areas often reflect their respective professional biases. Thus leisure counseling is sometimes an "educational" process, sometimes a "counseling" process, and sometimes a "therapeutic" process. An obvious question comes to mind: who cares? The basic idea is that leisure counseling (or education or therapy) is supposed to help people obtain leisure mental health. If that goal is achieved, will the clients ever really care what the process was called?

Wise sayings often fall on barren ground; but a kind word is never thrown away.

Sir Arthur Helps

A final and much more pragmatic problem in attempting to define leisure counseling is the extremely large number of activities that might legitimately be used in leisure counseling. A good definition not only reflects a theoretical base but also gives behavioral implications. In other words, a good leisure definition should provide indicators for what leisure counselors are supposed to do.

Unfortunately, a definition which would cover all such implications for leisure counseling would be so long as to be incomprehensible, and therefore useless in any practical sense. Consequently, definitions of leisure counseling have by necessity had to focus on only a few broad categories of counseling behaviors. It is unlikely that this limitation will ever be resolved since the numbers of appropriate leisure counseling activities continue to rise.

Some Previous Definitions

In spite of these problems, some professionals have presented definitions of leisure counseling. These definitions show wide variation in terms of both complexity and quality. It should become obvious, however, that the relationship between complexity and quality is not linear. The most complex leisure counseling definitions are not necessarily the best ones.

Overs (sometimes in conjunction with associates) favors the use of the term "avocational counseling" instead of leisure counseling. He has presented several definitions of avocational counseling. These include:

> Avocational counseling is concerned with the choice of one or more avocations and with adjustment to the avocation. (Overs, 1975, p. 36)
>
> Avocational (leisure) counseling assists individuals with leisure attitudinal and/or behavioral problems with choosing and effectively participating in an avocation. (Overs, 1977, p. 85)
>
> Avocational counseling, sometimes called recreational counseling or counseling for leisure activities, helps individuals with their choice of, and adjustment to, avocational activities. (Overs, Taylor, and Adkins, 1977, p. 1)

Overs' definitions are obviously derived from a work-related definition of leisure. Implicit also is a focus on activities, as opposed to time or intrinsic value definitions of leisure. The major limitation of Overs' definitions is that they provide few implications for leisure counselor behaviors, save those associated with client decision-making. Perhaps the major contribution of Over's definitions is that they emphasize the difficulty in simplistically defining leisure counseling.

O'Morrow (1970) provided a definition reflecting more complexity as well as a much different perspective. He defined "recreation counseling" as:

> ... a technique in the rehabilitation process whereby a professional person uses all the information gathered about a person prior to release or discharge to further explore interests and attitudes with respect to leisure, recreation and social relationships to enable him to identify, locate and use resources in the community and thereby become an active community participant. (p. 14)

O'Morrow's definition is based on a therapeutic perspective of leisure counseling. It is significant in that it emphasizes the social context of leisure. It also emphasizes information collection and processing as leisure counselor behaviors. No particular leisure definition is implicit in O'Morrow's definition, with the possible exception of vague reference to activity. A subtle, yet unique, aspect of this definition is that it incorporates leisure (recreation) counseling as a "technique" to be used in the context of another type (i.e. rehabilitation) of counseling.

A leisure counseling definition closely resembling other definitions frequently found in the professional counseling literature was presented by McDowell (1976). He defined leisure counseling as:

> ... a helping process which facilitates interpretive, affective and/or behavioral changes in others toward the attainment of their leisure well-being. (p. 9)

This definition is notable in its effort at comprehensiveness. That is, the cognitive, affective, and behavioral aspects of human functioning are alluded to. However, this definition does not imply a particular definition of leisure nor does it imply (even in general terms) particular leisure counselor behaviors. While this definition does not provide much specific direction, McDowell (1977b) has provided an elaboration of it which is more useful to leisure counselors. In brief, he suggested that there are four basic leisure counseling orientations. These include: *I. Leisure-Related Behavioral Problems,* in which the primary counseling focus is on therapeutic facilitation, *II. Leisure Lifestyle Awareness,* in which the primary counseling focus is on education and prevention, *Leisure Resource Guidance,* in which the primary counseling focus is on leisure activity exploration, and *IV. Leisure Skills Development,* in which the primary counseling focus is on developing integrative, normalizing leisure-related skills. When these orientations are combined with his definition, a much more comprehensive view of leisure counseling is apparent. However, the two specific limitations cited for his definition still apply.

A succinct yet comprehensive and descriptive leisure counseling definition has been presented by Gunn (1977). She defines it as:

> ... a process utilizing verbal facilitation techniques to promote and increase self-awareness; awareness of leisure attitudes, values, and feelings; and the development of decision-making and problem-solving skills related to leisure participation with self, others, and environmental factors. (p.22)

Her definition implies an activity based leisure definition, though this linkage is vague. More importantly, inherent in her definition are both goals of leisure counseling and some (general categories of) selected leisure counselor behaviors. This definition is a good example of condensing complex and comprehensive ideas into an easily interpretable statement.

> It is all right to hold a coversation but you should let go of it now and then.
>
> Richard Armour

Shank and Kennedy (1976), in their review of the literature on leisure counseling, present a statement of conclusion which is in effect a definition. They state that:

> Leisure counseling involves a careful examination of a person's background, beliefs, values, and attitudes and becomes a developmental education process as well as a remedial counseling service. (p. 259)

This "definition" has many of the shortcomings of the others presented previously; most notably no implied definition of leisure and no behavioral implications. However, it is unique in that it incorporates both "educational" and "counseling" aspects and both developmental and remedial perspectives for leisure counseling. These latter two are particularly important because they are only very rarely even implied in other definitions.

The more complicated leisure counseling definitions are exemplified in one provided by Hayes (1977). He stated that:

A professional person *with* specialized knowledge of:
* Leisure and recreation
* developmental, cognitive, and affective domains of individual growth and development
* individual and group facilitation techniques

helps the individual (the client) THROUGH
* establishment of a framework for communication
* facilitation of individual decisions and action through:
  * discussions
  * personal encounter
  * activity involvement
  * observation in activities and discussions
  * identification of community leisure resources
  * follow-up assistance through transitional phase and into the community

TO ACQUIRE
* personal values and attitudes
* individual goals and objectives
* self-confidence and self-esteem
* skills, knowledge, competencies
* successful experiences (p. 77-78)

Just about covers the waterfront, doesn't it? Unfortunately, it's a bit unwieldy to be of much practical value. However, it is significant in that it enumerates the potential scope of leisure counseling as well as its many potential activities.

The preceding definitions provide considerable food for thought. They emphasize the divergent nature of leisure counseling by exemplifying the many potential perspectives on it. Most importantly, they reemphasize the need to be aware of the preferred perspective being used by any individual professional. This of course leads to the current situation; namely, what definition will be used here?

One More for the List

As with definitions of leisure, a synthesis of (hopefully) the best of other definitions seems most appropriate.

Accordingly, the perspective to be used here is that:

> Leisure counseling is a process which uses verbal and nonverbal techniques to assist individuals to increase their affective, behavioral, and cognitive leisure awareness and to develop effective leisure activity selection and evaluation skills, thereby facilitating movement toward leisure mental health.

This definition has been carefully constructed to incorporate several important points. First and foremost, it holds leisure mental health as the consummate leisure counseling goal. In so doing, it necessitates consideration of the various facets of leisure mental health that were discussed earlier. Second, it reflects the activity based leisure definition offered earlier. Third, it allows for the use of both verbal and nonverbal (e.g. assessment) techniques in the leisure counseling process. Fourth, it emphasizes three types of human awareness and allows for both self awareness and awareness of others.

Fifth, it intentionally omits specific mention of either remedial or developmental counseling perspectivies and therefore potentially allows for its applicability to either approach. Sixth, it implies that both "educational" and "counseling" activities are appropriate within the leisure counseling context.

Seventh, it implies that the development of personal decision-making and problem-solving skills are important tasks in leisure counseling. Eighth, it emphasizes the importance of values and value based decisions in leisure counseling. Ninth, this definition exemplifies the multifaceted nature of leisure counseling.

The tenth and final point about this definition which merits attention is that the definition does not identify, necessitate, or even advocate any one particular counseling orientation. This intentional omission was derived from the fact that there is no substantive research nor any sound rationale to suggest that leisure counseling *should* be tied to a particular counseling orientation.

Indeed, it may even be that leisure counseling, at least at this stage of its development, *can't* be restricted to a single counseling orientation.

Leisure Counseling and Counseling Orientations

Literally hundreds of books describing various counseling orientations (theories) and their respective biases, idiosyncrasies, and applications have been written. It would therefore be ridiculous to attempt to provide even moderately comprehensive descriptions of them here. What can be discussed, however, are some of the more important concepts in the major counseling orientations as they apply specifically to the leisure counseling context.

> Generally the theories we believe we call facts, and the facts we disbelieve we call theories.
>
> Felix Cohen

Client-Centered Approaches

The client-centered (or "Rogerian" or "nondirective") counseling orientation seems to be the most popular among leisure counselors, as it seems to be among professionals in general. Popular is used not only to include its connotation of being liked, but also to include frequency of both use and advocacy.

If the professional literature is an accurate indicator, leisure counselors rely on client-centered counseling concepts and techniques much more than any other type. This popularity is not undeserved; client-centered counseling offers much that is useful for the leisure counseling process.

Self actualization is a key construct in the client-centered counseling orientation. In general, self actualization is a state where an individual has maximized all of the individual's strengths, abilities, and functioning capacities in ways that serve to maintain and enhance the individual. In other words, self actualization represents the highest, most effective psychological state a person can achieve. It is therefore the ultimate goal of not only the counseling process but of human development as well.

A self actualized person obviously would have achieved leisure mental health since the two would seem to be conceptually integrally related. It follows that leisure counseling, as a process that seeks to help people achieve leisure mental health, therefore has the potential to help people achieve at least a part of self actualization.

The relationship between self actualization and leisure may also be viewed from a somewhat more pragmatic perspective. Self actualization implies an inner contentment or peace. The complexities of a modern society make it unlikely that anyone can achieve inner contentment in all situations. What may be possible is inner contentment (self actualization?) in *some* situations. Leisure activities might just be those situations. Leisure counseling may therefore help people find situations where they can get at least a "taste" of self actualization.

A second key construct in the client-centered counseling orientation is that behavior is a function of perceptions. The ways that people behave are determined by the ways they look at the world around them. A significant portion of leisure counseling is devoted to helping people examine and evaluate the ways that they look at themselves and their leisure activities.

While this clarification process need not necessarily result in (leisure activity) behavior changes, at least it helps people understand the determiners of their behaviors. This understanding should in turn lead to greater self acceptance, and contentment, or the need to change (leisure activity) behaviors in the hope of achieving self acceptance and contentment.

> The ancient sage who concocted the maxim, "Know thyself" might have added, "Don't tell anyone!"
>
> *H. F. Heinrichs*

A third, and related, basic premise of the client-centered counseling orientation is that the clients are the ones who make the changes. Leisure counseling is provided for clients and they therefore have the ultimate reponsibility for the results of the process.

The most significant contribution of the client-centered counseling orientation to the leisure counseling process is the specification of counselor characteristics essential to an effective counseling relationship. These characteristics are empathy, genuineness, congruence, and warmth. In general, counselors who exhibit high levels of these characteristics are more favorably received by clients than those who exhibit low levels.

While people may have any of a number of expectations, one thing is certain—they at least expect the counselor to be receptive to their situations and to show humanitarian concern for them. The exhibition of these four characteristics is perhaps the best way for counselors to communicate their caring to their clients.

While the client-centered counseling orientation is very popular among leisure counselors and provides some useful constructs and techniques for leisure counseling, it is not without its limitations. Its primary shortcoming is its relatively slow pace. Since the major approach is to enable clients to find self insights and subsequent behavior changes, the pace of a client-centered counseling process is to a large extent contingent upon clients' abilities to proceed. These abilities are often slow to develop, particularly in early stages of the counseling processes.

A related limitation of the client-centered counseling orientation is its lack of reliance on other counseling tools such as assessment instruments, experiential activities, and other potential sources of information and assistance. The use of such counseling aids is inimical to the client-centered counseling orientation since information is provided by, or derived from, someone or something other than the client. However, such counseling tools are designed to expedite the (leisure) counseling process. Thus from a pragmatic viewpoint their use seems more justified and appropriate than strict adherence to the orientation.

Psychoanalytic Approaches

The psychoanalytic (or Freudian) counseling orientation, in direct contrast to the client-centered counseling orientation, is rarely viewed as one with much significant import in the leisure counseling context. The major reasons for this lack of interest and support among leisure counselors include the slowness of the psychoanalytic counseling process, its emphasis on sexuality as a primary determinant of human behavior, and its reliance on constructs that are almost impossible to define operationally. Thus the psychoanalytic counseling orientation suffers from the same lack of popularity among leisure counselors as it does among other types of counselors.

The psychoanalytic counseling orientation should not, however, be cast aside too quickly. While strict adherence to a psychoanalytic counseling orientation is probably impossible within the leisure counseling context, some aspects of it are potentially valuable. For example, it is another counseling orientation which strongly emphasizes the counselor-client relationship.

Another aspect of the psychoanalytic counseling orientation with potential implications for leisure counselors is the emphasis on interpreting the personal history of the client. Since current leisure activities are often simply a continuation of previous patterns (i.e. habits), explorations of how these patterns began may enable clients to gain significant insights into their current leisure activities. Thus leisure counselors might quite justifiably "borrow" the techniques of personal history interpretation from the psychoanalytic counseling orientations.

There's nothing wrong with a person's sex life that the right psychoanalyst can't exaggerate.

Laurence J. Peter

Finally, the psychoanalytic counseling orientation has provided the term "ego." The term ego has never been defined satisfactorily for scientific standards. That has not, however, hindered its colloquial usage. It is not at all uncommon to hear people speak of being "ego involved" or "ego defensive," or doing things that are "good for their egos."

Since clients will often use "ego" (related) phrases, leisure counselors are well-advised to examine their own (colloquial) interpretations of the term since it may well be that leisure counselors and their clients can use the term to mutual advantage during the leisure counseling process.

Jungian Approaches

The analytic psychology (or Jungian) counseling orientation is closely related to the psychoanalytic counseling orientation and therefore has many of the same liabilities and potential benefits for leisure counseling. This orientation does, however, emphasize one additional aspect which may be beneficial in the leisure counseling context. This aspect is the process of repression.

Whereas the psychoanalytic orientation holds that repressed thoughts are primarily sexual in nature, the analytic psychology orientation holds that any of a variety of thoughts (ideas, beliefs, feelings, etc.) may be repressed. Since in this orientation both conscious and unconscious thought processes trigger behaviors, it is reasonable to assume (in the context of the orientation) that at least some leisure activities are the result of "unconscious" motivations.

A common example would be the expression of (unconscious) hostility through participation in a vigorous, physical leisure activity. Such a situation is not necessarily bad. However, the analytic psychology counseling orientation suggests that people will be better adjusted (mentally healthy?) when they are aware of the causes of their behaviors. Awareness of the causes of behavior is seen as "freeing" people, regardless of whether behaviors change when awareness is achieved.

Gestalt Approaches

The Gestalt counseling approach (usually associated with Perls) has gained particular popularity among leisure counselors as more and more authors contribute potential techniques and activities to leisure counseling. This growing popularity is attributable to several factors.

First, it is yet another counseling orientation which places a heavy emphasis on the establishment of an effective interpersonal relationship between the counselor and client. Second, the Gestalt counseling orientation focuses almost exclusively on the present: what's past is history, cannot be changed, and therefore need not be worried about. The primary goal of this orientation is to bring about self awareness and understanding, especially as it relates to the present situation.

The Gestalt counseling orientation also uses "activities" estensively as part of the counseling process. These "activities" tend to make the counseling process more interesting for clients since they often feel they are "doing something immediately productive."

Many Gestalt counseling activities also are "fun." Client enjoy them and counselors feel good because their clients enjoy them. However, many of those activities are extremely powerful in terms of their psychological impacts on people.

Accordingly, it seems necessary to caution that the adaption of Gestalt counseling orientation activities and techniques to the leisure counseling process should only be done by professionals who have had extensive training and experience in the orientation.

Transactional Analysis Approaches

The transactional analysis (TA) counseling orientation (usually associated with Berne) is another one growing in popularity among professional counselors in general, leisure counselors in particular, and among laypersons as well. This popularity is primarily attributable to the "simplicity" of the major TA constructs.

The idea of the Parent, Adult, or Child within each person as controllers of various types of behaviors is a clever way of looking at human behavior. Since leisure activity (play?) is usually associated with children, leisure counselors using TA techniques attempt to help a person "let the child out" through leisure activities. It does, however, seem to be a very limited way of looking at leisure activities. Is there not also appropriate Parent or Adult play (leisure activity)?

The TA counseling orientation, like the Gestalt counseling orientation, also makes extensive use of activities and exercises. However, TA activities tend to be less intense than those for the Gestalt counseling orientation and therefore have less potential for being injurious. Even so, TA techniques are best used by those with comprehensive training and experience in its processes and potentials.

Behavioral Approaches

The behavioral counseling orientation is one which has been used very little in the leisure counseling context. This lack of utilization is not due to any inherent limitation in the behavioral counseling orientation. Rather, it is most likely due to the ways leisure counseling is conceived. In general, behavioral counseling uses reinforcement techniques to alter the frequencies of occurrence of rather specific human behaviors. Behavioral counseling may be used to decrease the frequency of a behavior deemed undesirable, or to increase the frequency of a behavior deemed desirable. The important question is *who* determines what is desirable or undesirable? Most professionals believe that leisure activities should be a matter of personal preference.

As an aside, it may be noted that leisure activities are often involved in behavioral counseling in a way different from the focus of this discussion. Leisure activity participation is often used as a "reinforcer" in behavioral counseling processes, particuarly with children. Thus the provision or withholding of leisure activity participation is used as a reinforcement technique for modifying other behaviors. "If you don't eat all of your supper, you won't be allowed to watch TV later. . . ."

Reality Therapy Approaches

The reality therapy (a la Glasser) counseling orientation is also one which has not been used extensively in the leisure counseling context. Two of the basic tenets of this approach are that people must accept the responsibilities of their behaviors and that a responsible person behaves in ways that provide for feelings of self worth as well as the worth of others.

Humankind cannot bear very much of reality.

T. S. Eliot

The reality therapy counseling orientaion therefore places heavy emphasis on how one person's behaviors might affect other people, particularly those who are important in the person's life.

The definition of leisure mental health presented earlier emphasizes the social context nature of leisure activity participation. Consequently, the primary potential benefit of the use of the reality therapy counseling orientation in the leisure counseling context is the opportunity to allow clients to examine how their leisure activities impact others. Consideration of the possible repercussions of leisure activity participation in turn influences whether the activity will be selected as appropriate.

RET Approaches

The rational emotive therapy (RET) counseling orientation is a cognitive approach which emphasizes logic, reasoning, and rational thought. It has not been extensively espoused as appropriate for the leisure counseling context. This is probably because it is often (inappropriately) viewed as a harsh and extremely confrontive approach. In addition, it does not emphasize the warm, caring counselor-client relationship so prominent in other counseling orientations.

A fundamental procedure in RET is the examination of the relationships among belief systems and behaviors. In general, RET holds that people "feel as they think." The RET goal is therefore to help people think in ways that are rational, logical, and reasonable, with the assumption that their feelings will subsequently be properly aligned. Since behaviors are related to the ways people feel, "inappropriate" behaviors will be changed when thinking is changed.

The interesting point about the general denouncement of RET among professional counselors is that the basic theoretical constructs of RET are in fact quite commonly used in other types of counseling. That is, many counseling orientations advocate careful examination of the relationships among beliefs, feelings and behaviors as well as the "rationality" of those relationships. The unique aspect of RET is the "directness" in which the examination is undertaken.

The distinction between criticizing RET techniques and possibly criticizing RET principles is an important one for counselors to consider. Often times in leisure counseling it is appropriate to evaluate whether a client's choice of a leisure activity "makes sense" (i.e. is rational) for the client, particularly when the choice seems to reflect other people's values more than the client's own.

Other aspects of the choice, such as cost, degree of anticipated proficiency, or time investment may also be "irrational" for the client. When this type of evaluation is made, a basic RET principle is being used.

Trait-and-Factor Approaches

The trait-and-factor counseling orientation, which was used very extensively in vocational counseling, is rarely espoused among professional counselors today. However, it is apparently alive and well among leisure counselors for its techniques are common in the leisure counseling literature. The essence of the trait-and-factor counseling orientation is achievement of a proper "match" between a person and an activity. This is accomplished by gathering as much information as possible about both the individual and various potential activities and then deciding the best person-activity pairing from among the possibilities.

If the shoe fits, you're not allowing for growth.

Robert N. Coons

This orientation necessitates that leisure counselors know a lot about a variety of leisure activities. As the world of work became more and more complex, it became increasingly difficult for counselors to keep abreast of current information about the many potential jobs and this orientation became an unsuitable approach to vocational counseling. However, even though there are a considerable number of potential leisure activities, there are still far less of them than there are jobs. It appears therefore that trait-and-factor counseling is still a viable approach in the leisure counseling context.

The trait-and-factor counseling orientation also necessitates that leisure counselors gain as much information as possible about their clients. This information gaining process is usually expedited through the use of various assessment instruments. These instruments are used to obtain information about client characterstics (traits and factors) such as leisure interests, values, and attitudes as well as about other personality characteristics. The resulting pattern of client characteristics is then "matched" to leisure activities known (or at least assumed) to be appropriate for the particular pattern.

The major advantage of the trait-and-factor counseling orientation for leisure counseling purposes is the emphasis on the use of assessment instruments. The use of such instruments greatly expedites the leisure counseling process. In addition, it has the potential to allow for (almost) simultaneous consideration of diverse types of information, thus allowing for more informed decision-making.

Unfortunately, the major advantage is also potentially the major disadvantage. The available leisure related assessment instruments are limited both in number and in quality (a point which will be discussed at greater length in a subsequent chapter).

Values Clarification Approaches

There is a one collection of activities which does not constitute a "counseling orientation" but which is worthy of note here because of its widespread use in the leisure counseling context. These are values clarification activities. They do not constitute a counseling orientation for several reasons.

> Man's judgments of value follow directly his wishes for happiness.
>
> *Sigmund Freud*

First, the emphasis is on a single human characteristic; namely, values. Second, they are intended to facilitate *awareness,* not change. Third, values clarification is theoretically supposed to be devoid of evaluation of the values considered, either by the clients or by anyone else.

Values clarification activities are helpful in the leisure counseling process because most, if not all, human decisions are based (in part) on values. Leisure activities selections, and the decision-making processes leading to those selections, will be expedited and facilitated if clients have accurate understandings (awarenesses) of their own values. In this regard values clarification activities serve a purpose somewhat similar to that of assessment instruments. In addition, values clarification activities are often "fun" for clients and therefore help to stimulate and maintain interest in the leisure counseling process.

Eclecticism

It is highly unlikely that any one counseling orientation can be singularly adapted and be totally effective. Some are too lengthy and time consuming. Others lack wide range applicability for clients at various stages of the life span. It seems appropriate, therefore, to adopt an orientation which is flexible enough to incorporate the best parts of each of these orientations while simultaneously ignoring or deemphasizing their limitations. Fortunately, the eclectic counseling orientation is one that provides such flexibility.

> When a man comes to me for advice, I find out the kind of advice he wants, and I give it to him.
>
> *Henry Wheeler Shaw*

The eclectic counseling orientation (usually attributable to Thorne) is based on the idea that people differ not only among themselves but also in their own lives over time. The goal of eclectic counseling therefore is to select a counseling technique which is appropriate for a particualr individual at a particular point in that person's life. Thus the counseling techniques used by an eclectic counselor may vary from person to person and also for a given person at different points in the counseling process.

It is important to emphasize that the eclectic counseling orientation is intended to be a deliberate, methodical approach even though a wide variety of techniques may be used. In order for a leisure counselor to use the eclectic approach effectively, it is necessary for the counselor to select each counseling technique on the basis of a sound rationale.

A counselor who simply uses a variety of counseling techniques with no apparent rhyme or reason is *not* following the eclectic counseling orientation. Unfortunately, there are far too many counselors who use techniques simply because they are interesting, or fun, or bring about a strong client reaction, and then call what they are doing eclectic counseling. Counseling eclecticism is not an excuse for a haphazard approach.

Discussion Questions

1. What are the major factors affecting mental health in our society today? How do these factors relate specifically to leisure mental health?
2. What can leisure counselors do to help their clients understand the goals of the leisure counseling process?
3. Do leisure counselors *really* have to adopt a particular leisure counseling definition in order to be effective?
4. Select any counseling orientation not discussed in this chapter. What are its advantages and limitations for use in the leisure counseling context?
5. What is your "personal" theory of counseling? What are its strengths and weaknesses?

Study Activities

1. Locate any three definitions of "counseling." Evaluate each of these definitions in terms of the criteria applied to leisure counseling in this chapter.
2. Ask any five practicing counselors to write down how they would define leisure counseling. Evaluate each of these definitions in terms of the criteria used in this chapter.
3. Find a counselor who uses a counseling orientation other than the one you prefer. Ask that person for the reason that person doesn't like the counseling orientation you prefer.
4. Ask any five people what behaviors they would expect from a leisure counselor if they were to participate in leisure counseling. Relate their responses to various counseling orientations.

Chapter IV

A Leisure Counseling Model

The counseling process may be likened to an abstract painting. At one extreme, there are those who look at it and believe they understand exactly what it is supposed to be. At the other extreme there are those who look at it and walk away in bewilderment, wondering how anyone can claim to understand it. Most people, however, fall somewhere between the extremes. Similarly, people look at the counseling process and comprehend small portions here and there, but don't really see how it all fits together. From a professional perspective, each of these lay perspectives is erroneous to some extent. No one *fully* understands the counseling process, but no one should be *completely baffled* by it. And no one should believe that counseling is simply a collection of "bits and pieces" that don't fit together.

Abstract Art: A product of the untalented, sold by the unprincipled to the utterly bewildered.

Al Capp

In order to help alleviate such situations and to clarify perspectives on the counseling process, the counseling profession has developed numerous models. These models are intended to demonstrate what the counseling process is and, sometimes, how it should be conducted.

While there are some models which attempt to explain the counseling process in general, most are developed to explain specific types of counseling. The professional literature is in fact replete with models for such things as family counseling, vocational counseling, gerontological counseling, premarital counseling, and so on. Unfortunately, however, leisure counseling models are conspicuously few in number in the literature.

Existing Leisure Counseling Models

The most commonly cited model in the leisure counseling literature is the Milwaukee Leisure Counseling Model. In fact, this model is presented under the same title in three different publications (Magulski, Faull and Rutkowski, 1977; Mirenda and Wilson, 1975; Wilson, Mirenda and Rutkowski, 1975). Yet while this model has enjoyed a relative degree of popularity, its utilitarian value for theorists or practitioners is at best suspect—at least in terms of what is provided in these publications.

> Modern art is what happens when painters stop looking at girls and persuade themselves they have a better idea.
>
> *John Ciardi*

For example, Mirenda and Wilson (1975) state that, "The key component in this model is the skill, expertise, and warmth of the counselor" (p.44). No further elaboration on this *key* component is provided. The model does describe the use of a leisure interest inventory and an avocational (leisure) activities file as part of the leisure counseling process. However, again, specific application guidelines are not provided. Several activities, including computerization of the interest inventory, telephone follow ups, and client feedback solicitation, are also described.

Overs (1970) and his associates (Overs, Taylor, and Adkins, 1977) have provided another leisure counseling model. This model is in essence an adaptation and synthesis of vocational counseling models (Overs, Taylor, and Adkins, 1977). There are three major components within the model: action (i.e. client or counselor activities), client choice points, and methods and instruments.

> Any work of art that can be understood is the product of journalism.
>
> *Tristan Tzara*

Although not explicitly stated as such, this model obviously follows (primarily) a <u>trait-and-factor counseling approach.</u> Heavy emphasis is given to the assessment of client characteristics and interests and to the provision of information about various avocational (leisure) activities. The model also suggests possible counseling techniques (e.g. assessments) which are particularly suitable for the model. Finally, a tentative sequence for the leisure counseling process is described and discussed.

> It is only an auctioneer who can equally and impartially admire all schools of art.
>
> *Oscar Wilde*

Hayes (1977) has presented a "leisure education and recreation counseling" model which is grounded in the "therapeutic recreation" perspective of leisure counseling. The model outlines eight major stages from program entry through counseling to termination. These stages are described only in general terms in the model and are in fact a reflection of Hayes' definition of leisure counseling (which was presented in Chapter III).

The discussion of the model suggests that it will be implemented most effectively if it is considered as part of the broader concept of life style counseling. The discussion also provides some general guidelines for how the model may be adapted to specific settings and for the role of a counselor who attempts to use it.

A somewhat more comprehensive model has recently been presented by Edwards and Bloland (1980). Although the article describing the model is coauthored, it is in fact a description of the model used by the senior author (cf. Edwards, 1980) and therefore will be addressed as such. Edwards' model is intended as (basically) a nontherapeutic leisure counseling approach. Her model contains four major components: an initial (plus additional as needed) interview(s), assessment, analysis, and referral.

The assessments recommended focus primarily on interests. The analysis portion includes information collection, evaluation of client interests, leisure activity selection and suggestions for pursuing potential leisure activities. The referral portion centers on implementing the results of the anaylsis phase.

The Edward's model is significant to the extent that it is presented for use as a counseling activity in and of itself. In other words, it does not present leisure counseling as a part of, or adjunct to, another (more comprehensive?) type of counseling. Thus it serves to accentuate the potential of leisure counseling as a functional specialty and provides some guidelines for how such specialization may be achieved.

McDowell (1977) has provided what is perhaps the most effective and comprehensive leisure counseling model in the professional literature to date. This model is grounded in McDowell's four leisure counseling orientations (which were described in Chapter III) and therefore contains several components. Each component is a slight modification of a basic approach, with the modification depending on the particular purpose (i.e. orientation).

> The worst thing about new books is that they keep us from reading the old ones.
>
> *Joseph Joubert*

The discussions of each of the components of the model incorporate overviews of theoretical constructs, primary facilitating foci, existential client characteristics, and identifiable models and facilitation techniques. Various counseling goals as well as examples of counseling processes and typical client concerns are also discussed in this model.

The models presented here are representative examples. The major considerations and concerns for evaluating leisure counseling models have been demonstrated already. In brief, the major elements of an effective leisure counseling model include: (1) a theoretical basis, (2) goals and objectives, (3) possible techniques, (4) potential or necessary resources, and (5) substantive examples of major points. Only a few of the available leisure counseling models include all of these major elements.

> If you're too lazy to start anything, you may get a reputation for patience.
>
> *Laurence J. Peter*

A Professional Challenge

The existing leisure counseling models (with the possible exceptions of Edward's and McDowell's) will not adequately or effectively serve the counseling profession. The vast majority of them are simply not substantive enough to withstand critical scrutiny by professional counselors. Neulinger (1977) aptly summarized the situation and issued a challenge to the profession when he wrote:

> At the threshold of a new discipline of leisure counseling, it's tempting to develop quick programs, easy solutions, and "workable" techniques. A simple solution would be ideal, but the nature of the problem is not likely to make such a solution possible, nor even desirable. Leisure counseling calls for a multiplicity of approaches. (p.28)

Needed: New Leisure Counseling Models

There are several important reasons why new leisure counseling models must be developed if professional leisure counseling is to achieve its potential. The most obvious reason is that many current models, in general, aren't very good. However, there are other significant reasons as well.

> If everybody contemplates the infinite instead of fixing the drains, many of us will die of cholera.
>
> *John Rich*

Freedom of Choice

The outstanding and probably most notable characteristic of the counseling profession is its dedication to the principle of personal freedom in choice. This principle is usually applied to clients, yet it is also true for professional counselors. Literally any task a counselor may undertake may be approached in a variety of ways, and counselors are usually free to choose from among them.

Unfortunately, however, the limited number of available models greatly restricts the possible approach choices counselors have for leisure counseling. Consequently, the development of new leisure counseling models should allow counselors to have personal choice flexibility similar to that for other types of counseling activities.

Professionalism

The simplicity of most existing leisure counseling models has a subtle effect which is another justification for the development of new models. That effect is that many of the models give the impression that just about anyone can do leisure *counseling*. In other words, even though many of the models give "lip service" to the need for effective counseling skills, their descriptions really don't justify how and why such skills are important for implementation of the models.

To use just one obvious example, the advocation of the use of an assessment instrument without any guidelines for its use and interpretation is against all professional counseling standards. There is a need therefore for leisure counseling models which are clearly based on established counseling standards and which necessitate that they be used only by qualified counselors.

Counseling vs. Education

A related justification for new models is derived from the fact that many so-called leisure counseling models are in reality leisure *education* models. Leisure education models focus primarily on information processing (i.e. provision and interpretation of information about leisure). Leisure counseling models include information processing but focus primarily on affect and behavior processing.

Certainly leisure education is important. However, there are significant differences between educational skills and counseling skills. Consequently, for counselors to use an *educational* model for a *counseling* purpose is inappropriate, and a disservice to clients. Therefore, if the educational models are removed from consideration among the existing leisure "counseling" models, the number of models suitable for counseling purposes is reduced even further.

Specialization

A final justification of the need for new leisure counseling models evolves from the belief that models are a direct reflection of the level of development of a counseling speciality. The development of an effective model necessitates careful synthesis of a variety of types of information such as theory, research, and practice.

> The purpose of learning is growth, and our minds, unlike our bodies, can continue growing as we continue to live.
>
> *Mortimer J. Adler*

Historically, such information relative to leisure counseling has been relatively limited. However, substantive and significant leisure counseling information is beginning to accumulate. As more information becomes available, new leisure counseling models should be developed to reflect current information. Accordingly, there is a need for new models because they serve, in part, to establish the credibility of leisure counseling as a professional speciality.

In summary then, new leisure counseling models are needed because of both the limited qualities of most existing models and their importances to the provision of effective leisure counseling services. The following leisure counseling model has been developed as one response to this need.

> Communication is something so simple and difficult that we can never put in in simple words.
>
> *T. S. Matthews*

The Triangulation Leisure Counseling Model

The model to be described here is intended to be appropriate and applicable specifically for leisure counseling purposes. Toward that end it is an outgrowth of much of the previous discussion. It relies on assumptions such as that leisure is potentially a unique human endeavor, that leisure is a highly complex phenomenon, that a myriad of factors influence leisure selection and satisfaction, and that leisure counseling must be uniquely adapted to the specific purposes of both clients and counselors.

> I've never been able to understand why it is that just because I'm unintelligible nobody understands me.
>
> *Milton Mayer*

However, it is readily acknowledged that parts of the model are similar to other counseling models. This "overlap" occurs because leisure counseling is a particular type of counseling and there are some commonalities among most types of counseling.

There are three major components to the theoretical basis of the model: triangulation, humanism, and holism. As they will be used here, these three concepts are integrally related. However, they will be discussed separately for purposes of clarity.

Triangulation

The concept of *triangulation* is used most commonly in the social sciences in the context of program evaluation discussions. Basically, triangulation means that the most effective program evaluations are obtained when three related but separate pieces of information about the program's functioning are available for consideration.

> Everything has been thought of before, but the problem is to think of it again.
>
> *Johann W. von Goethe*

An analogy may be drawn for the evaluation (or understanding) of human functioning in general. Thus a counseling process has a strong potential for success when the client and counselor effectively understand three major components of the client's functioning. These three components will be discussed subsequently. The concept of triangulation then is the primary basis for the name of the Triangulation Leisure Counseling (TLC) model.

Humanism

Humanism is used here to imply a positive attitude about, and respect for, each person. It also implies that each and every person is capable in a variety of ways. These include being capable to learn and understand, to make decisions, to have any conceivable emotion, to act as is personally appropriate and to accept or reject whatever the person sees fit.

Humanism has some direct implications for the counseling process. It implies that both the client and counselor have respect for each other, personal rights, commitment to the improvement of the client's functioning, responsibility for the success of the counseling process, personal preferences and values (which may not agree), and the potential to fail to achieve desired counseling goals.

In general, the humanistic perspective implies that the client and counselor have distinct but interrelated and complementary roles in the leisure counseling process. For the TLC model in particular, humanism means that an effective, bilateral counselor-client relationship is essential to the effective use of the model.

It may be noted that no intent is being made to suggest that leisure counseling can be effective *only* if this humanistic perspective is adopted. To be sure, many of the so-called less, or non, humanistic counseling orientations have strong potential for success in the leisure counseling context. However, this *particular* model is grounded in the humanistic perspective and other orientations may have less success potential if they are used with this model.

Holism

The concept of *holism* means that all aspects of human functioning are considered simultaneously. Again, this generalization may be applied specifically to counseling.

There are three primary dimensions of human functioning commonly discussed in the counseling literature. These are the affective, behavioral, and cognitive dimensions. These three may also be considered as potential focal points of counseling, and in fact one or more of them is usually seen as underlying any particular counseling approach (orientation).

Some "purists" suggest that there is a simple, linear cause and effect relationship between human functioning and any particular set of dimensions. For example, some suggest that human functioning is strictly a result of a person's affective dimensions (such as emotions, attitudes, values, etc.). Others suggest that human functioning is strictly behavioral and governed solely by behavioral principles (such as operant or classical conditioning). Still others see human functioning as a result of the person's cognitive dimensions (such as cognition, rationality, etc.). From purist perspectives, one of three possibilities exists:

Affective dimensions = human functioning

or

Behavioral dimensions = human functioning

or

Cognitive dimensions = human functioning

The holistic perspective is antithical to purist perspectives. The holistic perspective holds that human functioning is the result of complex interrelationships and interactions among the affective, behavioral, and cognitive dimensions. The complexity of these interrelationships and interactions (probably) would nullify the potential for understanding or modifying human functioning from within the holistic perspective were it not for one very crucial assumption. That assumption is that human functioning is the result of the dominance of a given dimension for any particular individual at any given point in time for a given situation.

In other words, sometimes one dimension is the primary determinant of human functioning while the other dimensions are secondary or tertiary determinants. It is therefore common to use the term "preferred mode of functioning," which is simply a way of describing which dimension is dominant. The three possible explanations of human functioning may therefore be diagrammed as follows:

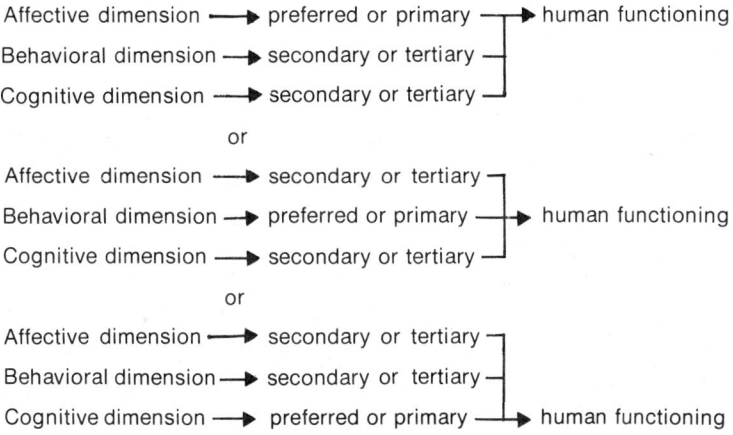

The tricky part of all this is, of course, figuring out which dimension is primary or preferred for any particular person. The situation is further compounded when it is recognized that the dominant dimension varies not only from person to person but also for the same person in different situations.

A Leisure Counseling Model

The holism concept is inherent in the TLC model in that all three dimensions are considered within the model. Since it is difficult, if not impossible, to determine with any degree of consistency a client's dominant dimension (preferred mode), the apparent alternative is to work with all three. This perspective not only "guarantees" that the client's preferred mode will be encountered, but also allows leisure counselors considerably more flexibility in their approaches and techniques.

The use of three different theoretical concepts (i.e. triangulation, humanism, and holism) as general basis for a single model may seem to be "a bit much." However, both leisure and leisure counseling are not easily explained in simple terms.

The Affective Dimensions

In society, and certainly within the counseling professions, there has been increasing emphases on emotions and feelings in recent years. Ranging from emotional displays by men in the popular media to affective (education or psychology) activities in the professions, a heightened awareness and acceptance of, and an increased willingness to express and share feelings, has become evident in the last two decades.

People's affective dimensions may have significant effects on many aspects of their views on leisure and their particular leisure activities. These dimensions may influence people's leisure in terms of levels of enjoyment, willingnesses to participate and/or experiment, potential benefits, levels of involvement, and interests. This is especially true for people whose preferred mode of functioning is centered in affective dimensions. Accordingly, careful exploration of the affective dimensions is essential to effective leisure counseling within the TLC model.

Feelings and Emotions

The major affective dimension is the individual's *feelings* about leisure activities. These feelings are unique and personal to each individual because they are a result of each person's particular past history of learning and socialization.

A person's feelings about leisure activities are often difficult to discern for two reasons. First, the expression of a feeling is often confused with the expression of an attitude. A statement clearly expressing a feeling has two essential components: a first person pronoun and a "feeling" word. The statements, "I don't like to rollerskate" or "Playing tennis makes me happy" are examples of expressions of feelings.

The second reason is that people simply don't make many "feeling" statements. Leisure counselors who are sensitive to clients' feelings statements will gain significant insight into clients' affect relative to their leisure activities. Such sensitivity is not easily achieved, however, and leisure counselors need to listen carefully to recognize clients' feelings statements.

Attitudes

An affective dimension closely akin to feelings is *attitudes*. An attitude statement is different from a feelings statement in that the former is usually much less personal. Attitude statements usually reflect a perspective that incorporates more than just a person's individual feelings. Typically, though not always, attitude statements are stated impersonally and refer to persons other than the speaker.

Some people feel with their heads and think with their hearts.

G. C. Lichtenberg

The statements, "Leisure helps you relax" or "Everyone should consider exercise daily" are examples of attitude statements. Leisure counselors should consider client attitude statements very carefully. They can be helpful in the counseling process if they in fact are an outgrowth of clients' feelings.

However, attitude statements are often merely a mimicing of what clients think other people think ought to be true. This type of attitude statement may be very misleading. When an attitude statement is encountered in the leisure counseling process, it should probably be countered with a request for a feelings statement to avoid confusion. Both types of affective dimensions then will be available for comparison.

Values

Values are another extremely important affective dimension. Values (i.e. basic belief systems) are usually viewed as the foundation of personal prioritizing. The understanding, exploration, and clarification of clients' values as they relate to leisure activities are therefore crucial aspects of leisure counseling under the TLC model.

There are three major ways clients can be helped to understand their values. The first is through counselor-client conversation, with particular emphasis on counselor feedback and clarification. The second is through the use of structured values clarification activities within the leisure counseling process. The third is through the use of a values assessment instrument. As a general rule, a major portion of the leisure counseling process is often devoted to achieving understanding of clients' values.

Expectations

Expectations are another part of the affective dimension. An important determination to be made in leisure counseling is what clients expect from their leisure. However, determination of what clients expect from leisure counseling is also of immense concern to leisure counselors. The clarification of each of these types of expectations is a necessary prerequisite to effective leisure counseling. Therefore, the exploration of expectations should be the major activity during the initial portion of the leisure counseling process. This clarification is best achieved through counselor-client verbal interaction, again with emphasis on counselor feedback.

Interests

Leisure *interests* are perhaps the most commonly acknowledged affective dimension. In fact, a considerable portion of the leisure counseling literature is devoted to the assessment, interpretation, and use of leisure interests. Similarly, almost every leisure counseling model gives heavy emphasis to interpretations of clients' leisure interests.

An "interest" in something implies a motivation to move toward, and at least some desire to engage in, the something. The understanding of clients' leisure interests helps leisure counselors and clients identify activities in which clients may want to participate. Since clients will often have at least some interest in a wide variety of leisure activities, the clarification of clients' leisure interests is usually accomplished through the use of leisure interest inventories.

Clients' leisure interests may of course also be evaluated through verbal interactions. However, given the potential number of activities to be considered, this process is likely to be inefficient, and therefore is not recommended. While consideration of interests is of major import in the leisure counseling process, caution should be exercised against placing too much emphasis on them. The *validity* of expressed (verbally or through an assessment instrument) interests in a leisure activity is primarily contingent upon clients' knowledge of the activity.

If the clients know little or nothing about an activity, or if clients respond from erroneous perceptions about the activity, then any expressions of interest (or lack of them) about activities will necessarily be invalid. A more complete discussion of leisure activity knowledge will be provided in the discussion of cognitive dimensions.

Personal Characteristics

Within the context of the TLC model, the affective dimensions conclude with consideration of clients' personal characteristics. Obviously the type of person that the client is has significance in the determination of the leisure activities which will be most effective and satisfying for the client. However, the history of human psychology is testimony to the fact that determining a person's nature is no easy trick. Nevertheless, some attempt should be made to determine at least clients' major (i.e. predominant) personality characteristics.

The assessment of clients' personality characteristics may be done either through verbal interactions or through the use of personality inventories. Unless leisure counselors have had extensive training and experience, the verbal interaction method is likely to produce less valid results, primarily due to counselor subjectivity and/or bias. On the other hand, the use of personality inventories also is by no means perfect. However, they do have a greater *potential* for reducing bias.

These then are the affective dimensions which should be considered in the context of the TLC model. In the TLC model sequence, the behavioral dimensions are next in line.

The Behavioral Dimensions

The study of human behavior is perhaps the most intriguing endeavor ever pursued. Literally everyone is a student of human behavior—from the person who makes casual mention of another person's speech pattern to professionals who devote their lives to trying to understand the causes of even the simplest human actions. This fascination is quite understandable. The colloquial phrase "Actions speak louder than words" epitomizes the basic rationale.

People often respond to other people more in terms of what they *do* than in terms of anything else about them; more than how they look, more than how they are perceived, and even more than what they say. Doesn't every "bigot" you know speak of at least one exception who doesn't fit the stereotype the bigot is biased against? That's because the exception's *behaviors* belie the stereotype.

The great end of life is not knowledge but action.

Thomas Henry Huxley

Within the TLC model particular attention is paid to both "real" and "potential" behaviors. Real behaviors are those that are characteristic of clients when they begin the counseling process. Potential behaviors are those that the clients would like to have be characteristic after completion of the counseling process.

It should not, however, be inferred that leisure counseling based on the TLC model must necessarily result in behavior change. Leisure counseling may be highly effective even when behaviors don't actually change. The most obvious example of this occurs when clients change feelings or attitudes about current (real) behaviors, but don't actually change behaviors.

In order to facilitate clarification and understanding of behaviors, four general categories of behaviors are considered within the TLC model. These include physical, personal, social, and environmental behaviors. The distinctions among these four general types are often "muddled" at best, but the distinctions are useful for discussion purposes.

Physical Behaviors

Physical behaviors are indicative of clients' general activity levels. Evaluations of clients' physical behaviors may be made both through observation and questioning. Leisure counselors may gain some impressions of clients' physical behaviors by observing clients' physical statuses.

Are the clients muscular? Are the clients heavy or slim? Do the clients appear to be in good physical condition? Such observations may be initially helpful, but they are typically only completely valid in extreme situations (e.g. excessive obesity). Accordingly, leisure counselors should validate initial impressions by asking questions. Such interaction will help both clients and counselors set the stage for decisions that will be made later on in the counseling process, particularly those relating to activity levels for clients' leisure activities.

Personal Behaviors

Personal behaviors are those which are, or could be, characteristic of clients when they are by themselves (i.e. alone). Unlike physical behaviors, personal behaviors can only be clarified through questioning. Leisure counselors may determine how clients behave when alone by asking questions such as: Do clients like to be sedentary or moving about when alone? If sedentary, do clients like to sit or recline? If moving about, do clients like slow or rapid movement? And do clients like to vary behaviors or be fairly consistent when alone? These questions are phrased as applicable to current (real) behaviors. With simple wording changes, they are also applicable to potential personal behaviors.

Think like a man of action, act like a man of thought.

Henri Bergson

Considerations of personal behaviors are important because of the multitude of leisure activities that are singular (i.e. participated in alone) in nature. Since most people have a variety of leisure activities, including some which are singular in nature, it is essential for clients to be aware of how they (would like to be able to) behave in their singular leisure activities.

Social Behaviors

Social behaviors are those which are, or could be, characteristic of clients when they are with other people (i.e. in social situations). Social behaviors are also best clarified through verbal interactions, though some social behaviors may be discerned through observations in group leisure counseling. Leisure counselors may gain understanding of clients' social behaviors by asking questions such as: Do clients initiate conversations in social situations? Do clients talk with groups of people or individuals? Do clients talk with many different people during social interactions? And do clients interact in various parts of a social interaction location or do they tend to stay put?

The importance of social behaviors in relation to leisure activities is essentially the same as it is for personal behaviors. In other words, many leisure activities are social in nature and typically people usually have (or want) some leisure activities of this type.

Environmental Behaviors

The last type of behaviors considered in the TLC model are what may be called environmental behaviors; that is, the ways clients interact with their various environments. In order to explore these types of behaviors, leisure counselors might ask questions such as: Do clients like to be indoors or outdoors? Do clients like "seasonal" activities? Do clients prefer any particular type of environmental setting (e.g. forests, beaches, clubs, etc.)? Do clients like to impact their environments (e.g. gardening) or enjoy them as is (e.g. bird-watching)? And do clients have preferences for time spent in various environments?

It is important to point out that leisure counselors should conduct questioning about various client behaviors in as tactful a manner as possible. This is because it is easy for clients to get the impression that the counselor is *advocating* a behavior change simply by virtue of the questioning process.

This is also possible in an analogous way for the affective dimensions. However, clients typically come into the leisure counseling relationship with the expectation that they will eventually be *doing* something different, which will in turn be accompanied or followed by affective changes. Accordingly, clients are typically more sensitive, at least intially, to potential behavior changes than they are to potential affective changes. Consequently it is important for leisure counselors to maintain a condition of objectivity during this portion of the leisure counseling process.

The affective and behavioral dimensions provide a comprehensive basis for understanding human functioning. However, this understanding is not yet complete until the cognitive dimensions are also considered. The next section completes the third corner of the triangle.

The Cognitive Dimensions

For those who reject the "you are what you do" philosophy, there's the alternative provided by Descartes, *"Cogito ergo sum"* (I think, therefore I am). Apparently, semblances of this philosophy are extremely popular in our society since many people place heavy emphases on cognitive abilities.

> It is only intellect that keeps me sane; perhaps this makes me overvalue intellect against feeling.
>
> *Bertrand Russell*

These emphases are sometimes subtle, as in the widespread popularity of crossword puzzles and word games in newspapers, and sometimes blatant, as in the extensive mental abilities assessments done in schools. Thus cognitive functioning is important throughout society, and of course extends into the leisure realm. Accordingly, the consideration of cognitive dimensions is a integral part of leisure counseling within the TLC model.

The TLC model addresses four general categories of cognitive dimensions: capabilities, accomplishments, thinking processes, and knowledge. As with the affective and behavioral dimensions, the cognitive dimensions are also complexly interrelated.

Capabilities

The assessment of clients' cognitive *capabilities* is important for both the leisure counseling process and the evaluation of potentially appropriate leisure activities. In the former regard, information about clients' cognitive capabilities enables leisure counselors to determine the most appropriate ways to interact with clients. For example, leisure counselors should adjust their vocabulary, use of media, and manners of speaking to be suitable for each of their respective types of clients.

Emotion has taught mankind to reason.

Marquis de Vauvenarques

Two types of cognitive capacities are considered within the TLC model. The first of these is *intelligence.* The word intelligence is used here (as it is in most places) to mean clients' general or global levels of mental abilities.

The second type is *aptitudes.* An aptitude is a specialized (or focused or limited) type of mental ability. For example, a person may have a musical, artistic, mechanical or mathematical aptitude which means the person tends to be able to do any of those kinds of activities relatively easily. Intelligence is thus sometimes construed as the "average" of a person's collective aptitudes.

Innumerable books and articles have been written on the assessment of human mental abilities and this attests to the difficulties inherent in the process. The controversies focus primarily on defining intelligence, how it should be measured, and how accurate the measurement can be. Within the leisure counseling context the first two controversies can be avoided by not requiring precise measurements of intelligence. In fact, leisure counselors should need only global or general estimates of clients' intelligence levels for the purposes cited earlier.

While leisure counselors could use intelligence tests to gain more precise estimates (which of course is in itself questionable), even that level of precision is not necessary. Leisure counselors can gain fairly good estimates through noting clients' vocabulary levels, asking about clients' academic records, inquiring as to clients' cognitive activities (e.g. do the clients read a lot?), and so forth.

The assessment of clients' aptitudes may be done in a manner closely akin to that for intelligence. In other words, asking clients what they are "good at" will usually provide sufficient information about aptitudes. Caution should be used, however, not to confuse an *interest* in an activity with an *aptitude* for the activity.

The ability to divorce one's mind from one's actions is a symptom of pyschological aberration.

Walter Goodman

Accomplishments

Closely related to the concept of cognitive capacity is the concept of cognitive *accomplishment*, which is usually referred to as *achievement*. The basic question to be answered is what are the clients' cognitive accomplishments (achievements) to date? Again, while formalized tests might be used to gain such information, that degree of precision is generally not necessary. Informal interactions will usually enable leisure counselors to be able to make fairly good assessments of clients' cognitive accomplishments; if not, the use of assessment instruments which measure achievement may be appropriate.

Thinking Processes

Thinking processes, the third cognitive dimension in the TLC model, may be divided into two types. The first is *information processing.* How do clients gain information (e.g. reading, conversation, media)? How do clients store information (memory, notes)? Do clients listen attentively? Do clients separate fact from opinion? The second type is *decision-making*. Do clients approach decisions emotionally or rationally? How comfortable are clients in making decisions? Who do clients let influence their decisions? And are clients capable of logical thinking? The assessment of thinking processes is primarily a result of observation and careful questioning by leisure counselors.

Logic is the art of going wrong with confidence.

Joseph Wood Krutch

While the assessment of thinking processes has some importance relative to potential leisure activities clients might select, its major import is for the leisure counseling process. Typically, large quantities of information and a considerable number of decisions will be encountered during the leisure counseling process. Consequently, it is in the best interests of both leisure counselors and clients to make effective assessments of clients' thinking processes as early as possible in the counseling process. This will enable leisure counselors to tailor counseling processes as much as possible to clients' thinking processes.

Knowledge

The fourth cognitive dimension in the TLC model is *knowledge*. The two most pertinent types of knowledge are knowledge of leisure activities and knowledge of resources for information about leisure activities. There are no tests or inventories currently available to assess clients' knowledge in either of these regards; the assessments must therefore be made on the basis of questioning.

Determination of clients' leisure activity knowledge is important since it has implications for the "flow" of the leisure counseling process. If clients have only limited knowledge of leisure activities, it is probably necessary to digress into a leisure education process. Clients cannot make effective decisions about leisure activities if they don't have accurate information about such activities.

The extent of this "educational" digression is contingent upon determination of clients' knowledge of leisure activity resources. If clients know of substantive resources, they may engage in "self instruction" about leisure activities. If clients don't know of such resources, leisure counselors should "educate" them about various possibilities.

Once clients are informed of resources, they can proceed with self instruction to obtain leisure activity knowledge. When clients have obtained sufficient leisure activity knowledge, the counseling process may be resumed.

Determination of clients' leisure activity knowledge is also an essential prerequisite to assessment of clients' leisure interests. If clients lack broad-based leisure activity knowledge, assessments of leisure interests will necessarily be invalid. This is because any identified preferences will be based on either (potentially) invalid perceptions of the natures of various leisure activities, or total lack of information about the activities.

Leadership is *action*, not position.

Donald H. McCannon

In either case clients are without an effective base from which to make preference decisions about specific activities. Of course it is neither necessary nor desirable for all clients to be informed fully about all possible leisure activities. However, typically clients will have relatively restricted informational bases and will need to engage in at least some leisure activity self education.

These four dimensions are the main ones considered in the cognitive dimensions section of the TLC model. Information about the cognitive dimensions is often (indirectly) obtained through discussion and consideration of the affective and behavioral dimensions. However, it should not be assumed that the cognitive dimensions are *entirely* covered in discussions of the other dimensions. They are important in their own right and should be treated accordingly.

Goals of the TLC Model

Presenting the goals at the end of the discussion of a model's elements rather than at the beginning is unusual, but in some ways it makes more sense. For one thing, it allows the reader's mind to think of possible goals without being biased by authors' "slanted" views. For another, it allows the reader to conceptualize the model in its entirety so that each of the components, and more importantly their interrelationships, can be related to each of the model's goals. Finally, it serves to allow for a variety of counseling orientations which might be suitable with the model.

> I am an idealist. I don't know where I'm going but I'm on my way.
>
> *Carl Sandburg*

In any event, the major goals for the TLC model are:

1. To enable leisure counselors and their clients to establish mutually acceptable, appropriate, and effective counseling relationships.

2. To enable leisure counseling clients to be aware of and understand their own affective, behavioral, and cognitive dimensions as they relate to current and potential leisure activities.

3. To help leisure counseling clients develop effective awareness and decision-making skills applicable to their current and potential leisure activities.

4. To help leisure counseling clients achieve the maximum possible satisfaction from their leisure activities.

> We are healthy only to the extent that our ideas are humane.
>
> *Kurt Vonnegut, Jr.*

The achievement of counseling goals is never a simple matter. The same is true of leisure counseling and leisure counseling goals. Further, the ways to achieve leisure counseling goals are myriad. Some initial suggestions on how these particular goals may be achieved, in part, have been incorporated into discussions of the various components of the model. Additional, more specific, suggestions will be provided in a later chapter (VI). However, since assessments are often an integral part of the leisure counseling process, some of the available leisure (counseling) assessment instruments will be discussed in the next chapter before additional suggestions are presented.

Discussion Questions

1. What other types of counseling "models" are you aware of? What would need to be changed in order to adapt them to the leisure counseling process?
2. What are the primary differences between counseling models and education models?
3. What is your preferred mode of functioning? What evidence do you have that it is your preferred mode?
4. Can all human functioning be defined in terms of three dimensions (i.e. affective, behavioral, and cognitive)? If not, what other dimensions should be considered?
5. How are the goals of the TLC model similar to and different from other counseling goals?

Study Activities

1. There are six affective dimensions, four behavioral dimensions, and four cognitive dimensions within the TLC model for a total of 96 different combinations. Identify what you consider to be the ten most important combinations for leisure counseling purposes and explain your selections.
2. Using the references provided in this chapter and any resources you may have available, develop a brief summary of any two of the models presented. Then compare and contrast those two models.
3. Develop a list of goals that you strive to achieve in any counseling process. Relate these goals to the ones for the TLC model.
4. Prepare a summary of the methods you would use to explain the principles and goals of the TLC model to a client. What procedure would you use to insure that the client understood your explanation?

Chapter V

Assessment in Leisure Counseling

Assessment (psychological and educational measurement and evaluation) is easily the most debated topic in the counseling profession. Other topics have been the "hot issues" at various times in the history of the profession, but no other topic has been discussed as often or as extensively as assessment, and none has as consistently defied professional resolution.

Yet in spite of all the rhetoric, assessment remains an important professional function and assessment instruments and techniques remain as primary counseling resources. It seems likely, therefore, that assessment will continue to play an important part in the counseling process. The same should be true for the role of assessment in leisure counseling.

There are several characteristics of assessment that make it particularly appealing to leisure counselors. Assessment expedites the leisure counseling process by allowing relatively large amounts of information (data) to be gathered in relatively short time periods. Assessment allows for inter and intra individual comparisons. Assessment processes reduce, to some extent, subjectivity in the counseling process.

And finally, assessment results introduce a degree of "concreteness" into the counseling process and often serve as the "reasons" for certain decisions or changes. Thus assessments often provide leisure counselors and their clients with information and perspectives that would be difficult, if not impossible, to obtain through other methods.

Assessment is not, however, without its limitations. There are the usual criticisms of invalidity, unreliability, and lack of representativeness about assessment instruments and techniques. There is also the potential danger of over reliance on assessment results to the point that the leisure counseling process becomes "depersonalized." Then, too, there is the tendency for clients to interpret assessment results as "facts" and to assume that these "facts" are irrefutable. Assessments may therefore also hinder the leisure counseling process.

Whether assessments will become a part of the leisure counseling process is a decision which must be made by each leisure counselor. It is true that most leisure counselors integrate assessments into their leisure counseling activities. However, there are many who do not.

There's a mighty big difference between good, sound reasons and reasons that sound good.

Burton Hollis

One of the aspects of being a *professional* leisure counselor is the ability to make *informed* decisions. An informed decision is one that uses the most current and accurate information available. The following material is an attempt to provide such information about leisure counseling assessment instruments.

Whenever possible, the information provided was from "primary" sources (e.g. test manuals, author correspondence, etc.). However, in some cases "secondary" sources (e.g. textbook summaries) had to be used because primary source information could not be obtained. It should also be noted that the assessment instruments covered are the ones most commonly cited as appropriate for leisure counseling purposes; instruments intended solely for research purposes are not covered.

Assessment of Leisure Attitudes

The assessment of attitudes, in general, is a difficult and complex process, but in the case of leisure the problems are even more profound. Attitudes are difficult to measure primarily because they are extremely difficult to define operationally. How would you know an attitude if you saw (or heard) one? Additional problems in measuring attitudes arise when the number of factors that could influence an attitude are considered. For example, does a particular attitude vary as a function of age, sex, race, educational level, income, geographic location or height?

Man is what he believes.

Anton Chekov

Still more problems in attitude measurement arise when it is acknowledged that stated attitudes sometimes change because of situational or contextual factors. Don't you know of someone who expresses different attitudes on the same topic in different situations? If not, follow the newspaper reports of the opinions (attitudes) of a national political candidate as the candidate traverses the country.

Each of these types of problems is inherent in the measurement of leisure attitudes, with the addition of at least one more very subtle problem. Many people really haven't spent much time *thinking* about their leisure and, consequently, their attitudes about leisure are not solidified. What then is being assessed in attempts to measure their leisure "attitudes?"

It is not my mode of thought that has caused my misfortunes, but the mode of thought of others.

Marquis de Sade

It is probably for these reasons that there have been few substantive efforts to measure leisure attitudes. And of these few efforts, most have been concerned with noncounseling (e.g. sociological) implications. The result is that only two leisure attitude assessment instruments have been mentioned frequently in the leisure *counseling* context: Neulinger's *A Study of Leisure* and Crandall and Slivkens' *Leisure Ethic Scale*.

A Comprehensive Measure

Neulinger's *A Study of Leisure* —Form 0769 (SOL), along with extensive technical and related research information, are presented in his 1974 book *The Psychology of Leisure.* According to Neulinger, the purpose of the SOL was:

> ... to develop a questionnaire that would enable us to deal meaningfully and quantitatively with various aspects of leisure, including specifically leisure attitudes. The assumption was that the multitude and diversity of questions relating to the leisure domain could be reduced to a relatively small number of basic leisure dimensions. (1974, p. 53)

To accomplish this goal an initial form of the SOL was revised twice, including both conceptual and technical changes. The current form thus reflects considerable effort and extensive analysis.

The SOL is a fairly long instrument which contains approximately 150 items covering a wide variety of leisure aspects as well as demographic information of the respondent. Several different types of response formats are used including Likert-type items, semantic differential format items, and forced-choice items. A factor analysis of 32 SOL attitude items yielded five factors: (a) Affinity for Leisure, (b) Society's Role in Leisure Planning, (c) Self-definition Through Work or Leisure, (d) Amount of Perceived Leisure, and (e) Amount of Work or Vacation Desired. Complete scoring instructions for the factor based and other scales are provided in Neulinger (1974).

Much of Neulinger's (1974) *The Psychology of Leisure* is in fact a discussion of the research results garnered from various administrations of the SOL. This discussion is therefore testimony to the *construct* validity of the SOL; the vast majority of the findings are in concert with theoretical expectations.

Additional support for the *empirical* validity of the SOL is found in the correlations of the SOL with other (psychological) instruments and the factor analysis of the SOL attitude items. Finally, the *content* validity of the SOL is attested to both by the large number of items included and by the (theory based) item selection procedures.

> The essence of belief is the establishment of habit.
>
> Charles S. Pearch

Information on the reliability of the SOL is limited. However the SOL does appear to be sufficiently reliable for at least research purposes and perhaps for individual evaluations (see Neulinger, 1974; Neulinger and Breit, 1969, 1971). The basic SOL norm group consisted of 335 individuals (198 males and 137 females), ranging in age from 18 to 65 (mean age = 35). Additional "comparison" groups may be found in the various reported studies which used the SOL.

As a counseling tool, the SOL has both significant advantages and significant disadvantages. On the positive side, the SOL has been developed using appropriate psychometric procedures and thus enjoys a degree of psychometric credibility. Additionally, the SOL results in a large amount of data on a wide variety of apsects of leisure. It is therefore a very comprehensive instrument and provides considerable information for counseling uses.

On the negative side, the SOL is relatively long and somewhat difficult to respond to (owing to the various response formats). It is likely, therefore, that many people would be reluctant to complete it fully and accurately (i.e. with consistent motivation throughout). In addition, the instrument would appear to be restricted to use with adults. In sum, the SOL could be a useful counseling tool if people can be motivated to complete it.

An Abbreviated Scale

Crandall and Slivkens' (1978) Leisure Ethic Scale (LES) is a dramatic contrast to Neulinger's SOL. The purpose of the LES is "to measure the positivity of attitudes toward leisure" (Crandall and Slivken, 1978, p.3). It therefore focuses on one selected aspect of leisure as compared to the many addressed in the SOL. The important contrast, however, is the number of items in each instrument. The LES is available in two forms, one with 19 items and one with ten items. The shorter form is the one now generally recommended by its authors (Crandall and Slivken, 1978, 1980).

> A belief is not true because it is useful.
>
> Henri Frederic Amiel

The LES items were derived from items on other similar scales, with particular attention given to items that were independent of work attitudes. The preliminary development of the LES is described in Slivken's master's thesis. The authors report that "versions of this scale have now been collected from over 1,000 people ranging from students in four states, to a community quota sample, to recreation professionals, and to heroin addicts" (Crandall and Slivken, 1978, p.3). The ten item scale is a result of data reductions from these administrations. Normative data for the 10 item version is, however, relatively limited at this point.

Several types of reliability coefficients for the LES are reported (Crandall and Slivken, 1978, 1980). Internal consistency (Cronbach's alpha) is .76 while item to total test (score) correlations range from .24 to .60. Test-retest reliability coefficients for periods of 1, 2, 3, 4, and 5 weeks were .82, .59, .80, .87, and .85, respectively.

Various types of validity information are presented by the authors (Crandall and Slivken, 1978). For example, a factor analysis of the scale yielded three factors (not named). The scale yielded predictable (i.e. theoretically expected) significant correlations with parts of other similar scales (notable Neulinger's SOL). The instrument also showed the ability to discriminate among the attitudes of selected groups (e.g. persons reporting satisfaction or nonsatisfaction with leisure) in expected directions.

> There is nothing commonplace in the world except the mental attitude of man.
>
> Charles Burchfield

The LES, like the SOL, has both strong and weak points for leisure counseling purposes. To its credit, it is a short, quickly administered, and easily scored instrument. It therefore has "practical" value. Unfortunately, the extremely limited number of items in the scale raises serious questions about its psychometric qualities.

Despite the reported reliability coefficients, it is unlikely that an instrument with such a limited number of items can achieve a sufficient degree of reliability for individual decision-making (cf. Anastasi, 1976). Relatedly, the emergence of three factors from a 10 item instrument contradicts both the internal consistency of the scale and the validity of the total score. In sum, the LES would seem to be most useful as a gross indicator of leisure attitudes.

The SOL and LES provide for diametrically opposed approaches to the assessment of leisure attitudes. Consequently, each leisure counselor must decide how important the assessment of leisure attitudes is to the leisure counseling process. Certainly some assessment of clients' leisure attitudes seems appropriate since the resulting information may provide insight into clients' (particularly initial) perspectives on leisure. However, whether that information is best obtained through informal verbal interaction or through the use of assessment instruments such as the SOL or LES is a decision that depends on each leisure counselor's purposes, circumstances, and biases.

> The moral world is as little exempt as the physical world from the law of ceaseless change, of perpetual flux.
>
> *Sir James Frazer*

Assessment of Leisure Values

The importance of values as determinants of behaviors is widely recognized and accepted in the psychological and counseling professions. Indeed, a voluminous amount of literature exists for counselors (leisure and otherwise) on how to understand and work with values in various counseling processes. This importance not withstanding however, only a few instruments for the assessment of values in general, and leisure values in particular, are available.

Values, like attitudes, are seemingly highly susceptible to situational factors and fluctuate widely across different circumstances (e.g. social, interpersonal, or familial contexts; specific environmental, political, or educational conditions; etc.). Additionally, values often fluctuate as a function of time, maturity, experience, and other developmental factors. These considerations suggest at least two general conclusions about the assessment of values: (1) in general, values are extremely difficult to assess validly, and (2), any values assessment is likely to be valid only for restricted circumstances and only for relatively short time periods.

One instrument that in part assesses values is Neulinger's SOL. That is, one subsection of the SOL requires respondents to rank order a series of statements relating to free time (leisure) activities. Although the SOL is presented as an attitude inventory, this particular subsection is clearly a "values clarification" approach to attitude assessment. It may therefore be used as a values assessment instrument. Since the characteristics of the SOL were discussed in the preceding section, they will not be repeated here.

What is moral is what you feel good after.

Ernest Hemingway

Another attempt at developing an instrument to assess leisure values has been begun by the senior author (Loesch, 1980c). The Survey of Leisure Values (SLV) was created to measure leisure values in a manner which would have wide range applicability for leisure counseling purposes. The SLV contains 40 items, with four items for each of ten leisure related values: interpersonal self-development, self-dependence, physical development, social recognition, accomplishment, intellectual development, self-expression, happiness, and creativity. Responses to the SLV items are made on a Likert-type, five-point scale ranging from strongly agree to strongly disagree.

During the field test of the SLV it was administered to 543 people ranging in ages from 14 to 52. The mean age of this norm group was 28.60. Validity and reliability data for the SLV are at present very limited. A factor analysis of the SLV yielded five factors, which were subsequently used as the basis for subscales: social recognition, personal happiness, autonomy, physical development, and interpersonal relationships. Cronbach's alpha coefficients for these latter subscales were .84, .79, .88, .85, and .76 respectively. Test-retest reliability coefficients for these subscales following a three week intervening period were .74, .70, .76, .72, and .60 respectively.

Although the SLV appears to have potential for leisure counseling purposes, it is clearly not yet sufficiently developed for more than research uses. The SLV will have to be improved and developed considerably further before it is suitable for individual decision-making (i.e. leisure counseling) purposes.

The conclusion which must be reached is that there simply aren't any substantively valid and reliable leisure values assessment instruments which would be appropriate for use in the leisure counseling context. The only option for leisure counselors therefore is the use of other, less structured methods of evaluating clients' leisure values.

Assessment of (Leisure) Psychological States

The assessment of psychological states as they relate specifically to leisure is an innovative and exciting approach to the use of instrumentation in leisure counseling. The uniqueness is derived from the attempt to evaluate the *totality* of personality (as it relates to leisure) rather than focusing on specific parts of personality (e.g. values, interests, etc.). Such an undertaking is of course an ambitious one. The process encounters not only the problems of assessing personality in general, but also the problems particular to leisure. It is probably because of these difficulties that only two efforts in this regard are commonly cited in the leisure counseling literature.

Every individual has a place to fill in the world and is important in some respect whether he chooses to be or not.

Nathaniel Hawthorne

Walshe (1977) developed the *Walshe Temperament Survey* (WTS) as an attempt to assess four psychological temperaments: melancholic, phlegmatic, sanguine, and choleric. According to Walshe (1977):

> Individual personality is seen as a blend of the four temperaments, occurring in manifold varieties, usually with one or two temperaments dominant. Thus the four temperaments are four discrete, all encompassing elements common to human beings which form the underlying basis for personality. They combine with infinite variety as catalysts to personality. (p. 94)

The basic aim of the WTS is to enable leisure counselors and their clients to evaluate which, if any, of the four temperaments is dominant in clients and, subsequently, to help clients select leisure activities deemed appropriate to the dominant temperaments.

Walshe (1977) has provided descriptive terms for each of the four temperaments. She has also provided examples of leisure activities potentially suitable for each of the four temperaments. The following are abbreviated examples of her information:

Melancholic

Descriptors—slow in movement and thought; sombre; introverted; sometimes lethargic, indifferent or passive

Activities—pet care, collections, memorabilia, volunteer service

Phlegmatic

Descriptors—lacking in vigor; often clumsy; introverted; comfort seeking; orderly; patient; meticulous

Activities—games, flower arranging, model making, crossword puzzles

Sanguine

Descriptors—extroverted; creative; carefree, full of good intentions; appreciative of art, beauty and culture

Activities—clubs, social events, artistic activities, dining out

Choleric

Descriptors—extroverted; firm; energetic; enduring; influential; courageous; sometimes quarrelsome and hard to get along with

Activities—auto racing, sports, flying, leadership roles

The WTS contains a total of 192 items. There are 48 items for each temperament. The response time varies depending on the respondent, but typically takes 20-30 minutes. Scoring is done using a template and usually takes 3-5 minutes per response (answer) sheet.

No man knows of what stuff he is made until prosperity and ease try him.

A. P. Gouthney

While the WTS offers an interesting approach to assessment in leisure counseling, it does, at present, have some severe limitations. Notable among these is a distinct lack of validity, reliability, and normative data. Two other considerations are more subtle but just as important. The use of the WTS necessitates that leisure counselors agree with the four temperament conceptualization of personality. Leisure counselors who prefer other personality conceptualizations will obviously have little regard for WTS results.

In addition, the relationships among personality types (i.e. temperaments) and satisfactions with suggested leisure activities have not been fully established. Thus the recommendation of various leisure activities as a follow-up to determination of particular temperaments is at best a tenuous proposition.

Walshe (1977) acknowledges the limitations of the WTS and is engaged in efforts to rectify its technical limitations. Should these efforts prove fruitful, the WTS will provide an interesting alternative for leisure counselors who accept its perspectives.

A much different approach to the assessment of psychological (leisure) states has been offered by McDowell (1979). He created the *Leisure Well-Being Inventory* (WBI) as an attempt to measure how well prepared an individual is to assume and maintain responsibility for enjoyable, healthful, satisfying, and dynamic leisure.

There is as much difference between us and ourselves as between us and others.

Michel de Montaigne

Leisure well-being, as defined by McDowell, has four major facets: coping, awareness-understanding, knowledge, and assertion. The WBI therefore is not based on a particular conceptualization of personality, but rather on a conceptualization of components of (leisure) "mental health."

The WBI contains four subsections with a total of 125 items. The item distributions are as follows: Coping - 29 items; Awareness-Understanding - 37 items (including Interests - 14 items); and Assertion - 26 items. Respondents answer Yes or No to each item in terms of personal appropriateness. Four subscale scores and a total score are computed.

The WBI suffers from many of the same limitations as other leisure instruments; namely, validity, reliability, and normative data are conspicuously absent. However, McDowell does recommend several score ranges indicative of "leisure well-being," or lack of it. Unfortunately, the decision information underlying the respective score ranges is not provided.

Unlike the WTS, McDowell's WBI would seem to have widespread usability among leisure counselors because it doesn't necessitate agreement with a particular theory of personality. However, it should be acknowledged that not all leisure counselors will agree with McDowell's beliefs about the components of "leisure well-being" and this could restrict its use.

McDowell's WBI is a "simplistic" instrument relative to other psychometric instruments. Yet therein may lie its greatest value. Leisure counseling clients should find it easy to use and understand. It should therefore be helpful for stimulating discussions within the leisure counseling process. As long as clients don't ask too many questions about how they compare to other WBI respondents, those discussions should prove productive.

In general, the assessment of psychological states as they relate to leisure is in its infancy. Some creative beginnings have been made and the futures of those efforts are promising. However, it must again be stated that the uses of these instruments must be cautious and tentative.

Assessment of Leisure Behaviors

The assessment of leisure behaviors has found much greater favor among researchers than among leisure counselors. This is probably because leisure counseling tends to focus on *potential* (as opposed to actual or current) leisure behaviors. Nonetheless, the assessment of leisure behaviors has some potential benefits for the leisure counseling process.

The major benefit is that it gives leisure counselors and clients insights into the "structures" of clients' lives. For example, the assessment of current leisure behaviors allows determination of how much time is available for leisure activities. Another benefit is that it requires clients to examine their current leisure activity patterns and to begin thinking about how those patterns might be altered.

The assessment of leisure behaviors is almost always done in an informal manner within the leisure counseling context. Leisure counselors often recommend that clients record or chart their behaviors over some time period. A common practice is to ask clients to monitor and record their major activities each day for one or two weeks.

As I grow older, I pay less attention to what men say. I just watch what they do.

Andrew Carnegie

The greatest value in leisure behavior assessment is the opportunity for clients to "reflect" on the results of the process. That is, leisure counseling clients can be asked to monitor their current behaviors and then to speculate on what they would like their behavior patterns to be. The comparison of current (actual) versus desired (potential) behavior patterns is very helpful in determining appropriate goals and procedures for the leisure counseling process. In addition, a discussion of current and desired (leisure) behavior patterns may help leisure counselors decide whether additional types of counseling (e.g. vocational, marital, familial, etc.) are appropriate.

Assessment of Leisure Satisfaction

The assessment of leisure satisfaction has been primarily an adjunct to, rather than an integral part of, the leisure counseling process. Leisure satisfaction is usually assessed prior to leisure counseling to identify persons in need of leisure counseling, or afterward to determine if leisure counseling has resulted in more (personally perceived) effective behavior patterns.

> There are some days I think I'm going to die from an overdose of satisfaction.
>
> *Salvador Dali*

The assessment of leisure satisfaction has several potential benefits for the leisure counseling process when it is conducted before counseling begins. Such an assessment may provide indications of clients' levels of motivation for leisure counseling. Theoretically, leisure satisfaction should be inversely related to motivation for leisure counseling.

Such assessments also should help (potential) clients *focus* on their leisure and therefore help them self evaluate one of the important aspects of their lives. And finally since most leisure satisfaction assessment instruments are multidimensional, assessments may identify those aspects of leisure satisfaction which are most in need of improvement.

The work of Ragheb and Beard (1980) is one of two attempts at developing leisure counseling assessment instrumentation that follow rigorous standards and guidelines (the other is by McKechnie, to be discussed later). They provide strong theoretical bases for their work and have used a variety of techniques to refine their instrument.

Their original instrument, (entitled the *Leisure Satisfaction Index*), contained 57 items designed to measure the extent to which adults perceive that personal needs are met through leisure activities. They have subsequently created the *Leisure Satisfaction Scale* (LSS) which has the same purpose but only 24 items. Consequently, since the LSS is now the one they recommend, it is the one which will be discussed here.

The LSS has six factor analytic derived subscales. The following are the subscale names and some descriptive phrases:

Psychological — - sense of freedom, enjoyment, involvement, intellectual challenge

Educational — intellectual stimulation, gaining self knowledge

Social — rewarding relationships with other people

Relaxational — relief from stress and strain of life

Physiological — - physical fitness, health, physical well being

Aesthetic — pleasing, beautiful, and interesting leisure activities

Each of the six subscales contains four items. The items have a Likert-type, five-point response format ranging from "almost never true" to "almost always true." Scores are the sums of the respective item weights.

The technical information on the LSS is impressive relative to that for most leisure counseling instruments. The LSS validity is based primarily on the results and refinements of a series of factor analyses. These resulted in items with more than adequate statistical properties. Additional construct validity is derived from a series of studies investigating relationships among LSS scores and subject characteristics (see Ragheb and Beard, 1980).

The reliability coefficients for the subscales range from .80 to .93, with the reliability coefficient for the total scale being .93. The six subscales are moderately intercorrelated (median coefficient = .46). Normative data for the subscales are provided in various articles describing the use of the instrument (see Ragheb and Beard, 1980).

The LSS should prove to be a valuable assessment instrument, both for researchers and leisure counselors. Its psychometric qualities allow it to be used validly and with confidence in a variety of situations. For the purposes here, the most important one is as a pre leisure counseling assessment. The particularly enticing characteristic of the LSS is that it assesses dimensions of leisure satisfaction which should be amenable to leisure counseling intervention.

A leisure satisfaction assessment instrument more in the vein of typical leisure counseling instrumentation is the *Milwaukee Avocational Satisfaction Questionnaire* (MASQ) developed by Overs, Taylor, and Adkins (1974) as part of the Milwaukee Avocational Counseling Project. The MASQ is roughly based on the *Minnesota Job Satisfaction Questionnaire*. It contains 24 items, with responses on a five-point, Likert-type scale ranging from "not satisfied" to "extremely satisfied."

Somebody's boring me... I think it's me.

Dylan Thomas

Validity, reliability, and normative data for the MASQ are minimal. That which does exist is based primarily on the data from the Milwaukee Project. It appears that the MASQ falls far short of the lead set by the LSS and therefore is of limited usefulness in the leisure counseling context. Its major value would lie in the discussions that might arise from examination of client responses to particular items.

An instrument which falls somewhere between the LSS and MASQ in terms of its current level of development is Rimmer's (1979) *Leisure Satisfaction Inventory* (LSI). The LSI was developed to measure leisure satisfaction in terms of intrinsic and extrinsic dimensions. The LSI contains 40 items and uses a five-point, Likert-type response format ranging from "Strongly Disagree" to "Strongly Agree."

The LSI was developed (i.e. initially normed) on a sample of approximately 1,800 high school students. This constitutes a relatively unique normative group since most leisure counseling assessment instruments are normed on adults. The factorial validity of the LSI was established through a factor analysis which yielded five factors. The concurrent validity was established through the results of correlations with the MASQ and the 57-item version of the LSS; correlations with each were positive and significant.

The reliability coefficients of the LSI were found to be statistically significant, but moderate in size. The moderate reliability coefficients may be a function of the nature of the norm group as well as the instrument itself. In sum, the LSI appears to have good potential as a measure of leisure satisfaction, but it is in need of further development before that potential will be fully realized.

A number of other leisure satisfaction assessment instruments have also appeared in the professional literature. These include ones by Haavio-Manila, 1971; London, Crandall and Seals, 1977; McIntyre, 1972; Orthner, 1975; and Winters, 1973. Most of these instruments were developed for research purposes and were not recommended for leisure counseling purposes.

While the assessment of leisure satisfaction may not yet be an integral part of the leisure counseling process, its potential should not be passed over too quickly. In addition to the possibilities offered earlier, it should be acknowledged that this is one of the areas of leisure counseling assessment where at least one substantive and credible instrument exists. Thus it may be that leisure counselors may have to turn to the assessment of leisure satisfaction to gain at least some valid assessment information about their clients!

Nothing is interesting if you're not interested.

Helen MacInness

Assessment of Leisure Interests

Instruments intended to assess leisure interests are by far the most common type cited in the professional leisure counseling literature. Several reasons seem evident for this predominance. First, interest inventories are used extensively in vocational counseling. When leisure counseling is considered as avocational counseling, it is logical to parallel the instruments used in vocational counseling.

Second, many people assume that interest inventories are easy to develop, primarily because the assessment process is seemingly "transparent." In other words, professionals often (erroneously) assume that the face validities of leisure interest assessment instruments are sufficient to merit their use.

Finally, an "interest" in an activity is assumed to imply a "motivation" to participate in the activity. Since motivation plays an important role in the counseling process, this assumption is readily accepted by leisure counselors.

In spite of the (relatively) numerous leisure interest assessment instruments available and in spite of the popularity of their uses, they still suffer from many of the limitations of other leisure assessment instruments. In fact, the ease and simplicity with which leisure interest assessment instruments are accepted may have set an unfortunate precedent.

The "shining star" among leisure interest assessment instruments is McKechnie's (1975) *Leisure Activities Blank* (LAB). The LAB is in fact the *only* leisure assessment instrument published by a major test publishing company. While this may not represent the epitome of psychometric credibility, it at least acknowledges that the LAB has achieved far greater credibility than other leisure assessment instruments. Nonetheless, the LAB is (to McKechnie's credit) still presented as a "research edition" which implies that it too is in need of additional refinement.

The LAB is presented as having three major purposes: (1) collecting standardized information on past leisure behaviors and intended future leisure activities, (2) providing normative data on the statistical organization of leisure activity patterns, and (3) exploring the psychological meanings and implications of self-reported involvements in leisure activities (McKechnie, 1975).

To achieve these purposes, respondents are asked to respond to 120 leisure activities under two different conditions. In the first, respondents rate the items on a four-point scale indicating their past involvement with each activity (1 = never tried, 2 = occasionally tried, 3 = used to participate but do not currently, and 4 = currently participating). In the second, respondents indicate their future intentions about each activity using a three-point scale (1 = do not expect to try, 2 = uncertain, and 3 = do expect to try). Thus the LAB provides information on "real" and "potential" leisure (behaviors) activities.

The LAB manual provides discussions of probable characteristics of high and low scores for each of the subscales. In addition, the LAB manual provides guidelines for interpreting various subscale score patterns.

The distinguishing feature of the LAB is the psychometric rigor used in its development. The LAB subscales are in fact derived from factor analyses of an initial pool of LAB items. Individual item statistics are also provided in the manual. Still more validity data is provided in descriptions of LAB subscale correlations with various other psychological measures.

The LAB test-retest reliabilities range from .7l to .92 for the Past subscales and from .63 to .93 for the Future subscales. Internal consistency coefficients for Past subscales range from .81 to .93 and for the Future subscales from .76 to .94. Normative data for each subscale for several norm groups are provided in the LAB manual.

The LAB has strong potential for use in leisure counseling. Its psychometric quality enables leisure counselors and their clients to use it with high degrees of confidence about its validity. Perhaps more importantly, since the LAB assesses both past and potential future leisure behaviors, it fits well into typical leisure counseling discussions. Thus the LAB is a good leisure counseling resource at both theoretical and practical levels.

We know nothing about motivation. All we can do is write books about it.

Peter Drucker

Hubert's (1969) *Leisure Interest Inventory* (LII) is another frequently mentioned in the leisure counseling literature. The LII assesses preferred leisure activities based on five (of six) typologies developed by Kaplan (1960): (1) Sociability - preference for activities involving other persons, (2) Games - preference for structured activities, (3) Art - preference for creative activities, (4) Mobility - preference for activities involving adventure, and (5) Immobility preference for sedentary activities.

The LII contains 80 items, each of which is a triad of leisure activities. Respondents identify which activity is "most liked" and which is "least liked" in each triad. Ten triads constitute a unit, in which each construct is represented in combination with each other construct. Each construct is represented six times within each unit. The constructs contain 16 items (activities), each appearing three times but not in the same combination. Five scores are derived, one for each construct (typology). Male and female forms of the LII are available.

The content validity of the LII is assumed on the basis of the representativeness of the sampling from each typology (Hubert, 1969). Additional content validity was established by juror validation. Concurrent validity has been established through correlating LII scores with other psychological instruments. Internal consistency and stability reliability coefficients are moderate to high for the various subscales. Normative data are available for several population groups including both students and adults.

The LII is modeled after the *Kuder General Interest Survey,* an instrument which has enjoyed a long and successful history in vocational counseling. If the LII is further developed, it could enjoy a similar history in leisure counseling. Its format is an accepted one and its theoretical basis is sound. If additional technical (particularly normative) data are provided, the LII should be a valuable leisure counseling resource.

Leisure is the most challenging responsibility a man can be offered.

William Russell

Edwards' (1978) *Constructive Leisure Activity Survey,* revised edition (CLAS-2), was developed specifically for use in the leisure counseling context (Edwards and Bloland, 1980). The CLAS-2 is an eight page instrument designed to survey a client's evaluations of past, present, and future leisure activities and interests and to clarify patterns of likes, dislikes, needs and leisure themes.

The CLAS-2 covers five general categories of leisure activities: physical and outdoor activities, social activities, arts and craftsmanship, learning, general welfare, and personal satisfaction. Administration time for the CLAS-2 is approximately twenty minutes. It is designed to be used and administered in an interview context.

The CLAS-2 will not find favor with researchers since its psychometric limitations are prohibitive for research purposes. However, the CLAS-2 is a relatively unique and potentially very effective instrument for leisure counseling purposes. Scoring of the CLAS-2 involves sorting and ordering. That is, the number of "would like to try" items are counted for each page and then the pages are arranged in order on the basis of those counts. This affords clients the opportunity to identify easily the respective "strengths" of their interests in the different leisure activity categories.

The scoring method emphasizes intraindividual (as opposed to interindividual or normative) comparisons and therefore limits the typical psychometric qualities of the instrument. However, the procedure does foster "personalization" of the leisure counseling process as much or more than any other assessment procedure does. The CLAS-2 also achieves its goal of being specifically appropriate for use in the leisure counseling context.

Just because everything is different doesn't mean anything has changed.

Irene Peter

The *Avocational Activities Inventory* (AAI) (Overs, Taylor and Adkins, 1977) was prepared as a means of systematically classifying avocational (leisure) activities. The AAI is patterned after the *Dictionary of Occupational Titles* and similarly uses a three digit code for classifying activities into interpretable categories.

There are over 800 leisure activities listed in the AAI (see Overs, Taylor and Adkins, 1977). The significance of the AAI here, however, is that it served as the basis of development for a series of leisure interest assessment instruments created by Overs and his associates.

The leisure assessment devices based on the AAI include the *Avocational Title Card Sort* and the *Avocational Plaque Sort* (Overs, Taylor and Adkins, 1977). The natures of these assessment devices are evident from their titles. The technical psychometric information available on these assessment devices is at best limited (cf. Overs, Taylor and Adkins, 1974). Consequently, they cannot be recommended strongly for general use.

These instruments, however, do have one enticing characteristic; they are not "paper-and-pencil" inventories. Thus they offer an assessment alternative for persons who would have difficulty responding to paper-and-pencil inventories. The most obvious example is persons with handicaps such as limited vision, physical disabilities, or poor reading skills. These instruments therefore allow leisure interest assessment to be extended to a greater potential leisure counseling clientele.

>The two most engaging powers of an author are to make new things familiar, familiar things new.
>
>*William Makepeace Thackeray*

Three other leisure interest assessment instruments frequently mentioned in the professional leisure counseling literature are worthy of note here because they are not currently available. These three are D'Agostini's *Avocational Activities Interest Index*, Hartlage's *Computer Research Avocational Guidance Program*, and McDowell's *Self Leisure Interest Profile*.

The instruments available for the assessment of leisure interests are, in general, the better developed of the leisure assessment instruments. Their use, in one sense, is therefore more justifiable. However, there are many, many limitations to the majority of the available leisure interest assessment instruments. Consequently, most of them can only be tentatively recommended for leisure counseling purposes.

State of the Art

The "state of the art" of assessment in leisure counseling can be summarized in a single word: poor. Of course everything is relative and so poor is better than terrible. But that's not good enough; leisure counseling assessment instruments are simply not sufficiently developed, in general, to merit a strong recommendation for their use. McDowell (cited in Walshe, 1977) offered a poignant comment on the situation:

> I am quite critical of instrumentation within leisure counseling, and am doing a lot of research soul-searching. Quite frankly, I think development is at the 'gimmick' stage to capture the market. I would like to approach the market with an instrument which meets the professional rigors and standards of the American Psychological Association. How else can I justify to students and practitioners that leisure counseling instrumentation to date is not classified in Burrows (sic)? (p.115)

The major problems of leisure counseling assessment instrumentation are similar to those associated with any psychological assessment instrument. For example, most of the instruments lack substantive theoretical bases. This may be a reflection of the lack of leisure or leisure counseling theories. However, this does not excuse the widespread *omission* of theoretical bases. Leisure counseling assessment instruments could at least be based on related (i.e. other than leisure) psychological theories. An exemplary case in point is Walshe's WTS.

> Doubt is not a pleasant mental state but certainty is a ridiculous one.
>
> *Voltaire*

The validities of leisure counseling assessment instruments also are not anywhere near what they should be. But they could be, as McKechnie's LAB exemplifies, if enough work is done in that regard. Finally, the normative data for most leisure counseling assessment instruments is sadly lacking. Unfortunately, the typical procedure is to administer the instrument to a group of several hundred people and then put it on the market for general use. Even that wouldn't be quite so bad if the instruments were identified as "research editions" in line with the American Psychological Association *Standards for Educational and Psychological Tests* (1974).

Since the state of the art of assessment in leisure counseling is not good, many of the instruments available (seemingly) have as much potential for harm as for help in their current stages of development. Hopefully many of these instruments will be refined as additional data are gathered. If they are, they could become valuable resources for leisure counseling.

Guidelines for Assessment in Leisure Counseling

The use of assessment instruments in leisure counseling definitely presents a conflict at this point in time. On one hand, the available instruments in general are not sufficiently developed to merit their use for individual decision-making such as in the leisure counseling process. On the other hand, assessment instruments have a history of facilitating and expediting counseling processes and it would be nice to be able to use them in the leisure counseling process. Given this latter situation, it seems safe to assume that these instruments will be used, regardless of the first situation. Consequently, some guidelines for the use of assessment instruments in leisure counseling are in order.

> When a man does not know what harbor he is aiming for, no wind is the right wind.
>
> *Seneca*

Leisure assessment instruments should only be used by leisure counselors who have had substantive training in educational and psychological assessment. Such training would allow leisure counselors to critique carefully the instruments they might use.

A second guideline is that leisure counseling clients should be informed of the limitations of the assessment instruments they are asked to respond to. It is particularly important to communicate limitations of interindividual (i.e. normative) comparisons.

It is also important to communicate that results of the assessments may be different at different times, owing to reliability considerations.

A third guideline is that the information obtained from leisure counseling assessment instruments should be "validated" through verbal interactions with clients. Given the current state of the art, if clients' comments disagree with the assessment results, it is probably best to assume that client statements are the valid information.

A final guideline is that assessment results should be used for the *discussion* of potential decisions rather than as the basis for decisions. This guideline would of course apply even if the leisure counseling assessment instruments were at higher and better stages of development. The important point here, however, is that assessment instruments can be effectively used for stimulating discussion even if their results are less than fully valid.

It is impossible for ideas to compete in the marketplace if no forum for their presentation is provided or available.

Thomas Mann

Although they have limitations, leisure counseling assessment instruments can be effective resources. However, they must be used as *resources*, not determinants of, or replacements for, effective counseling procedures.

Discussion Questions

1. Are any vocational counseling assessment instruments easily adapted for leisure counseling purposes?
2. What are the major problems involved in assessing a client's leisure values?
3. What are the major limitations of using client selfreports as the sole indicators of their leisure satisfaction?
4. Identify and describe a major trend in assessment in counseling. What are its particular implications for assessment in leisure counseling?
5. What are the major factors for and against the use of tests in counseling? How do these factors apply particularly to leisure counseling?

Study Activities

1. Compile an annotated bibliography of ten journal articles on the use of tests in counseling.
2. Select any leisure counseling assessment instrument and evaluate it relative to the APA *Standards for Educational and Psychological Tests*.
3. Compile a test battery appropriate for assessment in leisure counseling which would be compatible with your personal theory of counseling.
4. Identify and briefly describe three measures of personal characteristics (i.e. personality inventories) which would be appropriate for leisure counseling purposes. Defend your selections.

Chapter VI

Individual Leisure Counseling

The Triangulation Leisure Counseling (TLC) model presented in Chapter IV and the possible use of the assessment procedures presented in the preceding chapter may be adapted to a variety of leisure counseling situations. A good starting place in exemplifying these possible adaptations is to consider individual leisure counseling.

> Perhaps the most important lesson the world has learned in the past fifty years is that it is not true that "human nature is unchangeable."
>
> Bruce Bliven

The individual leisure counseling process utilizing the TLC model is composed of four stages. The first stage, *joining*, is a familiar part of all counseling processes. It is used here to mean that part of the counseling process which focuses on the development of rapport between the leisure counselor and client. The second stage, *exploration,* is concerned with clarification of the client's current and potential leisure in terms of the affective, behavioral and cognitive dimensions of the TLC model.

The third stage, *action,* involves client experimentation from both behavioral and psychological perspectives. The last stage, *termination,* is concerned with integration and culmination of the preceding stages. Before discussing these stages more extensively, it is appropriate to reconsider the goals of the TLC model because they also become the goals of the individual leisure counseling process. These goals are:

1. To enable leisure counselors and their clients to establish mutually acceptable, appropriate, and effective counseling relationships (stage 1).

2. To enable leisure counseling clients to be aware of and understand their own affective, behavioral, and cognitive dimensions as they relate to current and potential leisure activities (stage 2).

3. To help leisure counseling clients develop effective awareness and decision making skills applicable to their current and potential leisure activities (stage 3).

4. To help leisure counseling clients achieve the maximum possible satisfaction from their leisure activities (stage 4).

Leisure is the mother of philosophy.

Thomas Hobbs

Some Points Worth Repeating

Two points noted earlier also merit reemphasis. First, the individual leisure counseling process does not necessarily have to result in clients changing leisure activities. Such changes may, and most often do, occur. However, the individual leisure counseling process may be effective in promoting client leisure understanding and satisfaction even if leisure activity changes do not occur.

Second, the individual leisure counseling process is intended to help clients become more leisure self sufficient. That is, as a result of the individual leisure counseling process, clients should be better able to make effective leisure decisions, and therefore be able to move further toward leisure mental health. The individual leisure counseling process should therefore have both short and long term impacts on clients.

Stage I: Joining

The purpose of the joining stage is to develop rapport and an effective interactional relationship between the leisure counselor and client. In counseling vernacular, this means that an atmosphere of mutual trust and understanding must be created. Unlike the subsequent three stages, the success of the joining stage is almost entirely contingent upon the leisure counselor's behaviors.

The human understanding is no dry light, but receives infusion from the will and affections. . . .

Francis Bacon

Some Basic Skills

A number of counselor behaviors have been shown to facilitate the development of effective counseling relationships during the joining stage. These behaviors are intended to result in what have typically been called the "core conditions" of counseling. The four basic core conditions are:

1. Empathy — the counselor's understanding of the client's emotions (feelings) from the client's perspective.
2. Positive regard — the counselor's nonjudgmental acceptance of the client's affect, behaviors, and cognitions.
3. Congruence — the counselor's authenticity in words and behaviors.
4. Respect — the counselor's demonstration of understanding and acceptance of the client's dignity and worth.

The behavioral manifestations of the core conditions have been referred to as "facilitative responding" or "active listening" skills (among others). The primary skills in this regard are reflection (or understanding client feelings), clarification (or summarization) of client statements, and (open-ended) questioning. A complete discussion of these skills is beyond the scope and purposes of this book; for a succinct yet effective overview of these skills see Wittmer and Myrick, 1980.

The important point about these skills is that they are *responsive*. That is, they are skills used by leisure counselors in response to client verbal or nonverbal behaviors.

> The sum of behaviour is to retain a man's dignity, without intruding on the liberty of others.
>
> *Francis Bacon*

The process of using facilitative responding or active listening skills results in leisure counselors obtaining considerable information from and about clients. This information should be considered, and probably obtained, in a logical sequence by leisure counselors.

While leisure counselors are primarily "responsive" to client behaviors during the joining stage, there should be an attempt to insure that all pertinent information is obtained. This means that leisure counselors may sometimes have to direct (but not necessarily be "directive" in) the leisure counseling process. The obvious way to direct the counseling process is to ask open-ended questions which yield desired information.

Desirable Information

One important piece of information that leisure counselors must obtain is an indication of clients' feelings or attitudes about counselors. It would be naive to assume that clients go to counselors simply because they have high opinions of them; any of a considerable number of other factors may be sources of motivation. Consequently, leisure counselors should explore clients' opinions about (leisure) counselors so that misconceptions or misperceptions may be rectified as early as possible in leisure counseling processes.

Another important type of information obtained early in the leisure counseling process is a determination of the appropriateness of leisure counseling. A distinction is often made between "presenting" problems and "real" problems. A *presenting* problem is the one initially stated by the client as the reason for seeking counseling. A *real* problem is one that emerges after the client has become comfortable enough in the counseling relationship to state it.

Because of the connotations associated with the word "leisure," there is probably less (perceived) personal threat involved in seeking leisure counseling than in seeking other types of counseling. Leisure concerns may therefore be the presenting problem while in fact the real problems could be any of a myriad of other concerns. If the real problems are something other than leisure, then either referrals are appropriate or shifts in the type of counseling service being provided must take place.

Starting the Process

First impressions *are* important! Leisure counselors should therefore pay particular attention to their behaviors during the initial meeting. Promptness, friendliness, proper dress, and the conveyance of professionalism are major factors in initiating effective relationships.

It is also important for leisure counselors to communicate early in the joining stage that leisure counseling is purposeful activity. That is, clients should understand clearly that leisure counseling is intended to help them change in ways that will be personally satisfying.

One way to exemplify the purposefulness of leisure counseling to clients is to have them engage in a rather simple activity. The form on the next page may be used for this activity. Clients should be instructed to rate or evaluate leisure activities from each of two perspectives. The first is an evaluation of *current* leisure activities dynamics. The second is an evaluation of *potential* leisure activities dynamics.

The purpose of this activity is to help clients understand "where they are now" and "where they would like to be." If that purpose is accomplished, clients should also understand that the purpose of leisure counseling is to help them get from the former to the latter.

Leisure Activities Dynamics
Evaluation Form

Rate your current leisure activities in terms of each of the dynamics listed below by placing a check on one of the lines between each word pair. Then rate how you would like your leisure activities to be by circling one of the lines between each word pair.

Individual	Group
Intellectual	Nonintellectual
Competitive	Noncompetitive
Active	Passive
Physical	Nonphysical
Short term	Continuing
Parallel vocation	Avocational
Self oriented	Other oriented
Person centered	Product centered
High risk	Low risk
Expensive	Inexpensive
Essential	Optional

Initial Affective Information

Affective information from the client may be garnered both through verbal questioning and through interpretation of nonverbal behaviors. When questions are used, caution should be exercised against being too specific too early in the process. Asking for detailed information prematurely may have several negative effects.

For example, clients may not yet feel comfortable in divulging particular types of information. Relatedly, clients may not yet know how to respond. Third, clients may feel that they are being "psychoanalyzed." And fourth, they may not have expected to provide detailed information so soon.

Any of these situations will more than likely delay, if not preclude, successful completion of the joining stage. In essence, these and similar situations put the client "on the spot" and most clients will resist such pressure.

The interpretation of client nonverbal behaviors may also provide much useful information. Observations of body postures, mannerisms, facial expressions and the like can be important clues to clients' affect. Nonverbal behaviors are, however, highly personal in nature. A facial gesture by one client may not mean the same as the same facial gesture by another client. Caution should therefore also be exercised against "overinterpreting" client nonverbal behaviors.

The following are some questions about client affective dimensions which should be answered in *general* terms during the joining stage:

1. What is the client's general level of leisure activity satisfaction or dissatisfaction?
2. What are the general attitudes the client has about leisure and leisure activities?
3. Which of the client's values are most prominent?
4. What are the client's expectations for leisure activities?
5. What seem to be the client's general categories of leisure interests?
6. What type of person is the client?

7. How does the client feel about leisure counseling?
8. Which topics bring out the strongest affective reactions from the client?

The answers to questions such as these should provide clues for leisure counselors about how to proceed in interacting with their clients.

The genius of communication is the ability to be both totally honest and totally kind at the same time.

John Powell

Initial Behavioral Information

Behavioral information from clients may again be obtained through verbal questioning or nonverbal interpretation. Cautions about specificity and overinterpretation are applicable here as well. Verbal questioning should attempt to obtain general information, though the focus in this case is on leisure behaviors (activities). Nonverbal interpretations may be used to obtain some information about clients' personal behaviors (at least those present during the counseling situation).

The following are some questions about behavioral dimensions which should be answered in general terms during the joining stage:

1. What are the general categories of leisure activities now, or previously, engaged in by the client?
2. How much physical (i.e. nonverbal) behavior does the client exhibit when discussing various aspects of leisure?
3. How comfortable (in terms of reported behaviors) is the client in different environments?
4. Does the client suggest wanting to be more active or more passive in potential leisure activities?
6. What general nonverbal messages does the client send?
7. What general categories of leisure activities has the client failed to consider?

Initial Cognitive Information

Information about clients' cognitive dimensions may be obtained through careful listening and observation during the process of obtaining other types of information. The cognitive information obtained will be general in nature, and it rightly should be. Attempts to obtain specific information about clients' cognitive capabilities would probably be grossly premature and therefore highly threatening at this point in the process. However, this does not preclude leisure counselors from making subjective judgments about clients' cognitive functioning and abilities.

Intellect annuls fate. So far as a man thinks, he is free.

Ralph Waldo Emerson

The following are some questions whose answers will provide leisure counselors with general information about clients' cognitive dimensions:

1. What is the client's general level of intelligence?
2. What aptitudes does the client seem to have?
3. What are the client's major cognitive accomplishments?
4. What is the client's capacity for logical thinking and reasoning?
5. What is the extent of the client's knowledge of leisure activities?
6. What resources about leisure activities is the client aware of?
7. How effective are the client's decision-making skills?
8. What is the extent of the client's (leisure) vocabulary?

Ending the Joining Stage

The joining stage should conclude with a summarization by the leisure counselor. The summarization should allow both the leisure counselor and client to comprehend the many diverse types of information which need to be considered.

There are two major benefits to be derived from the summarization. First, the summarization allows both the leisure counselor and the client to evaluate how effectively the leisure counselor has "heard" and "understands" the client. Second, if the first benefit has been achieved, the leisure counselor's "credibility" with the client has been established. If these two benefits are achieved, then a mutually acceptable leisure counseling relationship has been developed and the joining stage has been successfully completed.

The summarization portion concludes with the leisure counselor providing a brief overview of the next three stages of the leisure counseling process. The leisure counselor should also provide a somewhat more specific introduction of what will happen during the next stage.

Stage II: Exploration

The purpose of the exploration stage is to investigate systematically each of the dimensions of the TLC model. The primary mode of interaction used by the leisure counselor during this stage is discussion, with the leisure counselor becoming less responsive and more active during this stage. Open-ended, probing questions are used extensively. In addition, the use of any of a variety of leisure counseling assessment instruments may be incorporated during this stage. The goal is for the leisure counselor and the client to have both a depth and breadth understanding of all factors pertinent to the client's potential achievement of leisure mental health.

> The more help a person has in his garden, the less it belongs to him.
>
> *William H. Davis*

The Affective Dimensions

As previously noted, the TLC model focuses on six components of affective functioning: feelings, attitudes, values, expectations, interests, and personality characteristics. These dimensions are explored in the order presented within the TLC model to insure that each of the dimensions is covered. However, it is readily acknowledged that there is considerable overlap among the affective dimensions and that it is difficult to make clear separations among them. Nonetheless, the attempt to focus on each of them in sequence adds structure and direction to the leisure counseling process.

Feelings. Simply stated, feelings are a client's emotional reactions to leisure and leisure activities. Feelings are highly personal in nature and clients often only disclose their feelings with difficulty. Consequently, leisure counselors should begin the explorations of clients' feelings slowly and carefully.

In many cases the leisure counselor will actually have to "teach" a client how to make feeling statements. This is typically accomplished through modeling behaviors, though in some cases a verbal explanation may suffice. Once the client has begun to make feelings statements, the leisure counselor should reinforce the client's behaviors.

As stated earlier, an effective feelings statement is one that contains the pronoun "I" followed by a word or words reflecting an emotion and a word or words to which the emotion applies. The following are some examples of feelings statements:

— I hate jogging.

— I am happy when I'm beachcombing.

— I would be afraid to skydive.

— I feel at ease when I read.

The use of the first person pronoun helps clients become more aware of, or personalize, their feelings. Leisure counselors should therefore strive to enable their clients to make feelings statements in this way.

The heart has its reasons which reason does not understand.

Blaise Pascal

For example, if the client says, "Badminton is for the birds!" (pun intended), the leisure counselor might reply, "What you're saying is that you don't like badminton" or "Can you make an 'I' statement about how you feel about badminton?" This type of intervention will help the client separate feelings from attitudes.

In the process of exploring a client's feelings, a distinction should be made between feelings about leisure (as a concept) and feelings about leisure activities. The two types of feelings may not, and often are not, synonomous. For example, a client firmly "entrenched" in the work ethic may hold generally negative feelings about the idea of leisure. However, that same client may have very positive feelings about particular leisure activities.

Affectation is as necessary to the mind as dress is to the body.

William Hazlitt

Exploring a client's feelings about leisure should be a relatively easy task, though responses can sometimes be long and involved. A simple question such as, "What feelings do you have about leisure?" will usually suffice.

If the client's feelings about leisure are generally positive, it can probably be assumed that the client will be more motivated in the leisure counseling process than if the client's feelings about leisure are generally negative. If the client's feelings about leisure are generally negative, it may be appropriate to explore the natures or "reasons" for those feelings. In rare instances, it may even be appropriate to terminate the leisure counseling process if the client's feelings about leisure are intensely negative. Exploring a client's feelings about personal leisure activities is similarly a relatively easy task. A few simple questions such as, "How do you feel when you participate in _____?" or "What leisure activities make you feel _____?" will usually suffice.

Sometimes a few "gamelike" activities can be used to help a client clarify feelings about personal leisure activities and also help to vary the nature of the leisure counseling process. For example, a leisure counselor might ask a client to identify a current leisure activity and then to identify the feeling words the client associates with that activity. This might be followed by having the client identify which of the feeling words listed are positive and which are negative. A discussion might follow as to the respective numbers of each type.

Another simple activity would be to have the client complete the statement: When I _____, I feel _____ and I want to _____. The words the client uses to fill in the blanks should provide clarification of whether the client wants to continue engaging in that activity.

The preceding discussion has focused on current feelings about leisure and leisure activities. With only slight modification, the same questions can be used to explore how a client would like to feel about leisure and leisure activities. This type of feelings exploration is in effect also a goal setting procedure.

Attitudes. There are three common characteristics of an attitude statement: (a) a focus on persons other than the one making the statement, (b) a value judgment, and (c) a "should" or an "ought to" which is stated or implied. The following are some examples of attitude statements:

1. Everybody should keep physically fit.
2. Playing chess is good for the mind.
3. Everybody needs to relax more.
4. I think people should stop watching sports on television and start playing the sports they were watching.
5. Exercising makes you feel better.

Inherent in statements like these is a reflection of values. Things *external* to the person have had significant influence on the person's attitudes.

The problem with attitude statements in the leisure counseling context is that it is difficult to separate the client's true beliefs from the client's perceptions of other people's beliefs. For example, if the client makes the statement, "People should meditate because it helps them cope with stress," the question arises as to whether the client truly believes he statement or the client is merely mimicking what others have suggested the client should believe.

One way leisure counselors can alleviate this quandary is by asking the client to make "I" statements. Thus the client may restate the point to be made as, "I believe meditation helps people cope with stress." A leisure counselor may help a client personalize attitude statements even further by requesting the client to make the statement personally applicable. The client would therefore respond, "I believe meditation helps me cope with stress."

Opinion has caused more trouble on this little earth than plagues or earthquakes.

Voltaire

Clarifications such as these are important because they help a client understand personal attitudes. They also help a client achieve a greater sense of personal identity. In general, such clarifications help to free a client from externally imposed goals and/or behavioral suggestions. Since leisure counseling is supposed to benefit each client individually, such clarifications must be achieved.

As with feelings, there are some relatively simple questions and activities that leisure counselors can use to help clients clarify their own attitudes. For example, some of the following questions will typically facilitate the clarification process:

— What do you believe about leisure?
— Is leisure important to you?
— What does your leisure do for you?
— What would you like your leisure to do for you?

Relatively structured activities can also bring about clarification of attitudes. For example, a client can be asked to state a leisure attitude and then to describe the history of the formation of the attitude. Similarly, a client can be asked to identify the major factors that influence leisure attitudes.

Values. A discussion and clarification of leisure attitudes leads directly into a discussion of values since attitudes are actually the results of value judgments. Values, or basic beliefs, are viewed by some as *the* determining factors underlying all human behaviors (cf. Simon, Howe, and Kirschenbaum, 1972). Even if this statement is not fully accepted, it seems obvious that values play major roles in guiding human behaviors. Leisure activities (behaviors), as a subset of human behaviors, are therefore in part a result of values. The clarification of a client's values is thus a crucial part of the leisure counseling process.

A leisure counseling client's values may be clarified through any or all of three processes. These include leisure counselorclient subjective interpretations, use of a values assessment instrument, and use of a values clarification technique.

Subjective interpretations of clients' values may be obtained through verbal interactions. The obvious place where such statements will occur is during the clarification of client attitudes. However, such statements are also "obvious" in other discussions. Value based statements made by clients should be mentally "filed" by leisure counselors so that they may be discussed directly during this portion of the process.

In addition to using previously made value statements as discussion stimuli, a leisure counselor may also focus discussion on a client's values by asking a few simple questions such as the following:

1. What are your most important values?
2. What values are reflected in your current leisure activities?
3. What values would you like to be reflected in your leisure activities?
4. How do your leisure values differ from those of your friends?

The discussions of the responses to questions such as these should help clients gain better awareness and understanding of their own leisure values. It is important in this context for leisure counselors to be wary of either interjecting their own values or subtly reinforcing some client values and not others. For example, leisure counselors often use behaviors such as smiling or seemingly innocuous mutterings such as "good" or "that's interesting" for the purpose of encouraging (reinforcing) continued talking.

However, if such behaviors are inopportunely used, they may serve to reinforce values clients are expressing, and therefore indirectly impose leisure counselors' values on clients. If leisure counselors want clients to say more about particular points, they should simply ask for clarification.

The use of assessment instruments to help clients clarify values has several distinct advantages. First, they allow for and in fact insure that a variety of values will be considered. Second, they disallow the possibility that leisure counselors will selectively reinforce expressions of some client values and not others. Third, they allow for normative comparisons, which might be desirable information for some clients.

Finally, they allow for comparisons between the relative strengths of values in a manner much simpler than can be achieved through discussion. Unfortunately, as noted in the preceding chapter, the instruments available to assess values in general, and leisure values in particular, aren't very good in terms of psychometric quality. Consequently, again, leisure counselors should only use such instruments with a great deal of caution.

Everything depends on what people are capable of wanting.

Enrico Malatesta

The use of values clarification activities as part of the leisure counseling process has enjoyed great favor among leisure counselors. Most of the "counseling" activities suggested in the professional leisure counseling literature are in fact values clarification activities.

Leisure counselors may select and adapt any of a wide variety of values clarification activities depending upon their personal and professional needs, skills, orientations and clients' situations. However, since (time) efficiency in the leisure counseling process is generally desirable, shorter and simpler activities are recommended.

For example, clients can be presented with a list of leisure values and then be asked to rank order them from most to least important. One possible list is the ten values from the SLV (Loesch, 1980) which was discussed in the preceding chapter. Another efficient activity is to have clients list their major values and then list several leisure activities that they think reflect the respective values. This latter activity can be particularly effective if the ensuing discussion focuses on whether any leisure activities are listed by more that one value.

Regardless of the procedure used to help clients clarify their leisure values, the culminating activity of this   portion of the process is a discussion of the relationships among leisure values and leisure activities. Clients should be encouraged to explore how they perceive certain leisure activities reflecting certain values, and vice versa. In addition, leisure counselors should help clients expand or extend these relationships by suggesting activities that clients may not have thought of in relation to a particular value, and by suggesting values that clients may not have thought of as being reflected in a particular activity. This type of discussion is extremely important because of the eventual implications it has for decision-making about leisure activities.

Expectations. A client's expectations about or from participation in a leisure activity will influence the   client's willingness to participate in the activity and   possibly the client's level of satisfaction from the activity. A straightforward way for clarifying expectations is for leisure counselors to identify a category of leisure activities and then to ask clients to summarize their expectations about participating in those activities.

For example, a leisure counselor might ask the question, "If you were to play board games, what are your expectations about what would happen to you?" In responding, the client should be encouraged to talk about personal perceptions. Discussion of the client's response to a question such as this should then help the client evaluate the "reasonableness"   of the expectation.

A question such as, "What evidence do you have (e.g. previous experience) that this expectation would come true?" is useful in this context.

This type of discussion can proceed across a variety of categories of leisure activities such as sports, crafts, social events, and so on. The composite effect is to gain an overview about the client's expectations for leisure activity participation which will eventually be useful in decision-making. It will also provide some possible areas for "reality testing" during the action stage of the leisure counseling process.

The expectations clarification process may also be achieved through the use of somewhat more structured activities. For example, the leisure counselor might ask the client to describe an "unexpected" experience in a leisure activity and then to discuss what caused the difference between the expectation and reality of the experience. A leisure counselor might also ask a client to describe what expectations the client has for participation in *any* leisure activity.

Interests. The assessment of client leisure interests, like the clarification of client leisure values, is a commonly recommended practice for the leisure counseling process. Since an "interest" in an activity typically reflects at least some motivation to participate in the activity, the exploration of leisure interests is one of the ways leisure counselors can evaluate client motivations.

There is a subtle yet vitally important aspect of interest assessment that is, unfortunately, often overlooked: The validity of expressed interests is contingent upon the person having some knowledge of the activity being evaluated. For example, if a client is asked to evaluate how much the client would like to play *Whist,* the client's response will be only as valid as the client's knowledge of *Whist.* Several potential response biases are evident. If the client knows nothing of *Whist,* the client's response will be essentially random.

If the client knows only that *Whist* is a card game, the client's response may be a relection of the client's evaluation of card games in general. If the client has a thorough knowledge of *Whist,* then the client's response will be fully valid. The implication is that a client's level of knowledge of various leisure activities needs to be *determined before* the client's leisure interests can be validly assessed.

The assessment of a client's leisure activity knowledge is by no means an easy matter. No assessment instruments designed for this purpose are currently available. It appears therefore that leisure counselors must rely on professional judgments. Such judgments can in part be made on the basis of information discerned from the preceding portions of the leisure counseling process. Additional information may be obtained by asking clients to evaluate their own levels of leisure knowledge. Once the evaluation of the client's levels of leisure activity knowledge have been made, the leisure counselor can then determine most appropriate subsequent activities in the leisure counseling process.

If a client has extremely limited information about various leisure activities, it is appropriate to digress from the leisure counseling process to afford the client the opportunity to learn more about leisure activities. The use of resources such as libraries, bookstores, educational programs, or "experts" are good examples of ways to proceed. Once the client has a good knowledge of leisure activities, the counseling process may resume.

> Ignorance is the night of the mind, a night without moon or star.
>
> *Confucius*

If a client has moderate levels of leisure activity knowledge, leisure counselor and client (verbal) interactions are probably most appropriate. This discussion should allow the leisure counselor and client to make evaluations of the client's leisure activity knowledge in various categories of leisure activities. The client can then focus on finding information about specific (types of) leisure activities.

When a client has relatively high levels of leisure activity knowledge, the use of an assessment instrument is recommended. Leisure interest assessment instruments almost in-

Individual Leisure Counseling 155

variably allow for evaluation of a large number of activities. They also allow for normative comparisons, which may be of interest to some clients.

Regardless of the method of assessment used, the ultimate goal of leisure activity interest evaluation is the identification of patterns or trends. Most people who are satisfied with their leisure have several different types of leisure activities which they enjoy. It is unlikely therefore that the selection of a few specific activities will ultimately be satisfying for the client. Most likely a few specific *categories* of activities will provide sufficient diversity and flexibility for clients to enjoy leisure satisfaction and mental health.

Personal characteristics. The last affective dimension explored in the sequence is the client's personal characteristics (i.e. personality). The exploration of personal characteristics is important because the selection of leisure activities will to a large extent be effective only if those activities "fit" the client. The term personal characteristics is used here to mean a composite description of the client. The purpose is therefore to obtain an overview of the client's general personality traits.

The assessment of personal characteristics is a fascinating, yet complicated, and perhaps threatening, activity for both leisure counselors and clients. The potential threat involved in assessing personal characteristics is derived from the fact that there are some things clients simply don't want to hear. A composite characterization of the client implies that both "positive" and "negative" (or strong and weak, or good and bad, etc.) characteristics of the client will be identified. Therefore, the exploration of a client's personal characteristics necessitates an optimum amount of "tact" on the part of the leisure counselor.

The method used for assessment of a client's personal characteristics should be determined by leisure counselors since clients typically will not be familiar enough with the alternatives to contribute effectively to the decision. Unfortunately, only two major guidelines can be given for aiding in this decision, and neither is very specific. The first is that leisure counselors must evaluate their own skills and the options related to them. For example, many leisure counselors will not have had training in the use of projective personality assessment techniques and so the use of projective techniques will not be an available option.

The second guideline is even more subjective. It involves evaluating clients' abilities for self insight and freedom to express those insights. If clients have good self insights, are willing to disclose those insights, and are open to feedback, then assessment of clients' personal characteristics can probably be achieved through discussions. Leisure counselors should strive for comprehensiveness in these discussions and clients should be encouraged to consider and evaluate as many of their personal characteristics as possible. The end result should be that clients have evaluated all their major traits and that leisure counselors concur with those evaluations.

If clients are deemed to be either ineffective in making self insights or unwilling to disclose self insights, an alternative procedure should be used. Most often this procedure will involve the use of a personality inventory. Leisure counselors should first identify those which are consistent with their own professional perspectives and then select from among those ones that are most appropriate for particular clients.

It is easier to fight for principles than to live up to them.
Alfred Adler

It is important to repeat here that definitive relationships among personal characteristics and satisfactions with participation in various leisure activities have not been established. Consequently, attempts to relate personal characteristics to specific leisure activities should be made cautiously, and with mutual inputs by leisure counselors and clients.

Up to this point six components of clients' affective dimensions have been considered. There should by now be awareness of the relationships between affective dimensions and leisure activities. Some further clarification of these relationships also occurs in the action stage. At this point, however, it is appropriate to consider the behavioral dimensions.

The Behavioral Dimensions

Four components of behavioral dimensions, including physical, personal, social, and environmental behaviors, are covered in the TLC model. The discussions and explorations of each of these components are considered in terms of both real and potential behaviors, as defined earlier. As with the affective dimensions, overlap and interrelationships among the behavioral dimensions are readily acknowledged. But again, sequencing and separating the dimensions facilitates their respective explorations.

Before beginning discussion of exploration of the behavioral dimensions, it should be noted that this discussion is a "logical" follow-up to discussion of the affective dimensions. That is, discussion of the behavioral dimensions should help clients clarify how their affective dimensions are manifested in their behaviors. This is an important linkage which must be made for eventual leisure activity satisfaction.

Physical Behaviors. The exploration of clients' physical behaviors should be a relatively simple endeavor. Leisure counselors may make cursory evaluations by merely observing their clients' physical statures. A more effective method, however, is for leisure counselors to ask clients to describe their physical behaviors. A simple question such as, "What types of physical behaviors do you now engage in?" will usually suffice. Clients should be asked to be as comprehensive as possible in their responses.

All human actions have one or more of these seven causes: chance, nature, compulsions, habit, reason, passion, desire.

Aristotle

In exploring current physical behaviors, two important points should be kept in mind. First, if the client is vocationally employed, physical behaviors during employment commitments should be considered since they have implications for leisure activities. For example, a client who engages in strenuous physical activity during employment may want less physical activity during leisure. Second, being sedentary (e.g.

sleeping, resting, etc.) is in fact a type of physical behavior. This point should be emphasized for clients so that the full range of physical behaviors may be considered.

Once the nature of the clients' current (real) physical behaviors have been clarified, the exploration should turn to *potential* physical behaviors. That is, clients should be encouraged to evaluate what they would like their physical behaviors to be.

When clients' real and potential behaviors have been clarified, a simple activity may be used to help client's comprehend further how they are and how they would like to be. Clients can be asked to think of "typical" days and then to list on paper the types of physical behaviors they engage in during those days.

Clients can then be asked to list next to each category the amount of time spent in each type during typical days. Finally, clients can be asked to reapportion the time allotments in ways the clients would like them to be. The ensuing discussion should clarify how much change, if any, clients desire as well as some relatively specific suggestions as to the types of changes desired.

Personal Behaviors. The exploration of personal behaviors (i.e. those a client engages in when alone) has the potential for providing some very unique information about the client. Within the leisure context, the client is "free" to do whatever seems most appropriate. Two important types of information should thus be considered.

The strongest man in the world is he who stands most alone.

Henrik Ibsen

The first is *how* the client makes decisions in a "free choice" situation and the second is the nature of the *limits* of free choice as the client interprets them. These two pieces of information have significant implications for determination of the most effective decision-making processes for the client.

In the individual leisure counseling process, the exploration of personal behaviors is highly subjective since it is based entirely on client self-reports. Consequently, leisure counselors should strive to have clients report personal behaviors in as objective, valid, and reliable a manner as possible. In addition, leisure counselors should seek as much clarity and "evidence" as possible for client evaluations of satisfactions with personal behaviors.

As with many of the other dimensions, both questions and activities may be used to facilitate the personal behaviors exploration process. Leisure counselors may use questions such as, "What do you do when you're alone?" or "What factors influence what you do when you alone?" A natural question to use concerning potential behaviors is to ask the client, "If you wanted to be more satisfied when you're alone, what would you do?"

Leisure counselors might also use an activity such as asking the client to list behaviors engaged in when alone, the respective amounts of time spent in each, and some indication of the degree of satisfaction from each activity. The client might then be asked to restructure the list using potential preferred behaviors.

Self-interest is but the survival of the animal in us.

Henri Frederic Amiel

Social Behaviors. Many leisure activities are social in nature (i.e. involve association and interaction with other people) and in fact many people seek leisure activities because of the potential for social interaction. Clients' social behaviors are therefore an important consideration in the leisure counseling process.

Social behaviors by definition necessitate that two or more people be involved, in this case the client and at least one other person. A subtle but important point in this regard is that the "involvement" in social behaviors is not always mutually voluntary. One person can "involve" another person in social behaviors by "forcing" that person to behave in certain ways.

For example, if one person "annoys" another person long enough, the second person will eventually react (behave) to the first person's behaviors. In the leisure context such extreme situations are not the rule. However, less obvious but similar situations are common. For example, it is not uncommon for two people, such as spouses, to engage in a leisure activity together and yet have widely different degrees of satisfaction from participation in the activity. This situation is technically social leisure behavior for each person, but it may not be mutually desirable in terms of effective leisure mental health.

The importance of the point just made is that a client's explorations of social behaviors are equally, if not more, subjective than those for personal behaviors. In exploring social behaviors, clients have to offer subjective perspectives and interpretations on their own behaviors *and* on those of others. To be sure, the emphasis is on the former in the leisure counseling context; however, neither the existence nor the importance of the latter can be completely overlooked.

Everyone thinks chiefly of his own, hardly ever of the public interest.

Aristotle

The explorations of a client's social behaviors proceeds in much the same manner as it does for personal behaviors. The leisure counselor might use a series of questions to elicit information about the nature, extent, and satisfaction levels of the client's social behaviors. The leisure counselor might also use an activity similar to the one used for personal behaviors.

The added dimension in the exploration of the client's social behaviors is consideration of the client's perspectives on other people's perspectives on the client's social behaviors. The client might be asked: How do people react to you in social situations? How would you like other people to react to you in social situations? Whose social behaviors have the greatest impact on your social behaviors? And how important is it for your social behaviors to be compatible with those of other people?

Individual Leisure Counseling

Environmental Behaviors. The exploration of environmental behaviors is intended to help clients clarify the ways they interact with their respective environments. A considerable amount of social psychology literature exists to suggest that different environments have different impacts on a person. More importantly, the converse is also true: a person interacts differently with different environments.

Since a leisure activity must be conducted in *some* environment, every leisure activity is in a sense an environmental behavior. In some cases the person-environment behavioral interaction is obvious (e.g. hiking) whereas in others it is very subtle (e.g. reading). Nonetheless, this interaction is present to some degree in every leisure activity.

Life is the continuous adjustment of internal relations to external relations.

Herbert Spencer

The exploration of client environmental behaviors is primarily achieved through verbal discussion and again is highly subjective. The leisure counselor should solicit a variety of information including the types of environments the clients interact with; natures of the client's interactions satisfactions with those interactions; and most importantly, which aspects of the environments have the strongest impact on the client.

The answers to questions about topics such as these will provide information about current environmental behaviors. It is then logical to proceed to a discussion of the environmental behaviors the client would like to have. Similar types of information may be covered in this regard. In addition, it may be helpful to explore what the client might have to do to bring about the desired environmental behaviors.

Since clients may have difficulty discussing environmental behaviors because of "lack of experience" (i.e. they're not a typical topic), it may be helpful to conduct an activity. The easiest way for the leisure counselor to do this is to have the client evaluate the environment currently (i.e. during counseling) around the client and also how the client may be reacting (behaving relative) to that environment.

This is also a good time for the leisure counselor and client to explore further the relationships among the affective and behavioral dimensions. It is important for these relationships to be understood before the cognitive dimensions are explored because the number of interrelationships increases during the next exploration. The exploration of cognitive dimensions "completes the triangle" and brings into focus all the possible combinations among the respective dimensions.

The Cognitive Dimensions

The importance of the relationships among levels of cognitive abilities and human functioning is undeniable. The extent of a person's cognitive abilities is a major determinant of both what and how well the person does things. Leisure is no exception to this generality. For example, leisure activities that are "beyond" a client's cognitive capabilities will rarely be satisfying, except in those instances where leisure activities are used as an escape from cognitive functioning. Consequently, the exploration of a client's cognitive abilities is an important part of th TLC leisure counseling process.

Four cognitive dimensions are considered within the TLC model: capabilities, accomplishments, thinking processes, and knowledge. As before, their interrelationships are readily acknowledged but they are considered separately to facilitate clarity and thoroughness.

It is important to emphasize that the relationships among the levels of cognitive abilities and levels of functioning also are by no means perfect. The strengths of those relationships must be evaluated in light of motivations. Whether motivation is an affective or cognitive dimension is certainly debatable. However, since motivations determine the extent to which cognitive abilities or dimensions are used, it is included here.

The evaluation of a client's motivations is an extremely difficult task. Literally, all leisure counselors have to go on during the exploration stage is what clients report. Some additional information about clients' motivations may be inferred from the clients' behaviors during the action stage. However, in the interim, leisure counselors should simply accept clients' self reported motivations as accurate and proceed as best as possible.

Capabilities. Included within this dimension are explorations of the client's intelligence and specific aptitudes. It is probably best to explore intelligence, as a reflection of general level of mental ability, first and then to move on to aptitudes, as reflections of specific mental abilities. This sequence is recommended because everyone has some mental abilities that are stronger than others and the later discussion of specific "strengths" allows the discussion of capabilities to end on a "positive" note.

As a general rule, informal assessments of a client's intelligence will suffice. At this point in the process the leisure counselor should have gained an opinion about the client's intelligence from the preceding discussions. Careful listening to the language (particularly vocabulary and sentence structure) and the "reasoning" used by the client are important clues in this regard. Relatedly, information about the client's previous behaviors and the intelligence necessitated therein help to form a judgment.

Leisure counselors may help to validate their impressions of clients' intelligence through discussions with clients. Many clients will have valid insights into their own intelligence levels. If an effective counseling relationship has been established, they will share such insights.

As an aid to facilitating exploration of clients' intelligence levels, leisure counselors should point out that most leisure activities are amenable to widely varying intelligence levels. Consequently, only global estimates are needed. They should point out that the purpose of obtaining this estimate is most often to "rule out" certain leisure activities rather than to identify ones to include for consideration.

In a few rare instances clients may be considering activities that require specific (usually high) levels of general intelligence. In these cases the use of standardized intelligence tests may be merited. It would seem most appropriate to use an "individual" intelligence test (e.g. one of the Wechsler scales) since they are usually considered to be more valid and reliable than "group" intelligence tests.

The exploration of client aptitudes follows the same pattern. Leisure counselors can make judgments based on careful listening, particularly from discussions reflecting specific aptitudes. These judgments can be evaluated further through discussions with the client. Similarly, if appropriate, selected aptitudes can be assessed through the use of specific aptitude assessment instruments.

Accomplishments. The exploration of clients' accomplishments (or achievements) is closely related to the exploration of clients' capabilities in that accomplishments are in fact manifestations of capabilities combined with motivations. An arithmetic analogy is obvious: accomplishments equal capabilities plus motivations. Simple manipulation of this "equation" reveals that motivations can be inferred from the differences between accomplishments and capabilities.

So in every individual the two trends, one towards personal happiness and the other towards unity with the rest of humanity, must contend with each other.

Sigmund Freud

An assessment of a client's cognitive accomplishments could be achieved through the use of a standardized achievement test. In rare occasions such precision may be necessary if the client is considering leisure activities which require specified levels of cognitive accomplishment (e.g. writing novels would seem to necessitate mastery of grammatical skills). In most leisure counseling situations, however, the use of a formal assessment will not be necessary. Rather, information gathered through verbal interchange will suffice.

Verbal discussions of client accomplishments should explore two realms: cognitive accomplishments in general and cognitive accomplishments in leisure activities. The former area can be explored by asking clients questions about how well they achieved in school, what (cognitive) activities have they been most successful at, and what other indicators they have of their levels of cognitive accomplishments. The latter area can be similarly explored through the use of similar questions applied to clients' current (or previous) leisure activities.

In addition, the levels of skills development for various leisure activities should also be considered. Clients may be asked how well they have learned the "fundamentals" of their leisure activities, how well they know the rules and guidelines of their leisure activities, or whether they have ever "studied" their leisure activities. Of course they can also be asked simply to evaluate their own accomplishments.

There are also ways to use activities to help clients explore their leisure activity accomplishments. For example, a client might be asked to list past accomplishments. Another (probably more fun) way is to have clients design awards for their leisure accomplishments and then develop awards speeches which recognize their accomplishments.

The exploration of a client's accomplishments should conclude with some discussion of the roles of motivations in leisure activities. This discussion should emphasize that motivations are highly personal and that no attempt is being made to specify what the client's motivations should be. This emphasis is important lest clients get the impressions that their accomplishments and/or motivations are not sufficient.

Thinking Processes. The way a client "thinks" has obvious implications for both the leisure counseling process and the eventual selection of potentially satisfying leisure activities. Consequently, exploration of a client's thinking processes is very important. Thinking processes may be divided into information processing and decision-making functions to facilitate exploration.

Information processing is concerned with how a client obtains (receives), categorizes, and retains information. Decision-making is concerned with the processes (i.e. methods and steps) a client uses to make decisions. Decision-making typically follows information processing in that decisions are made on the basis of information available. However, clients of course also make decisions about what information is processed.

The examination of a client's thinking processes is best achieved through verbal interactions. The exploration of a client's information processing may be begun by asking clients how they best obtain information.

For example, do they obtain their information primarily by hearing, or by seeing, or by a combination of both? This may be followed by questions about the ways they use to retain information. Do they read something several times if they want to memorize it? Do they have difficulty remembering things they hear? And so on. Since by this time in the leisure counseling process the leisure counselor has probably formed some impression of the client's information processing style, this is a good time for feedback to the client and discussion of the validity of the leisure counselor's impressions.

Client's decision-making processes can be explored in a similar manner. The client might be asked questions such as how do you make decisions, what factors affect your decisions, what types of decisions are most difficult for you to make, and how would you evaluate your decision-making skills? Discussion of the responses to questions such as these can be followed by feedback on the leisure counselor's impressions and further discussion of the client's evaluation of that feedback.

The exploration of client thinking processes should close with some discussion of the interrelationships among information processing and decision-making. This is a good time to help the client understand those relationships since it leads naturally into the next dimension to be explored.

Knowledge. The fourth cognitive dimension in the TLC model is knowledge. Within the model, two types of knowledge are considered: knowledge of leisure activities and knowledge of resources for information about leisure activities. There are no standardized tests available to measure either of these types; the assessments must therefore be made on the basis of verbal interactions.

Perhaps the easiest way to explore these types of knowledge is simply to ask clients to evaluate their own levels of knowledge. Most often clients will be fairly knowledgeable of some types of leisure activities and some types of resources. Relatedly, it is also likely they will not be extensively knowledgeable about many other types of activities and resources. Consequently, the discussion is likely to be an educational one in which leisure counselors inform clients of the various possibilities.

In keeping with the perspective that clients have a major responsibility for the leisure counseling process, the attempt should not be made to "educate" clients about all the nuances of all possible leisure activities. Most leisure counselors simply cannot be that well informed, to say nothing of the process inefficiency which would result. Clients should therefore be informed of the major types of resources and then be encouraged to use them. This approach has the added but subtle effect of fostering self sufficiency in clients.

> The greatest torture in the world for most people is to think.
>
> *Luther Burbank*

Some of the major types of resources clients might use include books, pamphlets, magazines, newspapers, bookstores, libraries, television, radio, and local speciality stores. In addition, people who are active participants in various leisure activities are important resources that are often overlooked. Effective leisure counselors will have identified the major local leisure activity resources before beginning leisure counseling processes. If this has been done, then the presentation of resources should be efficiently conducted and should be locally applicable to all clients.

> There is no difference of truth that doesn't make a difference of fact somewhere.
>
> *William James*

This concludes the explorations of the three major dimensions in the TLC model. It should be apparent that there are many commonalities among the various exploration processes presented. These commonalities were intentional because they help to maintain consistency within the leisure counseling process. Further, these commonalities can be diagrammed in order to add to the systemization of the leisure counseling process. The flowchart shown on pages 170-171 is one possibility.

This flowchart presents the major elements of the exploration of each of the dimensions. It is important to note that each part of the flowchart need not be used in each exploration. In addition, the elements fo the flowchart identify what needs to be done or considered, but not how to do it. That specificity is unique to each exploration. The flowchart is offered simply as an aid to conceptualizing the major aspects of each exploration.

> Even if you're on the right track you'll get run over if you just sit there.
>
> Will Rogers

Stage III: Action

The purpose of the action stage is to enable clients to move toward determination of the (potentially) most effective leisure activities. The result of the action stage should therefore be delineation of leisure activities that *should* be satisfying for clients. To achieve this result the stage begins with summarization, follows with consideration of several appropriate courses of action, and concludes with tentative decision-making.

> A life which does not go into action is a failure. . . .
>
> Arnold Toynbee

Summarization. The first portion of the action stage involves summarizing all the information that has been compiled to this point in the leisure counseling process. The easiest way to organize this summarization is simply to review, in order, the elements of the TLC model. Only the major types of information obtained need be covered since it would be highly inefficient to attempt to review everything.

After recapping the highlights of the client information obtained, it is important for the leisure counselor to solicit client feedback on the accuracy of the summarization. This feedback from the client is essential since it serves as the determinant of the most appropriate next portion of the action stage. Three courses of action are apparent.

Figure 2
A Flowchart Model of TLC Leisure Counseling

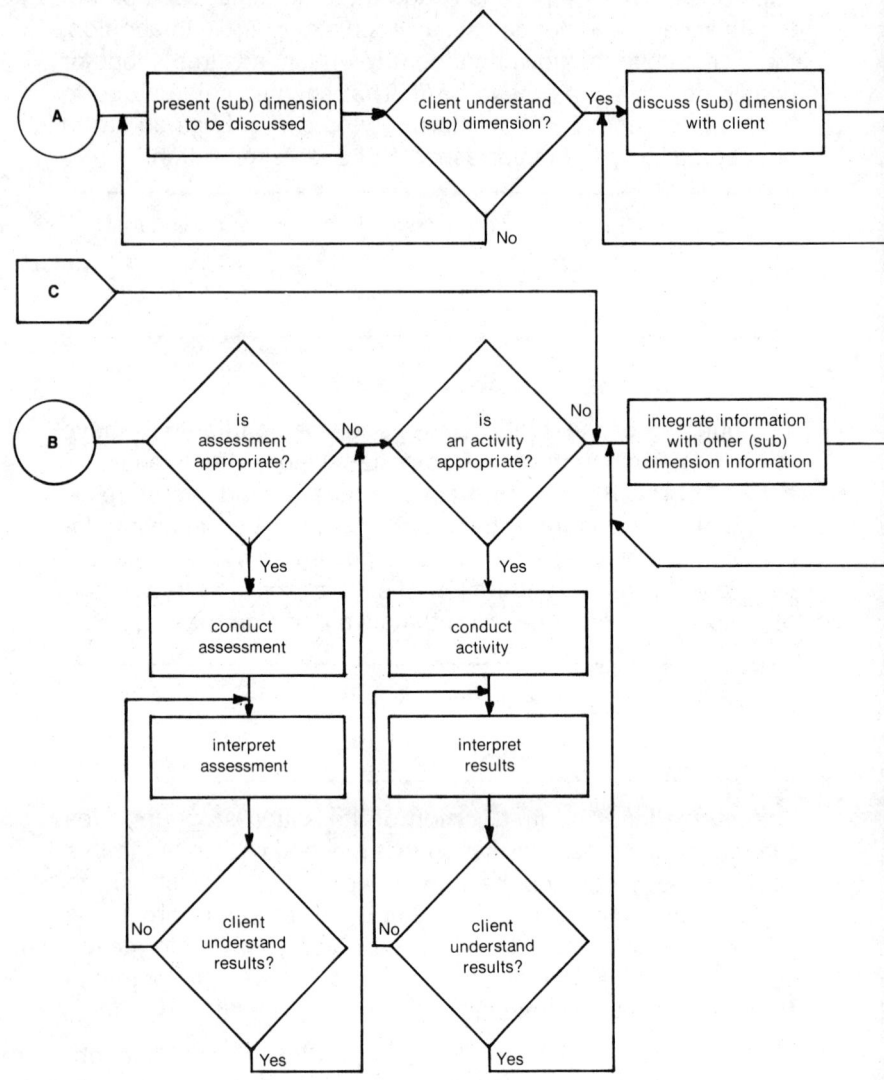

170 Principles of Leisure Counseling

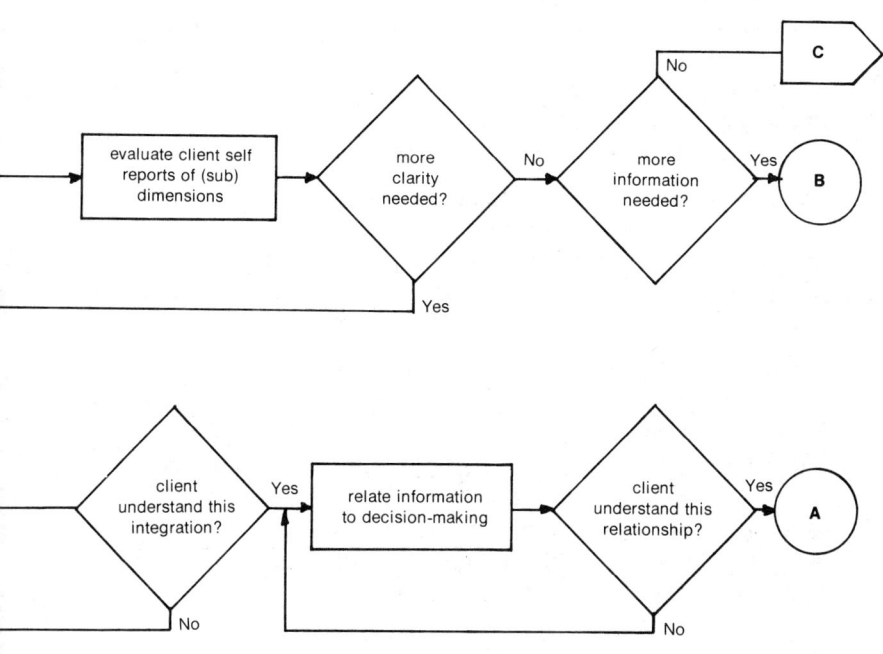

Reconsideration. If the client disagrees with any part(s) of the summarization, the most appropriate activity would be to reconsider the points of disagreement. This would involve reexploring any particular dimension(s) for the purpose of achieving clarity and consensus on the major aspects of the dimension(s).

Experimentation. This will be the most appropriate next step for the majority of clients. Having considered the summarization of the dimensions, some potentially appropriate leisure activities should be apparent. Accordingly, clients should be ready to begin exploratory involvements in those activities.

The experimentation process may proceed in one of two directions. The first involves having the client utilize available resources to learn more about the leisure activities under consideration. Clients should be encouraged to consider each of the TLC model dimensions as they investigate potential leisure activities. This is one of the ways clients can be encouraged, or taught, to be self sufficient for the exploration of potential leisure activities at future points in their lives.

All life is an experiment. The more experiments you make the better.

Ralph Waldo Emerson

The second possible direction is for clients to move directly into participation in some potentially appropriate leisure activities. This alternative might follow directly after summarization if clients feel they are knowledgeable enough about the activities, or if they simply want to "learn by doing." However, this alternative might also follow clients' investigations of potential leisure activities via the first alternative. In either case the purpose is to have clients gain some "first hand" experience in the leisure activities.

It is important for clients to understand that their first impressions of their participations may not be totally accurate. Experimentation involves participation on a limited basis and client evaluations of those participations may not be the same as they would be if they participated on continuing bases.

For example, if a client attempts a new sports activity, it may be necessary to rent equipment for the initial participation. The client might therefore decide that the activity is too expensive. However, if the client were to participate in the activity on a regular basis, it would probably be appropriate to purchase the necessary equipment and therefore reduce participation costs over extended use.

Movement to Termination. In a few rare instances clients will be ready to move to the termination stage after the summarization. The most common example of this is when a client has done some "self counseling" before entering the leisure counseling process and is essentially only looking for "confirmation" from the leisure counselor. Since clients with this degree of definitiveness at this point in the process are rare, caution should be used in selecting this alternative.

Decision-making. It is important to emphasize that decision-making in the action stage is somewhat tentative. The goal is to clarify *how* the client makes decisions rather than to finalize decisions. This part of the leisure counseling process should therefore be related to the decision-making discussion in the exploration of the cognitive dimensions.

The easiest way to help clients begin to make decisions about leisure activities is to ask them to "think out loud." This allows comparisons between the ways that clients described their decision-making processes and the ways they are actually making them at this point. It also allows for suggestions about how clients may make decisions more effectively.

To understand is hard. Once one understands, action is easy.

Sun Yat-sen

The action stage concludes with a statement and summarization of any decisions that have been made so far. This discussion should acknowledge that important decisions should not be made hastily and that no decision should be considered irreversible. Also, clients should be encouraged to adopt the perspective that there are not "bad" decisions; rather, that there are some decisions which are less effective than others.

This perspective is important for two reasons. First, it maintains a "positive" perspective on decision-making processes. Second, it helps clients allay fears about making "wrong" decisions and therefore having "failure" experiences. Together these emphases help to maintain client motivations both in the leisure counseling process and toward leisure self sufficiency.

Stage IV: Termination

The purpose of the termination stage is to bring closure to the leisure counseling process. Accordingly, two major activities occur during this stage: decisions about leisure activities are "finalized" and the counseling process is terminated.

If reason is a universal faculty, the decision of the common mind is the nearest criterion of truth.

George Bancroft

There is usually some time lapse between the action and the termination stages (as will be discussed shortly), so the termination stage begins with a review of what has been covered and experienced thus far.

The two important types of information to be reviewed at the beginning of the stage are the client's perspectives on what has happened relative to previously selected leisure activities during the intervening period and what decisions, if any, the client has made about the selection of leisure activities.

It is assumed that the client has continued experiential exploration of potential leisure activities during the intervening period. Therefore, the client should have at least some additional information and probably more definitive evaluations of those leisure activities. These two factors should again be related to the client's decision-making processes. It is likely that some of the potential leisure activities were evaluated more favorably than others. Therefore, the client should be helped to develop a prioritized list of those activities which have good potential for leisure activity satisfaction.

The resulting list is obviously not *the* definitive list of the only leisure activities which may be satisfying to the client. For one thing, the client may not have participated enough to have reached definitive conclusions. For another, it is likely (and probably desirable) that the client listed *types* of leisure activities along with a few specific examples. Thus the particular leisure activity a client chooses to represent the type may yet have to be determined. And finally, as before, no decision is irreversible.

This remaining tentativeness should not be over emphasized lest the client be given the impression that leisure counseling has been inconclusive, yet it should not be ignored either. The client should be informed that the decisions made were seemingly the most appropriate ones that could be made, but that they may change in the future depending on the course of the client's life. This should be followed by a review, summarization, and encouragement for the "self sufficiency" skills the client has developed during the leisure counseling process.

The next to the last step in the leisure counseling process is to obtain a client's evaluation of the process. Depending on particular needs and situations, this evaluation may be either oral or written. Regardless of the method used, the client should be asked to point out both strong and weak points in the process. Such information is vital to the continued improvement of leisure counselor skills and services.

The actual termination of the leisure counseling process should involve the usual social amenities appropriate for the situation. In addition, the client should be appraised of the opportunities for more leisure counseling at future dates should the need arise. And finally, the client should be encouraged to tell associates about leisure counseling and how it might be useful to them.

Scheduling. Effective and appropriate scheduling of the leisure counseling process is essential if it is to be successful. If the pace is too fast, the client may be overwhelmed, significant information may be overlooked or the client may misperceive the leisure activity evaluation and decision-making processes as overly simplistic. Conversely, if the pace is too slow, the client may become bored or misperceive the leisure evaluation and decision-making processes as too complex to merit the effort. Consequently, establishing effective leisure counseling schedules is an important leisure counselor skill.

The basic leisure counseling scheduling guideline is to let the client determine the most appropriate pace. This is of course in keeping with the theoretical premise of emphasizing the individuality of each client. The best and easiest way to let the client set the pace of the process is to ask the client for feedback on a periodic basis. Thus, at convenient points in the process the client might be asked, "Do you think we should proceed faster, slower, or about the same pace as we have been?"

A related question is, "Do you feel we have covered this topic thoroughly enough?" Questions such as this should at least be asked at the end of each of the respective stages. In addition, a similar question is appropriate at the conclusion of the discussions of each of the dimensions of the exploration stage.

The mind is the man, and knowledge mind; a man is but what he knoweth.

Francis Bacon

A specific guideline as to the number of sessions necessary to complete the leisure counseling process is not possible. However, assuming a session is typically about one hour, it is unlikely that the process recommended here could be implemented effectively in less than five sessions. Further, the sessions should probably be spread across three or more days. A shorter period will probably compress the process too much and therefore inhibit the client from (mentally) "digesting" the content of the sessions. A longer period between sessions may result in "forgetting" and therefore interrupt the continuity of the sessions.

The one exception to the preceding guideline is the period between the action and termination stages when the client should be "trying out" various leisure activities. The ease with which clients will find such opportunities is highly individualistic, depending on both motivations and circumstances.

The client should be encouraged to "try out" the various activities several times before making definitive evaluations of them. This may necessitate as much as a three or four week interim period. The client should, however, be advised against making the interim period more than about four weeks since again this will disrupt the continuity of the process.

It must be considered that there is nothing more difficult to carry out, nor more doubtful of success, nor more dangerous to handle, than to initiate a new order of things.

Machiavelli

A final word of caution is appropriate at this point. Clients will often want to know how long the leisure counseling process takes and will usually raise this question at the beginning of the process. A good tact is to provide the client with an overview of what is involved in the process and to state that the client will have a great deal of control over how long the process lasts. Experienced leisure counselors may of course also provide some information on the typical durations of their leisure counseling processes with other clients.

In the final analysis, the schedule for the leisure counseling process is dependent on two categories of factors. The first are those associated with or controlled by the client. These include such things as motivations, abilities, and opportunities. The second are those accociated with or controlled by the leisure counselor. These include leisure counseling skills, abilities, resources, and motivations.

Discussion Questions

1. The effectiveness of "facilitative responding" or "active listening" skills for establishing counselor-client rapport is well documented in the professional literature. Explain this effectiveness in terms of your favorite theory of human functioning (e.g. learning theory, needs theory, etc.).

2. What is the potential for the use of "confrontation" skills and techniques in the individual leisure counseling context?
3. What indicators might a leisure counselor use to evaluate whether the pace of the leisure counseling process is appropriate for a client?
4. What (professional) ethical issues are likely to arise in the individual leisure counseling context?
5. What should leisure counselors do if they believe their clients have prematurely terminated the leisure counseling process?
6. If a leisure counselor determines that a client has a "problem" outside the realm of leisure counseling, what techniques might be used to bring about an effective referral?

Study Activities

1. Compose a statement of how you would introduce yourself at the beginning of the individual leisure counseling process.
2. Construct a time schedule for individal leisure counseling that would be appropriate for one of your "typical" clients (now or in the future).
3. Develop a list of questions or statements that you could use to elicit an *objective* evaluation of your leisure counseling from your clients.
4. Form a triad with two of your peers. In a role-playing situation, have one person be the client, one the leisure counselor, and one an observer. Role-play the beginning of the action stage. Have the observer provide feedback to the leisure counselor. Rotate "roles" so that each person has the opportunity to play each of the roles.
5. Construct a flowchart model for the termination stage.

Chapter VII

Group Leisure Counseling

Group counseling is popular in the counseling professions primarily because it allows counselors to extend their services to more clients in the time available for counseling. Relatedly, group interactions allow for multiple perspectives which are not possible in individual counseling. These benefits are obviously desirable in the leisure counseling context.

What we cannot invent, we may at least improve.

Charles Caleb Colton

The TLC model discussed previously is amenable to a group leisure counseling format. Primary attention is again given to the affective, behavioral, and cognitive dimensions of leisure. The four basic goals remain the same (although as applied to each group member) and the group leisure counseling process contains the same four stages. The major differences between individual and group leisure counseling, when the TLC model is used, are thus not in terms of the major components of the counseling process, but rather in terms of the natures of the counselor-client(s) interactions.

Perspectives on Group Leisure Counseling

Group leisure counseling typically involves a leisure counselor and 6-10 persons (i.e. clients). Groups of less than six persons are of course possible, but they tend to diminish the potential benefits of group interactions by limiting the number of contributed perspectives. Similarly, groups of more than ten persons diminish the potential of group interactions by limiting the respective involvements of the individual participants.

Time Considerations

One of the primary differences between individual and group leisure counseling is the time necessary to complete the process. Group counseling typically takes longer because of the number of people involved. However, when this time extension is considered against the time it would take for a leisure counselor to work with each person individually, the "additional" time is indeed minimal.

Never be so brief as to become obscure.

Tyron Edwards

The longer time required for group leisure counseling is primarily attributable to the fact that a group which is *effective* for *each* participant should proceed only as rapidly as its "slowest" member. That is, the components of the group leisure counseling process must take as long as is necessary (within reasonable limits) for each participant to achieve the desired results from each stage.

Group Member Considerations

The major implication of this time consideration is that relatively homogeneous groups are usually desirable. Homogeneity should be in terms of how quickly group members function, both verbally and mentally.

However, groups may, and probably will, vary greatly in terms of other personal characteristics. Therefore, this suggestion for homogeneity should be regarded as a desirable but not essential consideration, since often times situations beyond the control of the leisure counselor (e.g. class schedules) will in fact be the major determinant of group composition.

Practical Considerations

While the time necessary for group counseling is longer than for individual leisure counseling, the time available is of course not unlimited. Practical and professional considerations dictate that the process should be completed as rapidly as possible. The ramification of time constraints is that the depth of exploration of topics in group leisure counseling is often less than in individual leisure counseling.

Leisure counselors may find it necessary to help particular group members fully complete their respective explorations during time outside the group. This may be accomplished either through individual attention from the leisure counselor or by having participants continue the explorations on their own.

The preceding paragraphs may seem contradictory in that one suggests taking all the time necessary while another suggests limiting the depth of individual group member explorations. In actuality, this is a reflection of the professional dilemmas facing leisure counselors; practical constraints conflict with ideological goals.

Professional Considerations

The resolution of this dilemma is for the leisure counselor to decide what is a reasonable depth of exploration to achieve in the time available. This determination is made through careful consideration of the characteristics and abilities of each group member. It should then be possible to determine an appropriate "pace" for the process, and also whatever outside activities may be necessary to supplement the process.

Advantages of Group Leisure Counseling

As alluded to earlier, the major advantage of group leisure counseling is that it allows for input from multiple perspectives. In the individual leisure counseling (i.e. dyadic) situation, two perspectives may be offered — one from the leisure counselor and one from the client. In the group situation there are at least as many perspectives as there are people in the group. This allows each participant to receive a wide variety of inputs or feedback on any point of discussion. More importantly, as any perspective is offered, it may "trigger" an idea in any of the other participants.

It is usually the case, therefore, that many significant and important perspectives on a discussion point are presented in the process. This is not only beneficial to each individual group member, but also to the group as a whole. That is, the group benefits in that the process is expedited by reducing or eliminating the need to reconsider or rediscuss points that were not sufficiently covered at some earlier point in the process.

Consult your friend on all things, especially on those which you respect yourself. His counsel may then be useful where your own self-love might impair your judgment.

Seneca

Another major advantage of group counseling is the opportunity for a climate of "psychological safety." Such safety is of course present in individual leisure counseling and clients are free to "experiment" in interactions with the leisure counselor. However, group leisure counseling extends the potential for safe experimentation to persons other than the leisure counselor.

Leisure counselors may establish psychological safety in a group through behaviors such as modeling, establishing interaction rules, and monitoring and redirecting inappropriate interactions. Once the feeling of psychological safety is established in the group, each member should have ample opportunity to "experiment" with any point of discussion with the other group members. If this occurs, the group members have in fact assumed part of the role of the leisure counselor, which should in turn provide for a more effective experience for each participant.

A final advantage of group leisure counseling is that the knowledge (i.e. human resource) base for each member increases as a function of the number of people in the group. Each group member brings to the group a wealth of information and, theoretically, that information is available to all group members. This pool of information is especially important in regard to knowledge gained from the personal experiences of each group member.

A Disadvantage of Group Leisure Counseling

The primary disadvantage of group leisure counseling is of course that the amount of "attention" afforded a participant by the leisure counselor is greatly diminished as compared to individual leisure counseling. This limitation may be significant for some clients, and group leisure counseling may not be appropriate for them.

The determination of which is most appropriate must be made on the basis of individual client needs and situations. Also, not all leisure counselors who are good at individual leisure counseling are good at group leisure counseling, and vice versa. When all of these factors are considered for a particular client, the choice of the most appropriate approach should be evident.

Guidelines for Group Leisure Counseling

All too often counselors assume that group leisure counseling is simply an extension of individual leisure counseling. That is, they assume that group leisure counseling amounts to doing the same things as in individual leisure counseling but with more than one person at a time.

This assumption has often lead to frustrating and ineffective experiences for both leisure counselors and clients. It is true that individual and group leisure counseling processes have similar components. However, the implementations of these components are often very different in the respective processes. The following suggestions are offered to help clarify some of the important differences.

> A man's reputation is the opinion people have of him; his character is what he really is.
>
> *Jack Miner*

Client Screening

An important part of group leisure counseling is client screening. However, client screening is done during the joining stage of individual leisure counseling, but it should be done prior to formation of the group in the group leisure counseling process.

Client screening is also a part of determining group membership. It is done to avoid placing clients in awkward, threatening, or embarrassing situations once the group process is begun. Such an occurrence would not only be detrimental to the person in question, but also to the other group members as well since they might form misperceptions about their own suitabilities for the group.

Screening begins with determination of the appropriateness of leisure counseling for the person. This part of the process is essentially the same as it is in individual leisure counseling. If leisure counseling is deemed appropriate, a second determination must be made as to whether individual or group leisure counseling is most appropriate.

This determination is based on the leisure counselor's evaluations of the client's willingness, motivation, commitment, and ability for participation in group leisure counseling. However, leisure counselors must also bring into play their own professional judgments.

Man's character is his fate.

Heraclitus

Assessments

Assessment activities (i.e. testing) are a potentially important supplement to group leisure counseling as they are to individual leisure counseling. However, assessment activities probably should not be incorporated directly into the group leisure counseling process. For one thing, the time needed to assess all group members will interrupt the "flow" of the group counseling process. For another, different clients will have different reactions to being assessed and some of these may be highly disruptive to the group process and/or to intra group cohesion.

We are all exceptional cases.

Albert Camus

One viable alternative is for the leisure counselor to conduct assessments prior to beginning the group leisure counseling process. This procedure has the advantages of fostering additional motivation for participation in the group leisure counseling process and of providing sufficient time for the scoring and evaluation of assessments.

Another alternative is to use assessments as temporally appropriate during the group leisure counseling process, but to conduct the actual assessments during non-group time. Either of these alternatives should allow for the effective use of assessment *results* in group leisure counseling without unnecessary disruption to the process.

Leisure Counselor Behaviors

The remaining major differences between individual and group leisure counseling are in regard to actual leisure counselor behaviors. As in individual leisure counseling, leisure counselors should use active listening and facilitative responding skills extensively. The leisure counselor's use of such skills serves as a "model" for how group members should interact among themselves.

Group discussion and cohesion can also be facilitated by the leisure counselor's use of linking, pairing, and contra-pairing responses. A linking response occurs when the leisure counselor identifies a "link" between comments offered by two or more group members. For example, if person A says,"I like to play golf" and person B says, "I like to work in a garden," the leisure counselor's linking response might be, "Both A and B like to be outdoors."

A pairing response is when the leisure counselor notes that two or more group members have said essentially the same thing. For example, if person A says, "I do pretty well in school" and person B says, "I work hard to get my grades up," the leisure counselor's pairing response might be that, "Both A and B get good grades in school."

A contra-pairing response occurs when the leisure counselor notes that two or more group members have made essentially opposite comments. For example, if person A says, "I'm uncomfortable at parties and stay by myself" and person B says, says, "I like mingling with people at parties," the leisure counselor's contra-pairing response might be, "A, you're more subdued in social situations, whereas B, you're more outgoing."

The number of people involved in group counseling places an even greater emphasis in staying "on task" than in individual leisure counseling. Consequently, leisure counselors should expect to make more discussion guiding responses in the group situation. Responses such as, "Thank you for sharing that; I hope we can discuss it further at some other time" help to keep the group from digressing from the purpose at hand.

Leisure counselors may also find it necessary to stop or "correct" group member comments when a group member makes a negative, derogatory or otherwise inappropriate comment to or about another group member. These types of responses also relate to the modeling phenomenon discussed earlier.

Process Balance

A group leisure counseling experience will be most effective when it contains a balance of action and discussion. Extensive, overly lengthy discussions among a few group members usually result in a loss of involvement and boredom by those not involved in the discussion. Relatedly, repeated use of activities without sufficient time for discussion (processing) of the purposes and results of the activities will cause members to lose sight of the purposes of the group leisure counseling experience.

Achieving an effective discussion/activity balance is thus a significant challenge to a group leisure counselor. As in individual leisure counseling, such balance is best achieved by thorough preparation by the leisure counselor. It is subsequently enhanced by the leisure counselor's sensitivity to the group members' psychological states during the process.

These guidelines provide a framework for group leisure counseling and help to differentiate it from individual leisure counseling. However, the actual group leisure counseling process proceeds in the same four stages as the individual leisure counseling process.

Stage I: Joining

Some of the most important leisure counselor behavior occur during the joining stage of the group leisure counseling process. In individual leisure counseling the leisure counselor's involvement level with the client is relatively consistent, and intense throughout the process. However, in group leisure counseling the leisure counselor's involvement level is initially very high but decreases across the process as other group members become more involved with one another (i.e. as the group becomes more self sufficient).

Starting the Process

The purpose of the joining stage again is to foster rapport and the development of effective interactional relationships. As in individual leisure counseling, this process begins with social greetings. The greetings are followed by a crucial phase of group leisure counseling: namely, the development of effective relationships among the group members. This important task is usually accomplished when the leisure counselor maintains a relatively high control over the nature of initial reactions. For example, the leisure counselor should carefully explain the purposes of the group and the types of activities to be used.

The first great gift we can bestow on others is a good example.

Morell

Setting Ground Rules

The leisure counselor's behaviors during the joining stage should also include an explanation of the "ground rules" for participation in the group. These ground rules typically include such things as that group members may participate to the levels they feel comfortable, that there should not be "put downs" or other derogatory comments, and that the ends to be achieved through the group are unique for each group member. These guidelines should be strongly emphasized to make the group members feel as comfortable as possible and to establish the "tone and environment" for subsequent interactions.

Building Rapport

The facilitation of rapport among group members during the initial stages of group leisure counseling may be accomplished through one of several methods. One approach is for the leisure counselor to lead an informal discussion on some topic (usually related to leisure) and to encourage each group member to participate to some degree in the conversation. During this discussion the leisure counselor should model active listening, facilitative responding, and other cohesion building skills as much as possible.

For some groups (e.g. children), it may be appropriate for the leisure counselor to explain the types of interactive statements or questions and responses being made. This should provide group members with insights and examples about how to interact in the group.

If you once forfeit the confidence of your fellow-citizens, you can never regain their respect and esteem.

Abraham Lincoln

The facilitation of rapport among group members may also be enhanced through the use of an "icebreaker" exercise. An icebreaker exercise is an activity designed to help group members get to know something about one another in a relatively short time period. Icebreaker activities are usually highly structured and typically involve some degree of self-disclosure.

It is important for leisure counselors to be thoroughly versed in the use of an icebreaker exercise prior to implementing it in a group. This will help to insure that particular group members will not be upset by the exercise. One possible icebreaker is *Vacation Fantasy*. Other examples of proven (i.e. shown to be effective and yet "safe") icebreaker exercises may be found in Pfieffer and Jones (1980).

Talk not of wasted affection; affection never was wasted.

Longfellow

Vacation Fantasy

The leisure counselor explains to the group members that each of them is going to have the opportunity to describe a "perfect" vacation. The group members should be encouraged to be as specific as possible about their "perfect" vacations. They are also told that they are not allowed to offer any comments until all members of the group have described their respective vacations. Each group member in turn then describes a vacation.

After each group member has presented, the group leisure counselor conducts a discussion about the vacations described. Particular attention should be paid to the similarities and differences among the presentations. Considerations of factors such as locations, times, costs, number of people involved, and specific activities are helpful in this regard.

> God asks no man whether he will accept life. That is not the choice. One must take it. The only choice is how.
>
> *Henry Ward Beecher*

Introducing the TLC Model

After the rapport building activities have been completed, the leisure counselor should focus the group discussion on the personal nature of leisure activities by introducing the dimensions of the TLC model. This may be accomplished through a brief explanation of the affective, behavioral, and cognitive dimensions and how they relate to human behavior in general and leisure behaviors in particular.

The subsequent discussion among group members can be developed by the leisure counselor asking some general, open-ended questions. For example, the leisure counselor might ask, "How do feelings relate to leisure behaviors?" or "What relationships are there between a person's mental (cognitive) abilities and that person's leisure activities?" It should be noted that the purpose at this point is simply to familiarize participants with the dimensions, not to begin full scale exploration of them. Consequently, the questions used should not require highly specific or personal responses.

The joining stage concludes with a summarization by the leisure counselor. It also should include a reaffirmation of the interactional ground rules so that they will be reinforced further. The summarization should then move to a brief overview of the next stage.

Stage II: Exploration

The exploration stage in group leisure counseling has essentially the same purposes as it does in individual leisure counseling. In general, these purposes concern having each group member explore the various dimensions in as personal a manner as possible.

The explorations of the dimensions are in many cases similar to those used in individual leisure counseling, with appropriate modifications for a group situation. Therefore, in order to avoid redundancy, the following discussions of each dimension will focus only on the aspects of the explorations specific to group leisure counseling.

Affective Dimensions

The affective dimensions relate to each individual's affective characteristics as they in turn relate to the individual's leisure activities. Because of the "social" nature of group interactions, as well as temporal constraints, the affective dimensions are not likely to be as thoroughly or deeply explored for each group member in group leisure counseling as in individual leisure counseling.

It will probably be necessary for some group members to do some exploration on their own. Thus the group process also contains an "educative" aspect. That is, the group interaction should enable each participant to be able to identify and conduct further self explorations outside the group. These outside activities should supplement, but not replace, intragroup interactions.

Feelings. The explorations of feelings and how they relate to leisure activities are facilitated primarily through the use of questions. Many of the questions suggested for individual leisure counseling may be modified for use in a group context.

The unique aspect of the group leisure counseling process is that the leisure counselor should encourage the group members to develop and ask the questions. Thus the process usually begins with the leisure counselor asking a few general questions (which in effect is a modeling of the behavior) and then becomes a situation where the group members question and respond among themselves.

This transition may be facilitated by a question from the leisure counselor such as, "What other questions could we ask ourselves that would help us understand how our feelings relate to our leisure activities?" It should be noted that in the course of the discussion, the differences between feelings and attitudes should again be emphasized.

Attitudes. The exploration of attitudes and their relationships to leisure activity selection and participation follows a pattern similar to that for individual leisure counseling. The important difference is that the group situation affords an excellent opportunity for discussion of the social influences and factors in attitudes.

Direct reference to what attitudes are present in the group and how they relate to group members may be a highly significant self insight experience for each group member. Such insights will be facilitated through the leisure counselor's use of linking, pairing, and contra-pairing responses. In addition, the leisure counselor's identification of "I" statements will help group members understand the sources of their responses.

Values. There are seemingly innumerable values clarification activities that could be adapted to the group leisure counseling context. Their use is highly recommended—for two reasons. First, the introduction of a structured activity at this point in the process helps to enhance group motivation by affording a "change of pace" for the group members. Second, structured values clarification activities are an efficient way of exploring a topic which might otherwise require quite lengthy discussion. However, two points of caution should be noted.

First, although a number of values clarification activities have been proposed, not all have been "tested." Accordingly, leisure counselors should carefully consider activities used.

Second, values clarification activities are rarely "self contained." That is, group "processing" in the form of discussion is almost always necessary following an activity in order for each group member to achieve the full, personal relevance of the activity.

Expectations. The exploration of expectations for leisure activities may be begun by an explanation of some of the potential benefits and liabilities of leisure activity participation (as covered in Chapter II) by the leisure counselor. This should lead to a discussion of expectations among the group members.

Interests. The exploration of all the possible leisure interests for each of the group members would obviously be an excessively time consuming activity were it achieved through discussion in the group. Accordingly, the use of a leisure interest assessment instrument or some other technique outside of the group is recommended.

The assessment of leisure interests can be effectively integrated into the final portion of the screening process. As noted, this would allow time for scoring, as well as leisure counselor review of the results, prior to the time the results are discussed in the group. The ensuing discussion could then focus on the interpretations of the results and the factors influencing the ways those results may be personally applied.

Everybody acts not only under external compulsion but also in accordance with inner necessity.

Albert Einstein

One important point in the discussion of leisure interests is the relationships between interests and motivations. The leisure counselor should help the participants understand that interests and motivations are related, but not necessarily synonomous. This typically involves the leisure counselor making a brief presentation for the group.

Personal Characteristics. In-depth explorations of the personal characteristics of each group member is usually not appropriate for group leisure counseling. For one thing, such exploration would be excessively time consuming. For another, and more importantly, some of the topics that could be discussed might be "sensitive" and therefore make some group members too uncomfortable in the situation. Given these limitations, an appropriate way for the leisure counselor to facilitate explorations of personal characteristics is to initiate a general discussion.

In other words, the leisure counselor can have the group members discuss how personal characteristics relate to leisure activities, without reference to particular group members. Each group member should then be able to ask questions or offer comments as is personally appropriate. This will alleviate the "threat" in the discussion but allow group members to discern what is needed for understanding of their respective personal characteristics.

It is possible that assessments of personal characteristics (e.g. personality inventory results) may be integrated into this exploration. If so, the procedures used should be essentially the same as those for leisure interests. However, extreme caution should be used in how the results of these assessments are shared in the group. In addition, leisure counselors should carefully explain the psychometric limitations of personal characteristics assessments.

The exploration of affective dimensions should conclude with a summarization by the leisure counselor. This summarization covers the major points that have been made relative to each dimension and reiterate appropriate cautions in interpretations. This part of the process allows for personal summarization by each of the group members. This may be accomplished by having each group member construct a "personal log." The group members should be instructed to write a few comments about each of the dimensions explored. A sample of what this log might look like is shown in Figure 3.

Figure 3

My Leisure

1. My feelings about my leisure activities:
2. My attitudes about my leisure activities:
3. My most important values:
4. My leisure activity interests:
5. What I want from leisure activities:
6. The kind of person I am:
7. How active I am:
8. What I do when I'm alone:
9. What I do when I'm with others:
10. Places I like to be:
11. Things I know a lot about:
12. Things I can do well:
13. Thing I have done well in the past:
14. How I learn best:
15. How I make decisions:
16. Leisure activities I know a lot about:
17. Places I can find information on leisure activities:
18. Leisure activities I would like to try:
19. People I know who like the things I do:

Behavioral Dimensions

The same four behavioral dimensions are explored in group leisure counseling as are explored in individual leisure counseling. These explorations generally should not be particularly threatening to group members since they will have a choice in selecting the specific behaviors they discuss and since behaviors are usually a less sensitive topic.

Temporal factors relating to group size come into play here, too, and the behavioral explorations are not as involved as in individual leisure counseling. It is therefore important to help group members be able to analyze their own behaviors during time outside of the group context. This is accomplished in part as an outgrowth of the group activities and in part as a function of instruction from the group leader.

Physical Behaviors. The exploration of physical behaviors is concerned with how much physical activity is exhibited by an member of the group. The exploration is usually begun with a discussion initiated by the leisure counselor. However, the group context allows for other types of activities to be used as well. For example, each group member could be asked to specify how much daily physical activity is appropriate for people in general and then to provide a "justification" for the recommendation. This could be followed by a (mini) "debate" as to the appropriate amount.

Of course the leisure counselor should emphasize that there are not right and wrong answers and that the activity is used to demonstrate peoples' different perspectives. The discussion and activity could then be followed by having each group member explain how much daily exercise is appropriate for oneself.

Personal Behaviors. The explorations of personal behaviors in the group leisure counseling context allows for an interesting contrast to be discussed. Personal behaviors are by definition unique to each individual. However, as the group members discuss their personal behaviors, commonalities are likely to emerge. This affords group members the opportunity to discern, in behavioral terms, how their behaviors are alike and different from other people's. This is another part of the process which is best achieved through informal discussion facilitated by the leisure counselor.

Social Behaviors. The group leisure counseling process provides an excellent opportunity for group members to examine how they behave in social situations. The exploration of social behaviors can be demonstrated by having group members carefully examine how they have been, and are, acting in the group—one type of social context. The group members can also be encouraged to look at how their behaviors have changed from the beginning of the group till the current time. They can then be asked how typical their current behaviors are of other social contexts. This discussion can then be generalized to leisure activity in other social situations.

A word of caution is in order here. In considering social behaviors within the group, the group members should be requested to consider only their own behaviors and not to analyze the behaviors of others. A group leisure counseling experience is not a sensitivity or encounter group, and should not even remotely resemble them.

Behavior is a mirror in which every one displays his image.

Goethe

Environmental Behaviors. In general, the explorations of the ways people interact with their environments and the ways those interactions relate to leisure activities are best conducted through discussions of questions such as those used for individual leisure counseling. This discussion may, however, be supplemented with an activity in order to add variety to the group leisure counseling process.

For example, group members could be asked to describe and share what they consider to be their "perfect" leisure activity environments. Other group members might be asked to comment on the "perfect" environments described and possibly even to suggest "improvements." Such an activity would of course involve reflections of the group members' respective values. The leisure counselor could use this point to emphasize how the various aspects of the leisure counseling process interrelate with one another.

The explorations of the behavioral dimensions concludes with a summarization by the leisure counselor, which includes highlighting the important points made during the various discussions and activities. The group members may again provide their own summarizations and make appropriate entries in their logs.

Cognitive Dimensions

The explorations of cognitive dimensions in group leisure counseling is a difficult task and one which places a heavy emphasis on leisure counselor skills for maintaining proper perspectives within the group. Asking group members to evaluate their own cognitive abilities is difficult and people are usually reluctant to do so.

The use of assessment instruments cannot be recommended because the results may be highly "sensitive" to some group members. Yet even in light of these difficulties, the cognitive dimensions should be explored because of their importance for effective leisure activity evaluation and selection. Consequently, leisure counselors must strive to achieve a situation where group members have insights into their cognitive abilities, but are not threatened or unduly uncomfortable in the process of gaining those insights.

Capabilities. The explorations in this portion of the process include considerations of both general intelligence and aptitudes. Perhaps the safest way to explore these dimensions is for the leisure counselor to make a brief presentation on intelligence and aptitudes, and then to initiate an informal discussion on how they are evaluated. This discussion should help the group members identify some ways they might determine and evaluate their own cognitive capabilities.

The methods which evolve from such a discussion will more than likely be informal in nature. Consequently, leisure counselors should stree the (psychometric) limitations of such methods. After the various methods have been proposed and discussed, the leisure counselor should lead the discussion toward the relationships between cognitive capabilities and leisure activities.

Accomplishments. The exploration of accomplishments is again a direct outgrowth of the exploration of cognitive capabilities. Accordingly, essentially the same tact should be followed in this exploration as in the previous one. A brief presentation, an informal discussion which does not cause group members to self disclose more than they wish, and some suggestions for self evaluation of accomplishments should suffice. This is, however, also a good place to discuss how motivation interacts with ability to produce a level of accomplishment. A few brief comments by the leisure counselor are usually adequate to emphasize this interaction and to stimulate appropriate discussion within the group.

Thinking Processes. The exploration of thinking processes focuses on the two major topics of information processing and decision-making. Concerns about the sensitivities of these topics and the time necessary for thorough exploration of them again suggest that they be covered in rather general terms.

It should be noted that the purpose of this portion of the process is not necessarily to help group members *improve* their information processing or decision-making skills. Rather, it is to help them become more aware of their own skills. This purpose involves considerably less time than the former.

In most cases a brief presentation by the leisure counselor about the ways people process information and make decisions, and an informal discussion will be adequate to facilitate awareness. The group members can then be encouraged to continue to analyze and evaluate their information processing and decision-making skills on their own.

Knowledge. The group leisure counseling process is particularly well suited to helping individuals both explore and gain leisure activity and resource information. The number of people in a group greatly extends the possible information to be shared over that in a dyadic counseling process. A simple yet effective activity that can be used is to have the group members both share the information they have about various leisure activities and "brainstorm" resource information sources. An informal group discussion can then be used to help each group member determine which information and resources are personally appropriate. The initial summarization of the explorations of the cognitive dimensions is essentially the same in format as those for the other dimensions. It includes a recapping by the leisure counselor, log entries by the group members, and leisure counselor responding to remaining questions and concerns. This summarization should be followed by another which has two purposes. First, the leisure counselor should provide a brief overview of the interrelationships among the three sets of dimensions and how they relate to leisure activity evaluation and selection. Second, the leisure counselor should provide a brief overview of what will happen in the next two stages so that group members do not assume the process is completed at this point.

Stage III: Action

The purpose of the action stage is to facilitate further exploration of potential leisure activities through experimentation outside the group context. The basic elements of this experimentation are similar to those in individual leisure counseling, but there are some aspects unique to the group situation.

Thought is the blossom; language the bud; action the fruit behind it.

Emerson

Summarization

The initial activity for the action stage is for each group member to summarize and synthesize the personal information obtained thus far. The summarization procedure is most easily accomplished through references to the personal logs completed by each group member. The goal of this activity is to have each group member determine the personally most appropriate next step in the process. This is usually accomplished through an informal discussion where each group member has the opportunity to relate immediate plans.

Action Planning

The typical course of action for group members will be the initiation of some activities which will further enhance their understandings of themselves and/or potentially appropriate leisure activities. Planning for this activity, usually through informal discussion, is therefore the next step in the process.

Experimentation

The activities potentially appropriate for the respective group members generally will fall into two categories: information gathering and trial participation. The information gathering activity involves having the respective group members find and evaluate information about leisure activities that might be of interest to them. This activity is particularly appropriate for group members who are considering activities of which they have little or no knowledge.

> Experience increases our wisdom but doesn't reduce our follies.
>
> *Josh Billings*

The trial participation activity involves having group members participate in (try out) activities they have selected as potentially appropriate. Trial participations should be engaged in by all group members, though some will be delayed until they have completed information gathering activities.

> The future is purchased by the present.
>
> *Samuel Johnson*

A unique advantage of the group leisure counseling process is that it allows participants to work together in the experimentation activities if they so desire. For example, several group members could visit a library or other resource center together to gather information. Similarly, if several group members all identified the same leisure activity as one they would like to try, they could try it together. Such group activities not only further enhance intragroup cohesion but also allow for more effective feedback for the initial portions of the termination stage.

The number of activities engaged in by the group members during this stage is contingent on the (relatively) unique situations and characteristics of the group members and the resources and opportunities available. However, it is essential that all group members have sufficient time to complete information gathering activities and at least one trial participation activity. Further activities beyond that should be on a time available basis.

> Friendship is always a sweet responsibility, never an opportunity.
>
> Kahlil Gibran

Stage IV: Termination

The purpose of the termination stage in group leisure counseling, as in individual leisure counseling, is to bring closure to the process. The activities used are therefore very similar to those suggested in the last chapter.

> Joys divided are increased.
>
> Josiah Gilbert Holland

The initial activity of the termination stage in group leisure counseling is to have each group member share individual experiences from the action stage. This sharing should include not only a description of what was actually done, but also the group member's reactions (e.g. feelings) about the activity. Group members should be encouraged to question or comment on each member's sharing as is appropriate. This feedback and input from the other group members should help to enhance the significance of the activity for the group member presenting the activity.

> Characters do not change. Opinions alter, but characters are only developed.
>
> Benjamin Disraeli

> All our final decisions are made in a state of mind that is not going to last.
>
> Marcel Proust

Next in the sequence is an informal discussion intended to help group members "finalize" their selections of potentially appropriate leisure activities. This discussion is the culmination of the counseling process in that it helps group members synthesize all that they have experienced previously. It should also allow them to have relatively definite plans about how they are going to proceed (at least in the immediate future) with their leisure activities.

Two final activities conclude the group leisure counseling process. The first is some form of evaluation of the process. Again, as in individual leisure counseling, this evaluation may be informal, as in verbal or written comments, or formal, as in the use of rating scales or other evaluation instruments. The second is the actual termination of the group which includes both the usual social amentities and any comments about future leisure counseling possibilities as may be appropriate for the group members.

Scheduling

The major points made about scheduling in the previous chapter are also pertinent here and therefore need not be repeated. One modification is appropriate however. Since leisure counselors should be the best judges of the varying rates in the group, they have the responsibility for determining the most appropriate progressions. In general, the group should proceed only as rapidly as is effective for the slowest group member. However, in some cases a few group members may be excessively slow and it would be unfair to the other group members to proceed at such a slow pace. In these cases it is probably appropriate to suggest individual leisure counseling for the slowest group members and to other group members.

Discussion Questions

1. What group counseling leadership styles would be most effective for group leisure counseling?
2. What group counseling process dynamics vary as a function of the number of the people in the group?
3. What are the major factors influencing the scheduling (ie. group meeting) pattern for a group leisure counseling process?
4. What are the advantages and disadvantages of using co-group leaders (i.e. two leisure counselors) for group leisure counseling?
5. What behaviors should be evaluated to determine whether a group has achieved sufficient interpersonal cohesion to allow for exploration of "sensitive" topics?

Study Activities

1. Select a client population of your choice. Develop a list of selection criteria you would use for inclusion or exclusion of those potential clients for group leisure counseling.

2. Select a client population of your choice. Outline a time schedule for group leisure counseling you feel would be appropriate for the potential clients.

3. Develop a list of "ground rules" you feel would be appropriate for the interpersonal interactions in the group leisure counseling process.

4. Interview (individually) two persons who have done group leisure counseling. Ask them: (a) what they believe to be the major factors influencing the success of group leisure counseling and, (b) how they evaluate the success of their group leisure counseling. Compare and contrast their responses.

Chapter VIII

Developmental Leisure Counseling

Throughout most of the history of the counseling profession, the term counseling has been colloquially interpreted to mean a process of correction or remediation. That is, when people think of "counseling," they think of something being done to "solve an existing problem." However, not too many years ago, some counseling professionals began speaking and writing of using counseling as a process for helping people either avoid problem situations or be prepared to cope with them as they arise. These processes are typically referred to as *developmental* counseling, although a variety of other terms have been used.

To exist is to change, to change is to mature, to mature is to go on creating oneself endlessly.

Henri Bergson

The importance and need for developmental leisure counseling is evident from several perspectives. However, any list of need justifications would most certainly include the following major points:

1. The changing "world of work" will have associated changes in the "world of leisure".
2. Societal changes (e.g. longevity) will result in more time and more options for leisure activity.
3. Technological changes will influence the natures and forms of leisure activities.
4. Economic fluctuations will influence leisure activity patterns.
5. If the history of the profession continues to follow the same pattern, there will not be a sufficient number of leisure counselors available to provide "remedial" leisure counseling services to all who need them.
6. Stress will continue to be a major mental health problem and leisure activity will continue to be viewed as a method of stress reduction. As these changes and situations arise, people will need to be more leisure self sufficient and to be able to cope in effective ways. For these reasons, developmental leisure counseling promises to be an important part of the leisure counseling realm.

A Perspective on Developmental Leisure Counseling

Developmental counseling processes and activities have been presented by numerous authors but the term is usually associated with Donald Blocher. In his 1966 book, *Developmental Counseling*, Blocher enumerated the basic tenets of the developmental counseling process. Most of the current professional literature on developmental counseling can be traced to Blocher's conceptualizations, even though his book is not typically referenced because of its age.

Perhaps the most important contribution of Blocher's work was his presentation of *generic* developmental counseling principles. In other words, the principles he espoused were not tied to a particular topic (e.g. values, vocations, leisure), but were adaptable to a variety of potential topics, including leisure.

Developmental leisure counseling is intended for use before "problems" occur. Thus developmental leisure counseling is intended to be educative or preventative, whereas other types of counseling are primarily intended to be remediative, adjustive, or therapeutic (Blocher, 1966).

Developmental (leisure) counseling, like "regular" (leisure) counseling, is based on several important assumptions. Primary among these is that people have a great deal of psychological and behavioral freedom (Blocher, 1966). In any given situation, a person has available a wide variety of options on how to think, feel, behave, and so on. People do not have *total freedom to do whatever* they please, yet in reality people do have many alternatives. Developmental leisure counseling strives to enable a person to select those leisure alternatives which are personally effective.

Never tell people *how* to do things. Tell them *what* to do and they will surprise you with their ingenuity.

Gen. George Patton

Another important assumption is that people can learn and obtain skills that will enable them to make effective decisions. Inherent in this assumption is the belief that people want more satisfying and effective lives, and will be motivated to move toward those ends. Developmental leisure counseling strives to enable motivated people to have effective leisure decision-making skills.

A third basic assumption is that people are, in general, mentally healthy (Blocher, 1966). Since developmental leisure counseling is intended for implementation before "problems" arise, it is reasonable to assume that people are functioning at least fairly effectively before the process is implemented. Developmental leisure counseling strives to continue and enhance existing effective leisure skills and behaviors.

A final relevant assumption is that awareness is an essential requirement for effective leisure (and indeed life) adjustment. The learning and refinement of personal skills will be useless if people are unable to determine the proper times to implement them. Developmental leisure counseling strives to enhance personal awareness of self, others, and situations in the leisure context.

These assumptions are similar to, and in concert with, those identified previously in the general discussion of leisure counseling. It should also be evident that the definition of leisure counseling presented in Chapter III encompasses developmental leisure counseling. Similarly, the goals and purposes presented for leisure counseling are general enough for, and readily adaptable to, developmental leisure counseling processes.

These close associations between developmental and so-called regular leisure counseling were intentional and are essential for conceptual continuity. However, it should not be assumed that the two processes are identical because there are some distinct differences.

The only completely consistent people are dead.

Aldous Huxley

Process Guidelines for Developmental Leisure Counseling

Since developmental leisure counseling is an educative/preventative process, all participants in the process should be aware of this perspective. Developmental leisure counseling is not a substitute for remediative leisure counseling. Consequently, some screening of participants should occur before the developmental leisure counseling process is begun. In most cases a simple question such as, "Do you feel *very* dissatisfied with your leisure?" directed at each potential participant will suffice. Persons responding in the affimative to the question should be encouraged to seek remediative leisure counseling, or perhaps some other type, as opposed to developmental leisure counseling.

The educative aspect of developmental leisure counseling necessitates that effective teaching principles be incorporated into the process. A good discussion of these principles from a perspective consistent with the one here may be found in *Facilitative Teaching* by Wittmer and Myrick (1980).

The educative aspects of developmental leisure counseling also necessitate that particular attention be paid to the ways ideas and information are presented, and the ways they are learned. The methods of presenting information may be divided into two general categories: didactic and experiential. Didactic presentations include lectures, readings, handouts, charts, figures, audio and videotapes, and so on. Experiential presentations include activities where people "learn by doing", such as through group activities, field trips, practice and so on.

In most developmental leisure counseling processes, both didactic and experiential presentations will be used. An important decision is, therefore, whether didactic presentations should precede experiential ones, or vice versa. The preferred order is contingent on the counselor's "style" and the nature of the participants. However, as a general rule of thumb, both types of presentations should be used to convey the most important ideas and information.

The ways people learn may similarly be divided into two general categories: visual and aural. The visual mode of learning is most appropriate for people who learn by seeing things, such as through the use of pictures, slides, films, videotapes, observations, and so on. The aural mode of learning is most appropriate for people who learn by hearing things, such as through the use of lectures or other verbal presentations, audiotapes, and so on.

Since the determination of an individual's preferred learning mode necessitates rather sophisticated evaluations, most counselors will not be able to make such determinations because of practical limitations. Additionally, any group of potential participants in developmental leisure counseling is likely to contain some persons with each type of preferred learning mode. Accordingly, it is again suggested that activites allowing for either type of learning on the same topic be incorporated into the developmental leisure counseling process.

The two types of information presentations, didactic and experiential, and the two types of learning modes, visual and aural, allow for four possible combinations. Participant interest and motivation in the developmental leisure counseling process will be enhanced when the various combinations are all used and balanced throughout the process.

Since the developmental leisure counseling process is future oriented, there is at least some time lag between the end of the process and the ultimate "test" of its effectiveness; that is, the actual attempt to implement the skills learned. Learning within the developmental leisure counseling context is akin to other types of "academic" learning—skills that aren't periodically practiced or otherwise continued are soon forgotten. (Can you still diagram a sentence correctly?)

In order to help people retain at least the basic information and ideas from developmental leisure counseling, the provision of materials for future reference is strongly recommended. These materials might include such things as handouts summarizing important points, reference lists, charts, diagrams, test profiles, and so forth. These materials will provide handy resources for participants who may need to "refresh their memories" in the future.

Only the educated are free.

Epictetus

The "psychological atmosphere" for the developmental leisure counseling process should be maintained as a positive one. Since the experience is intended for persons without serious leisure problems, it should not be threatening, anxiety provoking, or otherwise negative for any participant. The maintenance of a positive atmosphere may be facilitated in several ways.

First, an open and clear discussion of the distinctions between developmental and remediative leisure counseling should be provided at the beginning of the process. Second, participants should be encouraged to participate only to the extent they are confortable doing so. This is particularly relevant to activities that involve sharing and other types of self-disclosures.

Third, examples used during the process should be such that they are not threatening to any participant. Fourth, participants should be encouraged to provide input and feedback at any point in the process. This allows any participant to have some feeling of "control" over the process. Finally, counselors should be responsive to any input or feedback received during the process and adjust the process as much as possible to it.

These process guidelines for developmental leisure counseling must be adjusted for specific application to any particular group of participants. Such adjustments are most effectively made by careful planning and preparation. This preparation should include consideration of the following important factors:

Types of Participants

To the greatest extent possible, developmental leisure counseling should "tailored" to the participants. For example, vocabulary adjustments may have to be made depending on the educational backgrounds of the participants.

A small man can be just as exhuasted as a great man.

Arthur Miller

Facilities

All too often potentially effective developmental leisure counseling processes are "defeated" by failure to take into account the advantages or limitations of the physical setting for the process. For example, while small group discussion activities are typically desirable, they will be inhibited by a room that "scrunches" the groups together.

Resources

Possible resources for developmental leisure counseling include people, materials, and equipment. The respective availabilities of each of these types, as well as their qualitative characteristics, will define the potentials for their uses in the process.

Counselor characteristics

Not all leisure counselors work well with all types of people. A suitable "match" between the leisure counselor and the participants is essential for an effective developmental leisure counseling process. The suitability of the "match" should take into account factors such as the leisure counselor's training, experience, "style," personality, and preferred type(s) of participants.

TLC Developmental Leisure Counseling

The Triangulation Leisure Counsling (TLC) model described in Chapter IV may be readily adopted for developmental leisure counseling purposes. The three basic dimensions (affective, behavioral, cognitive) again provide convenient and significant focal points within a developmental perspective. In addition, some of the previously suggested counseling activities may be used for developmental purposes. However, before beginning a description of TLC developmental leisure counseling, a few comments about its applications are in order.

At a theoretical level, developmental leisure counseling processes can be implemented with any number of people. In actual practice, however, developmental leisure counseling often is done in small groups (e.g. 4-8 persons), or even more commonly with "classroom size" groups (e.g. 20-35 persons).

The use of groups for developmental leisure counseling is particularly desirable for one vary pragmatic reason. After the process has been concluded, it is likely that the leisure counselor will not be available as a resource for most "routine" leisure evaluations and decisions. The use of groups in the developmental leisure counseling process therefore enables each participant to test and evaluate various interactive behaviors relative to using other people (who are not leisure counselors) as resources for leisure considerations.

In sum, the use of group interactions for developmental leisure counseling is both a better "modeling" procedure and a closer approximation of the participants' eventual real life situations than is one-to-one interaction.

The preceding two chapters have discussed some of the basic considerations and activities for leisure counseling with individuals and small groups primarily from a remediative perspective. Since the basic leisure counselor skills needed for developmental leisure counseling are similar, the implementation of the skills primarily involves changing the purposes and activities used.

In most cases these modifications are easily made; they amount to focusing on the future more than on the past. In order to avoid redundance as much as possible, the following discussion of TLC developmental leisure counseling will be made as if the process were being used with a relatively large group (say 20 or more). This will allow for the use of leisure counseling principles with yet another size group.

Stage I: Joining

The large group, TLC developmental leisure counseling process begins by the leisure counselor's self introduction. The realtionships between the leisure counselor and the participants themselves will not be nearly as personalized as in individual or small group situations. Consequently, leisure counselors should make every effort to insure an effective beginning for the process.

The goals of the introduction should be to make everyone feel as "comfortable" as possible and to establish the "psychological atmosphere" for what will follow. These goals are usually accomplished in two ways. First, the leisure counselor should make a personal (self) introduction which conveys expertise (training and experience), a sense of professionalism, preparedness, understanding, sensitivity, and receptivity.

The second method for achieving these goals is through the use of "icebreaker" exercises. These exercises usually amount to subdividing the large group into small groups of 4-8, having the small groups work on some task, and then having each small group report on the results of their efforts. The purposes and goals of icebreaker exercises are the same here as they were in the previous chapter, only with applications to a larger group of people.

The leisure counselor's personal introduction and an icebreaker activity constitute the sum total of the joining phase of TLC developmental leisure counseling. Given the limited natures of these experiences, it is obvious that leisure counselor-participant rapport will be at best limited.

> No pleasure is fully delightsome without communication; and no delight absolute unless imparted.
>
> Montaigne

Accordingly, leisure counselors must continue to develop rapport with each participant throughout the process. While this is true for all leisure counseling processes, it is even more crucial in the large group situation, since the initial attempt at relationship building is so restricted.

> At best, the renewal of broken relations is a nervous matter.
>
> Henry Brooks Adams

Stage II: Exploration

The purpose of the exploration stage again is to investigate systematically each of the dimensions of the TLC model. The focus is primarily on future situations, through references to current and past situations are often used as examples.

The leisure counselor has two primary roles during this stage: teacher and activity leader. The teaching function involves presentation of information through any of a variety of procedures as well as responding to participant concerns or questions as they arise. The activity leader function involves coordinating various activities and insuring that participation is as effective as possible.

The Affective Dimensions. The exploration of affective dimensions begins with consideration of feelings. The actual process should probably begin with a presentation by the leisure counselor. This presentation should incorporate (but not necessarily be limited to) the following discussion topics:

1. "Definitions" of feelings.
2. Relationships among feelings, behaviors, and cognitions.
3. Differences between feelings and attitudes.
4. Uses and misuses of feelings words in interpersonal communications.
5. Internal and external "causes" of feelings.
6. Verbal and nonverbal methods of expressing feelings.
7. Methods of improving self awareness of personal feelings.

The presentation should of course center on these topics as they relate to leisure (as a concept) and to leisure activities. It should also allow for discussion and questions from the particiants.

The presentation might be followed by, or paired with, an activity that helps to clarify and reinforce the points made in the presentation. For example, the participants might be asked to list ten feelings that they currently have about their leisure activities.

They could then be asked to list ten feelings that they would like to have about leisure activities. Finally, volunteers could be asked to share some of the words from each of their lists. Activities such as this allow people to "practice" the use of feeling words and also to focus on their own feelings about leisure activities.

Attitudes

The next affective dimension for consideration is attitudes. In order to allow for variety in the process, this portion might be begun with an activity. One possibility is to have participants volunteer attitude statements about leisure activities, or leisure in general. Each volunteer could also be asked to identify a "source" for each statement (e.g. self, friend, relative, group or organization, famous person, and so forth).

These statements could be written on a chalkboard for the participants to allow for identification of commonalities and differences in both the statements and the sources. Such a discussion should effectively lead to a presentation about leisure related attitudes.

A presentation on attitudes should "key off" the activity and cover at least the following discussion topics:

1. Definitions of attitudes.
2. Relationships among attitudes, behaviors, and cognitions.
3. Differences between attitudes and feelings.
4. Sources of attitudes.
5. Relationships between attitudes and stereotypes.
6. Verbal and nonverbal expressions of attitudes.
7. Methods of improving self awareness of personal attitudes.

A similarity to the presntation on feelings should be apparent. This similarity is important because it should help participants be able to compare and contrast their own feelings and attitudes.

Values

The next affective dimension to be considered is values. Unfortunately, developmental counseling activities concerned with values are all too often simply limited to the use of a "values clarification" activity. The *potential* benefits of values clarification activities cannot be denied. However, the limits of the potential benefits are restricted if it is erroneously assumed that values clarification activities are *necessarily* beneficial in and of themselves.

In other words, mere participation in a values clarification activity does not guarantee that each participant will gain the maximum benefit from the activity. Often something else is needed to help participants be aware of the benefits to be derived from their participation. This is particularly true in large group situations where the potential for "personalization" is reduced.

With this caution in mind, the logical adjunct to leisure values clarification activities is a presentation. Discussion topics which should at least be covered in this presentation would include:

1. Relationships among values, behaviors, and cognitions.
2. Relationships among values, feelings, and attitudes.
3. Identification of the most common types of leisure values.
4. Sources and reinforcers of leisure values.
5. Methods of improving self awareness of personal (leisure) values.

A presentation such as this will enhance the effectiveness of values clarification activities by helping participants understand the "nebulous" yet highly personal nature of values. Such understanding is also desirable because values tend to be "sensitive" topics, and a misinterpretation of a values clarification activity could have severely detrimental effects on the developmental leisure counseling process.

There are many values clarification procedures which can be adapted for developmental leisure counseling purposes. For example, one relatively simple procedure is to have the participants list fifteen things they like to do, then to rank order their lists, and finally to specify a value reflected by each activity listed. These lists can then be shared with the large group for discussion and feedback (e.g. other opinions on the values reflected by each activity).

Some others suitable to (developmental) leisure counseling purposes have already appeared in the leisure counseling literature (cf. Connolly, 1977; Edwards, 1980). Still others which are easily adaptable may be found in the numerous books available containing values clarification activities (e.g. Simon, Howe, and Kirschenbaum, 1972; Howe and Howe, 1975).

Expectations

The fourth affective dimension to be considered, expectations, is probably best explored by first using an activity. Since expectations are highly personal in nature, it is probably best to establish a personal "frame of reference" before a presentation is made. This will help alleviate the possibility of some participants getting the impression that their expectations are "inappropriate," either too high or too low.

One potentially appropriate activity would be to subdivide the participants into small groups and then to have them generate a list of potential benefits from leisure activity. Each person in each group could then be asked to identify and perhaps rank order those benfits which are personally most appropriate.

There is no duty we so much underrate as the duty of being happy.

Robert Louis Stevenson

Another possible activity would be to present the participants with a list of potential leisure activity participation benefits and then have them rate each one on a scale of 1 to 10 for personal appropriateness. Either of these activities and others like them should in turn be followed by large group discussion, sharing, and questioning to personalize further the basic concepts involved.

A presentation on expectations from leisure activities should follow. This presentation should specifically emphasize that (a) expectations are highly personal and (b) that there are no "good" or "bad" expectations. In addition, this presentation should address at least the following discussion topics:

1. Potential benefits from leisure activity participation.

2. Potential disadvantages of leisure activity participation.

3. Methods of evaluating personal expectations from leisure activity participation.

4. Methods of coping with unanticipated results (positive or negative) from leisure activity participation.

Some large group discussion would follow this presentation since participants may have concerns about what are (personally) *appropriate* expectations.

Interests

The exploration of leisure interests is the fifth step in the affective dimension sequence. Under "ideal" conditions, it would be effective to have had the participants complete a leisure interest inventory prior to beginning the TLC developmental leisure counseling process. This would allow the exploration of leisure interests to begin with a large group "interpretation" of the results of the respective assessments. Explanations of trends and patterns could be provided and concerns about validity and reliability could be discussed.

In most typical situations, however, it will not be possible to have participants complete an inventory prior to the process. In this case activities will have to be used to facilitate leisure interest exploration. On possible activity would be to subdivide the participants into small work groups. The group tasks would be for each participant to identify some leisure activities not yet participated in but that one might like to try. This would be followed by the group members sharing their identifications and evaluations (to the extent they are comfortable doing so).

The future is the past returning through another gate.

Arnold Glasow

Another possible activity would be to present the participants with lists of general categories of leisure activities and then to have them evaluate individually how much they think they might like to try some of the activities. This could be followed by large group discussion of each of the categories and "strawvote" counting of the participants interested in each category.

A presentation about the nature and characteristics of leisure activity interests should accompany the activity. This presentation should include (but not be limited to) the following discussion topics:

1. Subjective aspects of leisure interests.
2. Relationships between interests and motivations.
3. Methods of evaluating leisure activity interests.
4. Relationships between leisure activity knowledge and interests.
5. Temporal stabilities of interests.
6. Factors influencing leisure activity interests (e.g. social/-cultural facotors, feelings, attitudes, values, personal characteristics, resources, etc.)

Personal Characteristics

The last affective dimension to be explored is personal characteristics. This is another "sensitive" topic. It must be handled cautiously in the large group situation lest some participants start playing "amateur psychologist" either with themselves or others. Such a situation must be avoided, even if it means omitting this step in the sequence.

> The only thing worse than an expert is a person who thinks he's an expert.
>
> *Aly A. Colon*

Because of the potential for psychological harm from inappropriate interactions, activities should not be used for explorations of personal characteristics. An appropriate tact is for the leisure counselor to make a general presentation and to allow each participant to interpret it for themselves.

This general presentation should occur in one of two ways. First, if the leisure counselor has a preferred perspective on human functioning, this presentation is essentially a coverage of one theory of personality, particularly as it relates to leisure.

Second, if the leisure counselor uses several different perspectives on human functioning, this presentation is an overview of the highlights of several theories of personality. In either situation at least the following topics should be discussed for every perspective presented:

1. Determinants of human behavior as they relate to leisure activity.
2. Characteristics of a mentally healthy personality.
3. Resources for obtaining more information about the theory.
4. Sources for more in-depth evaluations within the context of the theory.
5. Methods for maintaining"objectivity" in interpreting a theory as it pertains to self.

This presentation should be followed by large group discussion since there will more than likely be questions from the participants. This interaction should emphasize that "explanations" (i.e. theories) of personal characteristics merely attempt to describe human functioning; they do not "dictate" how people should behave. The information provided should then be related to the ways people select and use leisure activities.

The explorations of the affective dimensions should conclude with a brief recap by the leisure counselor. This recap should include the most important points made for each dimension. Finally, any remaining questions from the participants should be addressed before the second set of dimensions are explored.

The Behavioral Dimensions. The exploration of behavioral dimensions follows the same sequence as in individual or small group leisure counseling processes. Accordingly, it beings with exploration of physical behaviors after a few introductory comments about the behavioral dimensions in general.

The exploration of physical behaviors could begin with an activity intended to help participants become more aware of the types and extents of physical behaviors in their lives. One possibility would be to subdivide the participants into small groups with the task of generating a list of types of physical behaviors (e.g. strenuous, nonstrenuous, "work" behaviors, leisure behaviors, rest, and so forth).

The members of the group could then be asked to evaluate how much of each type they have in a "typical" week. They could then be asked to reapportion the amounts as they would like them to be. Finally, the group members could share and discuss their respective listings with the other group members.

A presentation on physical behaviors after the activity should include at least the following discussion topics:

1. That a person is *always* behaving in some way.
2. Relationships between physical behaviors and psychological states.
3. Methods of categorizing physical behaviors.
4. Methods of assessment and evaluation of personal physical behavior patterns (e.g. personal behavior "logs").

This presentaton should also allow for large group discussion at its conclusion.

We visit others as a matter of social obligation. How long has it been since we visited with ourselves?

Morris Adler

Personal Behaviors

The consideration of personal behaviors may be initially confusing to participants and so it should probably begin with a presentation. This presentation should start with a definition of personal behaviors and then incorporate at least the following discussion topics:

1. Psychological advantages and disadvantages of personal behaviors.
2. Distinctions between personal and social behaviors.
3. Methods of assessing and evaluating personal behaviors.
4. Distinctions between work and leisure personal behaviors.

In addition to being responsive to questions, the discussion following this presentation should emphasize that personal behaviors vary widely from individual to individual.

One possible activity related to the latter point in the discussion is to have the participants respond individually to several questions. For example, participants might be asked to assess how much time they spend, and how much time they would like to spend, in personal behaviors. They might also be asked to identify their own benefits and disadvantages from personal behaviors. Finally, those who are comfortable doing so could be asked to share some of their responses with the large group.

Jealousy is all the fun you think they had.

Erica Jong

Social Behaviors

Since personal and social behaviors are in some ways conceptually related (i.e. one is the converse of the other), one appropriate approach to the exploration of social behaviors is to parallel the approach for personal behaviors. Thus a presentation on social behaviors would begin with a definition and include at least the following discussion topics:

1. Psychological advantages and disadvantages of social behaviors.
2. Distinctions between personal and social behaviors.
3. Methods of assessing and evaluating social behaviors.
4. Types of social behaviors (e.g. casual, intimate, functional, etc.).

As before, individual variations in preferences for social behaviors should be emphasized in the discussion following the presentation.

An activity which may be used is one that "repeats" the one used for personal behaviors but focuses instead on social behaviors. If this activity is used, a subsequent discussion could enable participants to compare and contrast their perceptions of their own personal and social behaviors.

Environmental Behaviors

Since environmental behaviors are another type that might be initally confusing to participants, their exploration also should start with a presentation. This presentation should include discussion topics such as the following:

1. Psychological reactions to varying environments.
2. Methods of evaluating different types of environments (e.g. open, closed, indoor, outdoor, etc.).
3. Factors influencing environment selection (e.g. type of leisure activity, resources, availability, etc.).

The discussion following this presentation should be responsive to participant questions and also help participants to understand that they are always in some type of environment.

One possible activity for exploring environmental behaviors is to subdivide the participants into small groups and have each group "evaluate" the current environment in terms of its impact on the participants. This activity can be repeated after slightly modifying the environment through changes in such things as lighting, seating arrangements, and so forth. A final task might be to have the group members identify and share their favorite leisure environment(s) with the other group members.

This concludes the exploration of the behavioral dimensions. As before, the leisure counselor should provide a brief recap of the important points made during this segment of the process. Any remaining questions also should be answered at this time.

The Cognitive Dimensions. The exploration of cognitive dimensions within a developmental perspective is similar to the previous ones in that a presentation and an activity are associated with each dimension. However, a greater emphasis is given to the presentations because the cognitive dimensions are not easily assessed validly in a large group context and because some of these dimensions (e.g. capabilities) are "sensitive" topics.

Capabilities

The exploration of capabilities should probably begin with a presentation in order to avoid having them considered, discussed, or evaluated from invalid, unfair, or unreasonable

perspectives. The presentation should emphasize the highly personal natures of capabilities and cover at least the following topics:
1. Methods of conceptualizing intelligence.
2. Distinctions between intelligence and aptitudes.
3. Problems in evaluating intelligence and aptitudes.
4. Relationships, or lack of them, among intelligence, aptitudes, and behaviors (i.e. performance levels).
5. Sources of information about intelligence and aptitudes (both personal and general information such as school records).
6. Motivation as it affects human performance.
7. Relationships among intelligence, aptitudes, leisure activities, and relative levels of performance therein.

The discussion following this presentation should be conducted carefully so as not to imply that certain leisure activities must be "ruled out" on the basis of self perceived capability limits.

One possible activity following this presentation would be to have the participants individually evaluate some of their own capabilities. This might be accomplished by presenting each participant with a list of aptitudes and then asking them to evaluate themselves for each aptitude listed.

They might also be asked to identify their "strongest" aptitudes, and even to include some not on the list distributed. The discussion accompanying this activity should insure that participants understand that aptitude levels are not "good" or "bad," they just are.

Accomplishments

Accomplishments might be initially explored through the use of an activity. One possibility would be to have the participants list the major "accomplishments" of their lives. Such a list would obviously contain many different types of accomplishments, some of which would be in the leisure realm and some of which wouldn't (e.g. vocational accomplishments, professional accomplishments, and so forth).

The participants could then be asked to divide their respective lists into leisure and non leisure categories of accomplishments. At this point the participants could be asked to (self) evaluate their leisure accomplishments and to compare theirs to others.

Finally, this could be followed by asking the participants to identify what they would like their leisure accomplishments to be in the future. The discussion with this activity should emphasize that this is essentially a goal setting procedure.

This experiential activity could then be followed by a presentation. The presentation on accomplishments need not be lengthy, but it should incorporate at least the following topics:

1. Relationships among accomplishments and capabilities.
2. Methods of self evaluations of accomplishments.
3. Types of accomplishments.
4. Questions relating to whether leisure activities should be evaluated as "accomplishments."

The discussion following this presentation should strive to insure that participants do not feel "lacking in accomplishments." This is best achieved by pointing out that accomplishment is a *relative* word, and that each person has many accomplishments.

Thinking Processes

The exploration of thinking processes should begin with a presentation since participants will not always understand exactly what is implied by the term. The presentation should be divided into two major parts. The first part should focus on information processing and should incorporate, but not be limited to, the following topics:

1. Brief overviews of various learning theories.
2. Sources of information (e.g. sensory, verbal, written, visual, etc.).

3. Preferred modes of information receiving (e.g. verbal and auditory).
4. The current "information explosion."
5. Resources for information processing.

The second part should focus on decision-making and should include at least the following topics:

1. Types of decision-making processes and styles.
2. Factors influencing decisions (e.g. values, resources, capabilities, etc.).
3. Sources of information about decision-making.
4. Relationships among information processing and decision-making.

The discussion following this presentation should incorporate examples of information processing and decision-making from the previous presentations and activities in order to personalize the presentation.

All human activity is prompted by desire.

Bertrand Russell

Of the many appropriate activities, one would be to subdivide the participants into small groups for the purpose of discussing individual information processing and decision-making styles. The instructions to each group would be to have individual group members share their preferred modes of receiving information, primary methods of processing and retaining information, and most common methods of decision-making.

This could be followed by asking group members (who are comfortable doing so) to share whether they would like to change their information processing or decision-making styles, and if so, how. These instructions should of course be put in the contexts of leisure and leisure activities. The discussion following this activity should again emphasize these processes are highly personal in nature and that there is not necessarily a "best" way to process information or make decisions.

Knowledge

The fourth and last cognitive dimension is knowledge of leisure activities and resources about leisure activities. Its exploration could begin with a large group activity. This activity could amount to asking the participants to generate a list of possible resources about leisure information. The list could be written on a chalkboard or newsprint so that it could be copied by the participants and also to emphasize the diversity and extensiveness of possible resources. The participants could also be asked to evaluate which of the listed resources are most appropriate for their individual needs.

The presentation accompanying this activity would simply be a completion of the list already generated. That is, the leisure counselor would identify any other resources that had not been previously listed. The exploration stage should conclude with a summary of the major points discussed for each of the dimensions, with particular attention paid to skills identified and exemplified. The creation and distribution of summary lists, charts, diagrams and so forth by the leisure counselor would be especially helpful at this time. The major intent of the summary is to help the participants begin to understand the various relationships among the dimensions. Accordingly, the summary should be more than just a presention; it should allow for whatever discussion and large group interaction are appropriate.

Action to be effective must be directed to clearly conceived ends.

Nehru

Stage III: Action

In remediative leisure counseling the action stage is intended to help clients select and evaluate leisure activities which have good potential for personal satisfaction. By contrast, the action stage in developmental leisure counseling is intended to help participants begin to use and refine selection and evaluation skills that may be used at a later time. This is accomplished primarily by allowing participants to "practice" skills in situations where "immediate" results are not necessarily desirable.

The primary activity in the action stage of TLC developmental leisure counseling is experimentation. The participants should be directed to "try out" the ideas and skills they have been exposed to in whatever ways are personally most meaningful. The effectiveness of the experimentation is obviously contingent on each participant's level of self awareness. Consequently, the action stage should begin with a discussion of self awareness.

The self awareness discussion should focus on *what* to be aware of and *how* to be aware of it. The what in the present context are the dimensions previously discussed. The *how* is more complicated. At a minimum, participants should be instructed to "stop and think" during or immediately after their experimentation activities to allow them to "become aware of" what factors are in operation.

Perhaps an even better way is to have participants keep a "log" of their activities and their reactions to the activities. This log might include the dimension being considered, a brief summary of the activity, the factors deemed to influence the nature of the activity, and personal reactions to (i.e. feelings about) the activity.

A myriad of experiential activities are potentially appropriate. The general instructions for the activities would be to have the participants identify those dimensions each is interested in exploring and then to identify activities which would allow exploration of those dimensions.

The activities identification and selection process may be facilitated through the use of small group interactions. For example, participants could individually identify preferred dimensions for exploration and then meet in small groups of persons interested in exploring the same dimension, for the purpose of identifying mutually appropriate activities. This procedure has the advantage of allowing those participants who would like to do so to engage in activities with others who have similar purposes.

The easiest way to find more time to do the things you want to do is to turn off the television set.
J. Harold Smith

Time is the obvious limiting factor in the action stage. Time constraints are necessary for both theoretical and practical reasons. The extension of the TLC developmental leisure counseling process beyond reasonable limits is self defeating; participants will lose motivation if the process is too lengthy. On the practical side, leisure counselors typically will not have the flexibility to lengthen the process to limits of their own choosing. Consequently, a reasonable time period should be identified for the action stage before participants begin their activities. Relatedly, participants will need to prioritize their activities in order to meet the time constraints.

If at all possible, the leisure counselor should be available at least periodically for individual consultation during the action stage. This allows participants to obtain help as needed, which in turn maximizes the potential effectiveness of the activities.

Stage IV: Termination

The purpose of this stage in the TLC developmental leisure counseling process is to help the participants gain clarity about their experiences during the action stage. This may be accomplished through three types of activities.

The first activity involves subdividing the participants into small groups. These task groups share perspectives on the results of activities during the action stage. Each group member could relate the nature of the activities conducted, purposes for the activities, results of the activities, and personal reactions to the experiences.

The other group members could offer comments and insights as appropriate. In essence, the small group activity should be relatively informal where gorup members feel comfortable, both sharing and receiving feedback on personal experiences. The process should be kept in a positive perspective. Participants should not be allowed to criticize the experiences of others and should be encouraged to help others understand their experiences more clearly.

The second activity is a large group discussion. In this discussion the participants share experiences which were particularly effective and some which were not very effective. When sharing these experiences, the participants should also be asked to describe some of the feedback they received on their reactions to their experiences. This latter activity is especially important because it helps to emphasize how personal the process is, and how different people may react to the same situation in very different ways.

The third activity is an optional one. This activity allows for individual consultation with the leisure counselor. The small and large group activities are "public" in nature and some participants may be reluctant to share their experiences or reactions in such situations. Thus this latter activity attempts to insure that each participant has had an opportunity to discuss personal activities with someone. Procedurally, this activity is often conducted after the "formal" termination of the developmental leisure counseling process.

The TLC developmental leisure counseling process should conclude with the opportunity for the participants to evaluate the process. In its simplest form this evaluation might be asking the participants to write (anonymously) their comments about the process and the leisure counselor's conduct of it. More sophisticated procedures might involve the use of rating scales or specific questions about particular parts of the process, or the leisure counselor's performance. Such evaluations are vital for effective refinement of the process and improvement of a leisure counselor's presentation and leadership of the process.

Implementation

The preceding description of the TLC developmental leisure counseling process was intentionally general. The intent was based on the belief that a general presentation allows for greater flexibility in interpretation and implementation by leisure counselors. This point has particular significance for scheduling the TLC developmental leisure counseling process.

The process described may be modified in any of a wide variety of ways. For example, the presentations may range from brief to rather extended and detailed descriptions of the various topics. Similarly, the activities can be changed to varying lengths and other activities added or substituted as appropriate. In other words, the process described is a general model which can be easily adapted to a variety of circumstances.

> If you can't answer a man's arguments, all is not lost; you can still call him vile names.
>
> *Elbert Hubbard*

The particular adaptation used for a particular situation is contingent on several factors. The most obvious one is the amount of time available. Under optimal conditions, the stages should be broken down into time blocks spread over several weeks. For example, the first two stages might be scheduled as 1-2 hours a day for a convenient number of consecutive days, the third stage could cover several weeks, and the final stage could be one last 1-2 hour time block.

This type of schedule might be convenient for use in schools or community programs such as adult education activities. Another possibility is to use a workshop format where part of the process is covered in one day and the rest on another day. Regardless of the schedule used, however, it should be determined before beginning the process.

A second, and perhaps more important, factor is the nature of the potential participants. Characteristics such as participants' ages, education levels, and reasons for participating will strongly influence what could, and should, be done. Characteristics such as these also will be major determinants of the schedule even if "unlimited" time is available.

> I have always thought the actions of men the best interpreters of their thoughts.
>
> *John Locke*

Resources are another factor that influence the appropriate form of the process. Physical resources such as room sizes and locations, material resources such as handouts or chalkboards, and human resources such as "assistants" all need to be considered in an effective process plan.

Finally, the characteristics and skills of the leisure counselor are important factors. Given the potential complexity of the process, it is likely that leisure counselors will be more skilled for some parts than for others. Thus the leisure counselor is a key component since these variations will influence the natures of the participants' experiences.

Life is like music. It must be composed by ear, feeling, and instinct, not by rule.

Samuel Butler

The exact nature of the TLC developmental leisure counseling process will be determined by how these factors "come together." Typically, the most effective combinations will result from experience. However, effective planning, with attention given to all important factors, will help to insure that even initial efforts will be effective.

Discussion Questions

1. What are some other common types of developmental counseling? Who are their major proponents? How are those types similar to and different from the model presented in this chapter?
2. Among the combinations of didactic and experiential educative modes and visual and aural learning modes, which is your preferred combination?
3. What are the similarities between teaching and counseling? What are the differences?
4. What methods are you aware of that could be used to evaluate the effectiveness of developmental leisure counseling?
5. Which counseling orientations (theories) are most amenable to developmental leisure counseling?

Study Activities

1. Develop a profile of the pertinent characteristics of a group of people with whom you would like to do developmental leisure counseling.

2. Interview a counselor who has done some type of developmental counseling. Ask about that person's perceptions of the experience in terms of theoretical bases, activities, and evaluations of the worth of the experience. Ask also about perceptions of the participants' attitudes, responsiveness, and evaluations.

3. Design an evaluation procedure which would allow you to investigate the effectiveness of a developmental leisure counseling activity you might conduct.

4. Develop a plan for identifying and soliciting participants for developmental leisure counseling.

5. Identify a clientele of your choosing and then develop a rationale for developmental leisure counseling for that clientele.

Chapter IX

The Fine Points of Leisure Counseling

The preceding chapters have provided basic theoretical perspectives and process guidelines for leisure counseling. They should enable counselors to provide "adequate" leisure counseling services if the information in them is implemented as presented. The leisure counseling services thus rendered certainly would be of benefit. Unfortunately, however, those services would probably be boring (for both leisure counselors and clients) and also probably not be as effective as they should be. Fortunately, leisure counseling services don't have to be boring.

Invention is the mother of necessity.

Thorstein Veblen

The achievement of the full effectiveness of the leisure counseling process, and the "excitement" associated with that achievement, are to a large extent contingent upon the characteristics and abilities of the leisure counselor. The leisure counselor must be *sensitive* to the uniqueness of each leisure counseling circumstance, *creative* in the implementation of the leisure counseling process, and *positive* in all interactions with clients in order to achieve maximum effectiveness.

It is impossible to prescribe *how* leisure counselors should be sensitive, creative, and positive. Such characteristics exist uniquely within each person and therefore are manifested uniquely by each leisure counselor. It is, however, possible to identify some aspects of the leisure counseling process which are particularly well-suited to behavioral manifestations of sensitivity, creativity, and positiveness. These aspects then are what may be called the "fine points" of leisure counseling.

Coping With Negative Attitudes

Since leisure mental health is probably not among the more popular topics of discussion in society, it is likely that many people (i.e. real or potential clients) will have neutral or negative attitudes about leisure counseling. In fact, many will think it is unnecessary, frivolous, or reserved for people who have nothing better to do.

> The most manifest sign of wisdom is continued cheerfulness.
> *Montaigne*

Leisure counselors may therefore expect considerable attitudinal resistance in their efforts to initiate leisure counseling. The elimination, or at least significant reduction, of client resistance implies that leisure counselors may have to attempt to change client attitudes. Historically, many counselors have been trained to behave as if they were "valueless" as far as clients were concerned. It has been considered "inappropriate" for counselors to change or significantly influence client attitudes. However, such generalizations are invalid for several reasons.

First, it is impossible for people to be totally "valueless"; leisure and other types of counselors are constantly displaying values and attitudes in counseling processes. Second, many people are unhappy or maladjusted *because* they hold inappropriate or ineffective attitudes and perspectives. Many counseling processes therefore have the readjustment of client attitudes and perspectives as a primary goal.

The question is therefore not whether counselors should attempt to change client attitudes, but rather in what contexts and in what ways should counselors influence client attitudes.

To be sure, it is not recommended that leisure counselors go around trying to convince everyone that they need leisure counseling. However, for those who *might* benefit from leisure counseling, leisure counselors should help them put leisure counseling in proper perspective. Moreover, counselors will often encounter situations where leisure counseling is deemed an appropriate procedure in lieu of, or in addition to, some other type of counseling.

Creative minds always have been known to survive any kind of bad training.

Anna Freud

Leisure counselor resistance reduction (i.e. attitude change) activities place a premium on creativity. All too often it is assumed that the mere presentation of information is sufficient to effect attitude change. Such is not the case: witness the continuing resistance to reduction in racial prejudice even in light of the evidence refuting significant differences in human characteristics solely on the basis of race. Tactics other than insight facilitation must be used in order to achieve resistance reduction.

A general rule of thumb is that attitude change is most easily accomplished when clients are convinced that changes of attitudes are in their own best interests. In other words, a fundamental counseling precept applies in this context also: (leisure) counseling is most effective when it is uniquely personalized for each client. This personalization should help clients achieve positive attitudes about leisure counseling both before and during the process, and therefore maximize the potential of the leisure counseling process.

Extremists think "communication" means agreeing with them.

Leo Rosten

Differentiating Counseling From Therapy

In addition to client resistance to the need for leisure counseling, leisure counselors must also contend with common stereotypes about counseling in general. The problems in this regard center on the perception of counseling as synonymous with therapy. People often think of therapy as something appropriate for people who are "sick", "crazy", or "weird."

Anybody who goes to a psychiatrist ought to have his head examined.

Samuel Goldwyn

This leads to the supposition that therapy (or counseling) is not something that "normal" people need, or can benefit from. Thus counseling is a term which carries with it a history of attitudinal and perceptual inaccuracies, and this history leads people to resist counseling. Consequently, leisure counselors also often need to overcome negative perceptions about counseling in general in order to provide effective leisure counseling services.

The reduction of negative stereotypes about counseling in general may be accomplished in creative ways to convey the idea that people don't have to be "crazy" to benefit from counseling. The process reflecting this creativity should again result in personalized attention, information, and application for each client.

Using Audio-Visual Materials

A primary way to pique interest in the leisure counseling process is to vary the nature of leisure counselor-client interactions. Typically, a suggestion such as this is interpreted to be a recommendation for the use of experiential leisure counseling activities. They are of course a valid method for introducing process variation. However, another viable method is the use of audio-visual resources. Modern technology coupled with some simple ideas often results in very interesting leisure counseling processes.

Audiotape recorders (particularly cassettes) are now readily available to most leisure counselors and therefore can be an effective resource. For example, audiotape recordings of leisure counseling sessions may be used to help clients "really listen" to themselves. Taping counseling sessions enables clients to hear not only what they said, but also *how* they said it. An activity of this nature may be particularly beneficial during exploration of the affective dimensions of the TLC model. Tape recordings of sessions may also allow clients to review entire sessions at their convenience. This could help to insure that significant and unique aspects of clients' situations are not overlooked or covered too quickly.

Experience enables you to recognize a mistake when you make it again.

Franklin P. Jones

Videotape recorders are available to some leisure counselors and therefore may be used in similar ways. Further, the video aspect may serve to provide even more dramatic "feedback" to clients, particularly in regard to exploration and discussion of nonverbal behaviors.

A wide variety of other audio-visual resources may also be effectively integrated into the leisure counseling process. For example, multi-media presentations, slides, magazine pictures, overhead transparencies, charts, tables, figures, and "staged" photographs all may be used to emphasize, stimulate, or clarify various aspects of the leisure counseling process.

Two points of caution are in order here. First, the use of audio-visual resources, like the use of experiential activities, is not a sufficient substitute for effective leisure counselor-client(s) interaction. Audio visual resources may be used to complement the leisure counseling process, but not to replace it.

Every style that is not boring is a good one.

Voltaire

Second, the use of audio-visual resources can result in "too much of a good thing" if it is not carefully, and sparingly, injected into the leisure counseling process. People can become bored by seeing or hearing "too much" just as they can in "talking" too much. Leisure counselors should strive for *balanced variety* so that the leisure counseling process will be as interesting as it can and should be.

Volunteerism

In the vast majority of cases, the leisure counseling process is, and should be, one which is voluntarily entered into by clients. Perhaps the only exception is when leisure counseling is incorporated into larger programs in certain (e.g. correctional) institutions, though even then "forced" participation is not recommended. Volunteerism is crucial to the eventual effectiveness of leisure counseling for two primary reasons. First, it allows clients to have feelings of control over the process and their roles and behaviors in it. Second, it places some of the responsibility for the success or failure of the process in the hands of the clients. Both of these reasons help to insure that clients will only be involved in leisure counseling processes in personally appropriate ways.

Life is what happens to us while we are making other plans.

Thomas La Mance

Leisure counselors should never coerce, cajole, or otherwise "force" or intimidate people into leisure counseling. Such behaviors are patently unprofessional. Further, persons who enter leisure counseling under such circumstances will likely be highly resistant and uncooperative. The process will then be unsuccessful and disappointing to all involved.

Leisure counselors should also be sensitive to client volunteerism as the leisure counseling process proceeds. All too often counselors become overly upset or rebuffed when clients "prematurely" terminate a counseling process. This is especially true when a client simply fails to show up for a scheduled appointment. However, it *is* the client's prerogative to terminate at any time. Thus while leisure counselors may believe some terminations are premature, they should not be overly strenuous in their efforts to get clients to continue.

Heredity is what sets the parents of a teenager wondering about each other.

Laurence J. Peter

Humor

Leisure counseling is "serious" in that it should be a meaningful and significant experience for clients. However, it does not have to be "serious" in the sense of being devoid of pleasantness and lightheartedness. On the contrary, the leisure counseling process should be enjoyable for clients and this enjoyment encompasses humor in interpersonal interactions. If not overused, levity serves to enhance leisure counselor-client(s) relationships and therefore to influence positively leisure counseling processes.

Humorous jokes and comments which are degrading or derogatory to individuals or groups of people should be studiously avoided. Humor which perpetuates stereotypes also does not have a place in leisure counseling. In general, humor which focuses on events or situations, as opposed to people, is the most appropriate type for use within the leisure counseling context.

Sexism

There are few (if indeed there are any) leisure activities which cannot be enjoyed by men and women alike. Therefore there is no substantive reason why a leisure counselor should vary the fundamental aspects of the leisure counseling process on the basis of the client's sex. Leisure counselors should in fact make every possible attempt to avoid sex role stereotypic behaviors and attitudes. Such behaviors and attitudes are derogatory to both male and female clients and are degrading to leisure counselors. Professionalism dictates that clients are persons, not males or females, as far as the leisure counseling process is concerned.

Sexism (i.e. sex role stereotyping) may, however, be an important theoretical consideration in the leisure counseling process. That is, leisure counseling may be an excellent way for persons to be freed from "sex-role stereotypes" if they so desire. For example, a male may not perceive himself as having the freedom to pursue a "female" vocation (whatever that is. . .), but may pursue such an interest in leisure activities. Thus leisure counseling may enable clients to find satisfying activities without (self perceived) undue emphasis on those activities being sex role stereotypic.

Racism

The comments made about sex-role stereotypes are similarly appropriate for racial stereotypes. There is simply no substantive evidence nor any good reason to believe that some leisure activities are more appropriate to some racial groups than others. Consequently, again, there is no basis for altering the basic leisure counseling process because of the client's race.

In the manner similar to that for sexism, leisure counseling may be used to help reduce racism. Many leisure activities are social in nature and foster interpersonal relationships among people who enjoy similar leisure activities. It is therefore possible for a person to encounter people of other races in the pursuit of a leisure activity. Such interactions can and should lead to better interracial and interpersonal relationships and therefore help to reduce racism.

About the only thing that comes to us without effort is old age.

Gloria Pitzer

Ageism

One type of stereotyping receiving greater current attention is that based on age. Stereotyping on the basis of age has been particularly detrimental to older persons. They have been stereotyped as generally being nonselfsufficient, incompetent, senile, or otherwise unable to care for themselves. Fortunately, ageism appears to have begun a decline (albeit a moderate one) primarily because more and more older people have demonstrated that they are in fact competent in many different ways.

Older people's participations in leisure activities is no exception to this trend, and it shouldn't be. Since many, many older persons are competent and capable in leisure activities, ageism has no place in the basic procedures of leisure counseling. As with sexism and racism, leisure counseling may even be helpful in reducing ageism.

Confrontation

The success of any counseling process is largely contingent upon the formation of an effective leisure counselor-client(s) interpersonal relationship. In leisure counseling this means that the leisure counselor and client(s) have a relationship wherein each is free to be open and honest with the other without fear of termination of the relationship. If such a relationship is established, the leisure counselor is free to use whatever counseling skills are deemed appropriate.

The manifestations of these skills may even be initially disconcerting to the client. However, if these skills are used because they are particularly appropriate to the situation, the client should eventually benefit from their use. Obviously skills which may initially be disconcerting to clients should be used only sparingly and only after an effective relationship has been established. Confrontation is a skill which falls in this category.

Diplomacy: The art of jumping into troubled waters without making a splash.

Art Linkletter

In general, confrontation means helping clients understand that they have made statements or exhibited behaviors which are contradictory, invalid, misinformed, or discrepant. Confrontation does not mean that leisure counselors should be harsh, mean, intimidating, or unnecessarily blunt with their clients.

The purpose of confrontation is to help clients understand that their words or behaviors are not consistent and therefore not effectively contributing to successful resolution of their situations or concerns. The most powerful and effective confrontation behaviors of leisure counselors are often those made gently and without further comment.

Co-lead Groups

It was mentioned in Chapter VII that "modeling" is one of the important functions served by leisure counselors in the group leisure counseling process. That discussion was based on the presumption of a single group leader (i.e. leisure counselor), as will most often be the case. However, there are some occasions where it may be possible to have co-leaders for group leisure counseling. While this situation is relatively infrequent, it does present some interesting possibilities in regard to modeling behaviors.

In co-lead group leisure counseling, the two group leaders may implement modeling behaviors in either or both of two ways. The most common tact is for the two group leaders to interact with each other and then to lead discussion about what was done. This is modeling in the purest sense of the term since it is simply a demonstration of certain behaviors. A less common variation is where one of the group leaders interacts with a group member and the other functions as a process "observer." The "observer" usually leads a discussion following the modeling enactment although sometimes the observer will comment as the modeling is being conducted.

Care should be taken, however, not to let modeling "over-structure" the group process. That is, the group members should not be given the impression that *only* the behaviors modeled are appropriate. Such a misimpression will stifle creativity and spontaneity in the group. Unfortunately, the potential for this type of misimpression is intensified when co-leaders are in the group. This is because the impact of the modeling is increased as a function of the professional credibility of two leisure counselors. Accordingly, co-leaders of group leisure counseling should be particularly careful not to give inappropriate impressions about "legitimate" intragroup behaviors.

One other caution is needed here. Co-leading leisure counseling groups involves a lot more than just having two leisure counselors in the same group. The co-leaders need to plan and coordinate their activities and styles in careful and conscientious manners. Uncoordinated and inadequately planned co-leading typically leads to intra-group confusion and bewilderment. Group members will not know when or how to interact. In general, unprepared co-leaders do a disservice to their clients and to themselves.

Homework

The complexities and subtleties of the leisure counseling process necessitate that every possible resource be used in order to achieve effectiveness. A valuable resource, yet one which is often overlooked, is the client. The process may be enhanced by capitalizing on the capabilities of the client. The client's abilities may be effectively used through activities outside of the actual leisure counseling sessions; activities which fall under the general rubric of "homework."

Homework activities have been considered previously in regard to the Action stage of the leisure counseling process. However, homework activities may also be beneficial supplements to other parts of the process.

> My education was the liberty I had to read indiscriminately, with my eyes hanging out.
>
> *Dylan Thomas*

Perhaps the most common homework activity clients can engage in is reading. Clients may gain significant information about not only leisure activities but also about themselves through reading. For example, clients might be asked to read a description of a particular theory of human behavior. The reading could then be discussed in the next leisure counseling session, with a focus on how the client personally applies the theory.

Other types of homework activities can also be beneficial. Clients can be asked to watch a particular program on television, to study another person's nonverbal behaviors, or to write some notes that relate to a topic to be discussed in a subsequent leisure counseling sessions. Activities such as these allow clients to enhance their own benefits from the leisure counseling process.

> If your capacity to acquire has outstripped your capacity to enjoy, you are on the way to the scrapheap.
>
> Glen Buck

The cautions in order for other aspects of the leisure counseling process are also appropriate for the use of homework activities. Homework supplements, but doesn't replace, parts of the leisure counseling process; too much of a good thing may be self defeating; and so on. In addition, it should be remembered that clients will need to have clear and explicit instructions in order to complete homework activities successfully. Further, clients should not be harshly reprimanded if they don't complete the homework activities. The use of homework activities can be both effective and fun, but it needs careful planning and cooperation in order to achieve those ends.

Comprehensiveness

Determination of how much of the client's "total being" should be covered in a counseling process is a major difficulty confronting counselors. Some counseling processes literally span several years. Others may take an hour or less. Either of these extremes is inappropriate for leisure counseling. An overextended counseling process is ineffective by virtue of being inefficient. An extremely brief counseling process rarely is effective in covering all significant topics, issues, or dimensions. Obviously the appropriate tact lies somewhere between these extremes. But the question remains, how much coverage is enough?

> Scientific and humanist approaches are not competitive but supportive, and both are ultimately necessary.
>
> Robert Wood

There is no *right* answer to the question posed since the answer depends on each leisure counseling situation. However, some of the factors which influence the answer for any given situation can be identified. These factors are reflected in the following questions, which must be answered by each leisure counselor for each leisure counseling situation:

1. How much time (do)es the client(s) have available for the leisure counseling process?
2. How much time (do)es the leisure counselor(s) have available for the leisure counseling process?
3. What (human or material) resources are available for the leisure counseling process?
4. How capable is (are) the client(s) in facilitating and aiding the leisure counseling process?
5. What time or monetary factors need to be considered for the leisure counseling process?
7. What is the immediacy of need for completion of the leisure counseling process?

The answers to these questions are not always easily found, but they must be determined since they are a major factor in the personalization and subsequent effectiveness of the leisure counseling process.

It was stated earlier, and merits reiteration here, that effective use of the TLC model necessitates that each aspect of the model be addressed. It is erroneous to assume that parts of the model can be "skipped" without losing effectiveness. The model is an integrated one and all parts need attention. However, this should not be construed to mean that all parts need equal attention. On the contrary, the various parts of the TLC model should be attended to as is appropriate for each client.

This is another major aspect of personalization. It should be remembered, though, that personalization encompasses clients actively participating in the leisure counseling process. Thus clients may do significant portions of "attending" to the aspects through activities (e.g. homework or reading) which are not part of the leisure counseling sessions. Specifically addressing each part of the TLC model does not necessarily imply that leisure counseling must be an extremely lengthy process. It all depends on leisure counselors, their clients, and their unique interaction combinations.

Evaluations

Evaluation activities are typically the last part of the leisure counseling process, if they are included at all. They are therefore often conducted hurriedly as both clients and leisure counselors are anxious to finish the process. The unfortunate result is that evaluation activities are subtlely deemphasized and perhaps even negated. Two simple recommendations are evident: Don't rush through evaluation activities and don't deemphasize their importance. The future of leisure counseling depends on effective and valid evaluations.

Why should we subsidize intellectual curiosity?

Ronald Reagan

These then are the major "fine points" of leisure counseling. They are little things that mean a lot as far as the effectiveness of leisure counseling is concerned. Each leisure counselor must individually consider and implement them. In many cases this amounts to "thinking" about them, and making minor behavioral adjustments. Leisure counselors who take the time to think about them and to make the adjustments will move their leisure counseling efforts from adequate to effective.

Discussion Questions

1. Are there any other "fine points" of leisure counseling? If so, how should leisure counselors attend to them?
2. How may a leisure counselor determine what types of humor are appropriate in any given leisure counseling situation?
3. What methods besides the presentation of information may be used to change people's attitudes?
4. One of the biggest problems people have is admitting to others (and sometimes to themselves) that they have problems. This inhibition prevents many people from entering counseling or from being fully involved in counseling. How can leisure counselors help people admit that they have leisure problems or concerns?

Study Activities

1. Using pictures from magazines, make a collage that you might use as a leisure counseling resource.

2. Review various catalogs of counseling resources (e.g. films, slides, tapes, kits) and list ten resources that could be adapted for leisure counseling purposes.

3. Select a client population of your choosing and develop three "homework assignments" that could be used in conjunction with leisure counseling for those clients.

4. Select a client population of your choosing and develop a list of five "readings" that could be used in conjunction with leisure counseling for those clients.

Chapter X

The Complete Leisure Counselor

There are direct relationships among the consistencies and degrees of leisure counseling effectiveness and leisure counselor competencies. To be sure, some less than fully competent (so-called) leisure counselors occasionally provide services which might be deemed effective. However, such situations are the exception, not the rule. In order for leisure counseling to be provided *consistently* and with *maximum* possible effectiveness, leisure counselors must have and maintain a complete repertoire of up-to-date information, skills, and resources. Such a repertoire is in fact the feature that distinguishes *professional* leisure counselors from all the others. As with other facets of leisure counseling, there are several major factors contributing to the professional status of a leisure counselor.

I have never let my schooling interfere with my education.

Mark Twain

Professional Preparation for Leisure Counselors

If leisure counseling is to become a substantive functional specialty within the counseling profession, then leisure counselors must have appropriate and effective professional preparation. The need for such preparation has been discussed at some length in the literature (e.g. Epperson, 1977; Grossman, 1980; Hayes, 1977; O'Morrow, 1977; Overs, 1977), and so the need is not an issue. What *is* an issue is what should be the nature of that preparation. While a variety of perspectives have been offered, one consistent with the view of leisure counseling as a functional specialty within the counseling profession is the one of choice here. This perspective holds that professional preparation of leisure counselors should follow a pattern consistent with preparation for other counseling specialties. This pattern of training involves two major components: basic preparation and specialized training relating to leisure.

> Upon the subject of education, not presuming to dictate any plan or system respecting it, I can only say that I view it as the most important subject which we, as a people, can be engaged in . . . .
>
> Abraham Lincoln

The basic preparation of a counselor should include academic (i.e. classroom) education on a variety of counseling topics and training experiences for the development of a variety of counseling skills. A convenient delineation of this preparation is the *Standards for the Preparation of Counselors and Other Personnel Specialists,* which were developed by the Association for Counselor Education and Supervision (ACES, 1973). These *Standards* specify that all counselors should have preparation in at least the following areas:

1. Individual counseling—including basic and advanced helping skills, techniques and theories as applied to individuals.
2. Group counseling—including basic and advanced helping skills, techniques and theories as applied to groups.
3. Assessment—including psychological and educational measurement and evaluation.

4. Vocational counseling—including basic skills, theories, and resources.
5. Research—including statistics and descriptive and experimental techniques.
6. Consultation—including basic skills and theories.
7. Professional development—including ethics and other professional issues.
8. Supervised practice—including practicum and internship experiences.

These *Standards* also specify that all counselor trainees should receive preparation pertinent to the particular professional settings in which they anticipate working. Such training may focus on settings such as schools, colleges and universities, community agencies, correctional institutions, and so forth. Finally, these *Standards* specify that all counselor trainees should receive preparation pertinent to the types of primary clientele with whom they anticipate working. These clientele might include groups of people such as children, youth, adults, older persons, ethnic minorities, handicapped or disabled persons, and so on.

Natural abilities are like natural plants; they need pruning by study.

Francis Bacon

Collectively, the ACES *Standards* describe what should be the components of the *minimum preparation* for professional counselors. A counselor trainee who successfully completed preparation in these areas would therefore be assumed to have the minimum necessary skills for professional counseling of any type. However, since this type of training is considered minimal, the *Standards* also advocate that each counselor trainee receive additional preparation in a functional specialty of the trainee's choosing. Leisure counseling is obviously one viable alternative for a professional specialty.

The specialized training of a leisure counselor should include academic education on the various aspects of leisure as well as experiences for the development of leisure counseling skills (Grossman, 1980). In regard to the former, Grossman (1980), Hayes (1977) and Overs (1977), among others, have argued convincingly for an interdisciplinary educational approach. The major topics advocated for inclusion in this approach are:

1. Principles of recreation—including theories of sport and other types of recreation.
2. Leisure resources—including local and more distant resources.
3. Developmental psychology—including "life span" psychology.
4. Social psychology—including the social contexts of leisure.
5. Sociology—including sociological perspectives on leisure.
6. Educational psychology—including learning and teaching theories.

The experiential components of skill development are usually included as an extension of the basic counselor training sequence. That is, after a basic counseling practicum, counselor trainees should participate in another practicum and/or internship focusing specifically on leisure counseling.

> The best educated human being is the one who understands most about the life in which he is placed.
>
> *Helen Keller*

Collectively, academic and experiential training, as outlined above, should provide leisure counselors with sufficient skills to begin to function effectively. However, preparation programs are almost always limited in duration and therefore less than fully comprehensive in scope, primarily because of practical considerations (e.g. financial concerns). Consequently, in order for leisure counselors to become fully effective, two other factors must be incorporated into their professional evolutions: experience and continuing professional development.

The importance of experience in the leisure counseling process can not be overstated. While counselor trainees often receive effective supervised experience during their preparation programs, the amount received is rarely sufficient to bring about substantial "professional maturity." Such maturity is an essential component of effective leisure counseling, and it can only be gained through extensive and diverse experience in "real" situations (Edwards, 1977). This does not mean that "new" leisure counselors cannot be effective; rather, it means that experienced leisure counselors more consistently reach greater levels of effectiveness.

Nothing is a waste of time if you use the experience wisely.

Rodin

The second factor, continuing professional development, relates to the first in that it is another type of experience that leisure counselors should gain after completion of their preparation programs. It is difficult to make recommendations for practical experience beyond simply saying it is needed because the experiences must be determined by the circumstances and goals of any particular leisure counselor. However, there are several readily identifiable types of continuing professional development appropriate for all leisure counselors which merit extended discussion.

He who stops being better stops being good.

Oliver Cromwell

Professional Development for Leisure Counselors

Continuing professional development for leisure counselors is absolutely essential for the provision of effective leisure counseling services. As a new functional specialty, leisure counseling does not have the established history, and the corresponding established practices, which are common in other counseling specialties. Consequently, leisure counselors must keep abreast of the most recent literature and practices as they emerge in order to provide the best possible services.

Reading

A fundamental component of the continuing professional development process for leisure counselors is extensive reading (Edwards, 1980b). The appropriate reading materials may be divided into two general categories, books and periodic publications.

Obtaining books on topics relating to leisure counseling is not necessarily difficult, but it does necessitate some directed effort. A library is a good starting point. However, comprehensive collections of books on leisure and leisure counseling are not a part of most libraries. Accordingly, it may be necessary to "special order" many desired books.

The books that help you the most are those which make you think the most.

Theodore Parker

A good source for newer books is the publishers themselves. The *Directory of American Publishers* (available in most libraries and bookstores) is a helpful resource. Contacting those listed will usually result in receipt of numerous catalogs and informational pamphlets about their offerings. Another good source is *Books in Print* which is also available in most libraries or bookstores. Current titles are listed by author and title, and the names of publishers are provided.

A final source that may be used is recent books on leisure and leisure counseling. Perusal of the included references and bibliographies should identify appropriate related books. Two cautions are, however, apparent for this tact. First, references included in books are limited by the authors' biases and/or resources. Second, since it takes considerable time for a book to get into print from the time it was written; newer books may appear on the market in the interim.

Periodic publications include such things as journal and magazine articles, monographs, papers presented at professional meetings, and reports of grant activities. Periodic publications are best identified through computerized literature searches such as those available from the *Educational Resources Information Centers* (ERIC) and the *National Clearinghouse on Men-*

tal Health Information. The use of these searches and others like them is most easily accomplished through a library. The major advantages of computerized searches are their comprehensiveness and their provisions of information on how to find or obtain desired publications.

Subscriptions to professional publications may also be desirable. Professional journals relating to leisure, counseling, and leisure counseling are important for leisure counselors.

> It is with books as it is with men: a very small number play a great part.
>
> *Voltaire*

A third source of published information is the many persons engaged in private enterprise related to leisure counseling. Information on how to find these organizations is usually available through review of professional publications such as the *Leisure Information Newsletter* (published through the Recreation and Leisure Studies Department of New York University). In addition, most people in private enterprise are able and willing to provide information about others in similar endeavors. Thus contacting a few will often lead to information about many.

> Reading is a basic tool in the living of a good life.
>
> *Mortimer J. Adler*

Professional Organizations

A second component in effective professional development is involvement with appropriate professional organizations. The most appropriate ones are those relating to leisure, recreation, and counseling. The nature of the involvement should, however, be beyond mere membership. Professional involvement should mean attending professional meetings or conventions, providing input and feedback into organizations, contributing to the directions and functionings of organizations, and other activities that enhance the benefits of membership.

Compiling Resources

Compilation of personally relevant resources is a third component of continuing professional development. Counseling truly is intended to be a personalized activity, both for clients and for counselors. Accordingly, leisure counselors should accumulate resources which are appropriate to their particular counseling styles. Both material and human resources are included in this perspective.

Material resources include such things as assessment instruments, activity files, audio-visual aids, and record keeping procedures. Human resources include persons such as co-counselors, referral persons, and consultants who are knowledgeable of different types of leisure activities. Together, these types of resources enable leisure counselors to develop uniquely individual and personally most effective leisure counseling styles.

> There are more men ennobled by study than by nature.
>
> *Cicero*

Educational Activities

A fourth component of the process is formal educational experiences. These experiences would include continuing education courses, additional academic (post-degree) courses, and intensive workshops. Educational preparation of this nature has the decided advantage of providing structure for learning experiences. Since leisure counselors (like most other counselors) often find it difficult to conduct self instruction on a regular basis (because of other "priorities"), structured learning experiences often provide the necessary incentive and order for effective learning. The "commitment" made by virtue of enrollment in a formal learning process also helps leisure counselors strive to obtain the maximum possible benefits from the experience.

> Men learn while they teach.
>
> *Seneca*

Outreach Activities

The fifth component is what may be called outreach activities. The adage, "If you want to learn something, try teaching it" is certainly appropriate for professional development. Activities that could be included here include such things as consultation, provision of community programs, presentations at professional meetings and conventions, and speeches and other types of presentations. Activities of this nature necessitate that leisure counselors clearly conceptualize and integrate their professional perspectives and experiences. The process of planning one of these activities is therefore an excellent learning opportunity for leisure counselors.

Professional Writing

A sixth component, writing, is closely aligned with the fifth component. Leisure counselors may write for professional publications or for publications intended for lay audiences. In either case, the prerequisite processes and the subsequent benefits are very similar to those for outreach activities.

Research

The final component of the process is research, particularly personally relevant research. An effective research activity allows for careful, accurate, and objective evaluation of the leisure counseling process and/or factors relating to that process. Research on personal effectiveness is particularly helpful to professional self development. However, even more generalized types of research are personally beneficial in that they require preparation similar to that for outreach and writing.

The unexamined life is not worth living.

Socrates

The professional preparation and continuing professional development activities described above should enable leisure counselors to be highly competent in their professional activities. The heretofore unanswered question, however, is "what is all this training supposed to be able to help leisure counselors do?"

Professional Functions for Leisure Counselors

The direct service functions of individual, group, and developmental leisure counseling have been discussed at length in this book because they constitute the primary functions of professionals who identify themselves as leisure counselors. However, it is rare that a leisure counselor has the luxury of being involved only in direct service functions.

Further, professional organizations for counselors such as APGA and APA do not advocate such functional singularity for professional counselors. Indeed, these organizations recognize the need for, and advocate, functional diversity in the form of indirect service functions. This diversity not only helps counselors improve their direct service functions, but also helps them avoid "professional burnout" to some extent.

Consultation

Consultation is one of, if not *the* most important leisure counselor indirect functions (Edwards, 1980b). The term counselor consultation is a relatively new one and as yet has not been consensually defined (Myrick, 1977). However, in general, the term means a situation where a leisure counselor helps a second person help a client, or third person. The second person may be another counselor, a teacher, an administrator, a manager or boss, or anyone who could use assistance in helping another person. The third person may be a client (as when the second person is another counselor) or any person who is being helped by the second person (e.g. a student in a class when the second person is a teacher). The essence of the consulting situation is that there are reciprocal interpersonal relationships between the first and second persons and between the second and third persons, but not between the first and third persons.

Myrick and Moni (1972) have defined three major types of consultation. The first is called *crisis-consultation,* a situation where the consultee (i.e. second person) has an urgent problem. For example, a marriage counselor might be working with a couple who express an immediate need to change some of their leisure patterns. The leisure counselor might provide some suggestions as to how the marriage counselor might best handle the situation.

> A teacher affects eternity; he can never tell where his influence stops.
>
> *Henry Brooks Adams*

Crisis consultation is not likely to be a frequent activity for leisure counselors since leisure does not usually lend itself to the need for immediate, rather dramatic, intervention. However, leisure counselors should be prepared to offer this type of consultation should the occasion arise.

The second type is *preventive-consultation*. This is a situation where the consultee is not experiencing a crisis but senses that one may be forthcoming. Persons who work with incarcerated individuals such as prisoners or juvenile offenders are well aware that ineffective leisure may subsequently contribute to difficult, if not dangerous, activities in the situation. Consequently, a leisure counselor might provide preventive consultation to such persons to help them avoid problem situations.

> Precise knowledge is the only true knowledge, and he who does not teach exactly, does not teach at all.
>
> *Henry Ward Beecher*

The third type is *developmental-consultation*. Myrick (1977) distinguishes developmental-consultation from preventive-consultation by suggesting that the former is intended to help consultees facilitate conditions of learning and positive growth behaviors for others, as opposed to the latter which tries to prevent problems. This third type of consultation is the one which will be most frequently employed by leisure counselors. A good example of this situation is when leisure counselors help classroom teachers incorporate leisure and leisure mental health topics into their curricular activities (as opposed to the leisure counselor doing developmental leisure counseling directly with the students).

Specific consultation procedures, both real and recommended, vary almost as much as individual counseling styles. Readers who are interested in an approach particularly compatible with other principles cited here are referred to Myrick (1977). While Myrick's discussion focuses primarily on the elementary school setting, the principles described are easily generalized to other situations.

Referral

A second indirect function of leisure counselors has been alluded to earlier but merits additional discussion here. That function is referral. While the term referral is usually interpreted to mean a situation where a client is transferred from one counselor to another, a more generalized definition is preferred here. In the present context, referral is used to mean "shifting" the client from leisure counseling to another type of counseling, or from one counselor to another, or both.

Light is the task where many share the toil.

Homer

Since leisure counselors often do other types of counseling, this general definition is appropriate. Thus leisure counselors may refer a client to another counselor for typical reasons (e.g. counselor-client incompatibility, lack of appropriate skills for another type of counseling, etc.) or they may simply shift the counseling focus with the client from leisure to something else.

The importance of leisure counselors being sensitive to the potential need for referral cannot be overstated. To engage a client in a less than fully appropriate counseling process is not only to do a great disservice to the client but is professionally unethical as well. It is imperative, therefore, for leisure counselors to be continually evaluating counseling processes as to the need for a referral.

The need for a referral will most often be evident during the early stages of the leisure counseling process. Most notably, this need will arise when a discrepancy becomes evident between the client's "presenting" problem and the client's "real" problem. However, some clients may "persist" with their presenting problems well into the leisure counseling process.

Their "real" problems may become apparent only after they're fully convinced the leisure counselor is trustworthy, competent, caring and so on. One typical indicator that such a situation exists is when the client repeatedly digresses to the same topic throughout the leisure counseling process. Accordingly, leisure counselors should be ready to initiate a referral at any point in any leisure counseling process.

He that won't be counselled can't be helped.

Benjamin Franklin

Research

Research has been mentioned as an element of continuing professional development, but it is also an important indirect function for leisure counselors. Research in this context means that which is published or otherwise disseminated. While disseminated research may have direct relevance for a leisure counselor, its primary benefit in this context is to others and thus it is an indirect function.

What the nature and style of counseling research should be has been hotly debated in the professional literature (cf. Goldman, 1976; Mehrens, 1978). However, the one point of consensus is that professional counselors *should* engage in research activities, for either reasons of personal need or senses of professional altruism. Leisure counselors are no exception to this generalization. In fact, given the paucity of research on leisure counseling, the need is extremely great in this realm. Simply put, literally every topic in leisure counseling is in need of additional, if not seminal, research. This is, therefore, a potentially fruitful and rewarding function for leisure counselors.

Outreach

Outreach activities have also been noted previously in the discussion of continuing professional development, but they merit repeating here as the fourth indirect function. In addition to the personal benefits to be gained by leisure counselors, outreach activities are an important indirect function because they help to "spread the word" about leisure counseling. Any activity which helps to "advertise" the positive aspects of leisure counseling therefore serves to enhance its credibility.

Leisure counselors' outreach activities should be extended beyond the realm of professionals. All too often professionals are guilty of "talking only to one another." Leisure counseling in particular and counseling in general need to be "taken to the people" so that negative perceptions, attitudes, and stereotypes, as well as fears, about being in counseling can be allayed.

Since leisure counseling "sounds like" a nonthreatening activity, leisure counselors have the potential to have a strong, positive impact on the general public. Leisure counselors who do not attempt to manifest this potential do a disservice to themselves and to the counseling profession.

Program Development

The final indirect function of leisure counselors to be included here is program development. With the possible exception of the Avocational Counseling in Milwaukee Project (Overs, Taylor and Adkins, 1977; Wilson, Mirenda, and Rutkowski, 1975), citations of programs specifically for leisure counseling are few in the professional literature (Loesch, 1980a). More typically, leisure counseling has been included as part of more comprehensive programs such as life style or vocational counseling activities. It appears, therefore, that leisure counseling has been provided primarily as an independent service by leisure counselors. However, if leisure counseling is to achieve full status as a functional specialty, this situation will have to be changed.

The need for leisure counseling programs is similar to that for other types of counseling services. Programs provide much greater opportunity for comprehensive service delivery than do individual activities. Further, programs often provide for more effective services because of more efficient uses of available resources. Consequently, the development of leisure counseling programs is an important and meaningful indirect function of leisure counselors.

One obvious place where leisure counseling programs should be developed is within educational systems. Public and private schools, colleges, community and junior colleges, and universities are all excellent settings for leisure counseling programs. They have several distinct advantages in this regard including philosophies that are (usually) compatible with leisure counseling; concentrations of people, physical, material, and human resources; and the need and desire to extend their general realms of service offerings.

Another good place for leisure counseling programs is community social service agencies. Community mental health centers, hospital outpatient services centers, rehabilitation centers, drug and other abuse facilities, indigent and transient care facilities, and other types of human welfare agencies could all incorporate or benefit from leisure counseling programs. The major advantages of programs in community agencies are that leisure counseling is made available to people who might not otherwise be informed of its potential benefits and that leisure counseling can be provided to people who otherwise might not be able to afford it.

The final location to be suggested is in residential treatment facilities. Included here would be settings such as correctional institutions (for both youth and adults), mental disorder treatment centers, special learning environments (as for the retarded), nursing homes, and residential facilities for the elderly (such as seniors centers). The commonality among these settings is that the people in each spend most, if not all, of their lives in the settings. This implies that leisure counseling programs for these people must be conducted in those settings. The advantage of this implication is that the leisure counseling programs would be highly centralized. However, the disadvantage is that both the nature of the program and the potential leisure activity choices may be limited.

There are, then, at least five significant functions that leisure counselors can fulfill beyond their direct service functions. Certainly not every leisure counselor will be involved in all leisure counseling functions. However, it is equally certain that leisure counselors should be involved in one or more indirect functions.

Evaluation of Leisure Counseling

The evaluation of leisure counseling services and of leisure counselor performance are of paramount importance if they are to be improved. In actuality, service provision and counselor performance are inextricably linked. However, they may be separated for discussion purposes.

The evaluation of leisure counseling services is an attempt to answer the question how have people changed (if at all) as a result of leisure counseling? While the *methods* of deriving an answer are perhaps as diverse as leisure counselors and researchers, the *types* of answers that can be derived are much more distinct. Leisure counseling may change people in one or more of three basic ways: affectively, behaviorally, or cognitively. And isn't that familiar. . . ?

> The world hates change, yet it is the only thing that has brought progress.
>
> C. F. Kettering

Evaluating Affective Changes

Affective changes are those that relate to the dimensions inherent in the TLC model: feelings, attitudes, values, expectations, interests, and personal characteristics. Among these, feelings and attitudes are by far the most commonly assessed in the evaluation of leisure counseling services. However, leisure counseling may change any of the dimensions, and the most effective evaluations will encompass most if not all of these dimensions.

The method most commonly used for assessing affective change is client (or participant) self report. This is logical to the extent that people should be the best sources of information about their own affective dimensions. However, the validity of self report information is often questionable, particularly for people lacking self insight or who are defensive. Consequently, the use of (so-called) secondary sources, such as observational data, for information about affective dimension changes resulting from leisure counseling is highly recommended. This allows for pooling of clients' and others' perceptions of clients' affective changes following leisure counseling.

Evaluating Behavioral Changes

Behavioral changes also are those relating to the dimensions of the TLC model: physical, personal, social, and environmental. Physical behavior (i.e. actual leisure activity) changes are the most commonly evaluated in this realm. However, again, effective evaluation should allow for consideration of all four types. Behavioral changes are typically evaluated through either client (participant) self report or observation. In the majority of cases self report information is used even though its value is often questionable. A much better tact is to use self report information in conjunction with (preferably objective) observation information from others.

Evaluating Cognitive Changes

Finally, cognitive changes also are those relating to the TLC model dimensis of capabilities, accomplishments, thinking processes, and knowledge. Among these, accomplishments are the most commonly assessed for evaluation purposes. A tentative recommendation is made here also that effective evaluation should encompass all of the dimensions. However, the tentativeness arises from the fact that some of these dimensions are extremely difficult to assess. Self report has the least credibility in this realm since it is very difficult for people to assess changes in their own cognitive functionings. The use of formal, structured assessment instruments is probably the best procedure, though in some circumstances the judgments of others may provide useful information.

Among these three types of dimensions, leisure counselors are usually most concerned about affective changes. Leisure counselors like to have people "feel better" about their leisure activities. The desirability of positive affect change is undeniable, but such changes may not, and often do not, constitute sufficient evidence for the effectiveness of leisure counseling services.

For many people (e.g. program administrators, funding sources, etc.), the basic question is, "What do people *do* differently as a result of leisure counseling?" This question emphasizes behavioral changes; it seeks to determine if people actually behave differently after participating in leisure counseling. Cognitive changes frequently get overlooked in the debates over the values of affective and behavioral changes. This is unfortunate because the educational value of leisure counseling is minimized as a result.

Debates about which types of changes are most effective are futile since determination of the "best" type is contingent on specific goals for specific leisure counselor-client situations. Theoretically, leisure counselors want to help their clients change in all dimensions. Yet while such a situation is highly desirable at the theoretical level, practicalities often dictate that evaluations must focus on only one or two dimensions. Thus leisure counselors must establish their own priorities and use evaluation procedures which are in line with those priorities.

Separating evaluations of leisure counselor performance from evaluations of leisure counseling services, even at theoretical levels, raises an interesting question: Can a leisure counselor perform effectively yet not provide effective leisure counseling services, or vice versa? Logically, is it possible to answer yes to either form of this question?

The answer is a definite maybe! In other words, the linkages between performance variables and counseling outcome variables have not been clearly established. In fact, in some cases performance variables widely accepted in the profession (e.g. facilitative responding) have been shown to be unrelated to outcome variables (Rowe, Murphy, and De Csipkes, 1975).

The resolution of this situation lies in consideration of the types of outcome variables used. Counselor performance variables are often primarily affective in nature and therefore should affect a client's affective dimensions. They may or may not affect a client's behavioral or cognitive dimensions.

For example, consider a situation where a counselor helps a client "feel better' but the client doesn't actually change any behaviors. If counseling effectiveness is evaluated in terms of affective dimensions, this counselor would have performed effectively. However, from the perspective of behavioral dimensions, this counselor would have performed ineffectively. Thus the evaluation of counselor performance is linked to personal biases about what changes in outcome variables constitute effective counseling.

For the vast majority of clients, affective changes constitute effective counseling. In other words, clients will usually believe that the leisure counseling process has been effective if they "feel good" about what happened in the process. Leisure counselors can determine client perceptions in this regard through the use of any of a variety of counseling (process) evaluation scales.

Two scales with long and established histories are particularly appropriate for these types of evaluations. The first is the *Counseling Evaluation Inventory (CEI)* (Linden, Shertzer, and Stone, 1965). The CEI assesses three aspects of the (leisure) counseling process: counselor-client rapport, counselor professional competence, and (perceived) process benefits (Biersner, Bunde, Doucette, and Culwell, 1981).

The second is the *Barrett-Lennard Relationship Inventory* (Barrett-Lennard, 1962), which assesses client perceptions of counselor empathy, congruence, positive regard, and unconditionality of regard. Either of these instruments will enable leisure counselors to obtain valid information from clients about clients' perceptions of leisure counseling processes.

Behavioral indicators of counseling effectiveness may be obtained by recording how client behaviors have changed as a result of leisure counseling. For example, clients who engage in new (i.e. different) leisure activities after leisure counseling have made behavioral changes and those changes are easily noted (e.g. counted). Similarly, determining differences in the amounts of time clients invest in various leisure activities after leisure counseling is a type of behavioral evaluation of counseling effectiveness.

A third way to assess counseling effectiveness is for leisure counselors to have clients complete an instrument such as the *Leisure Satisfaction Scale* (Ragheb and Beard, 1980). This procedure probably should be used after some time (at least a month) has elapsed since the end of the leisure counseling process. This time lapse in important to allow sufficient time for clients to modify their leisure behaviors, and therefore be able to make valid assessments of their leisure satisfactions.

And in Conclusion

Leisure counseling promises to be an exciting new venture in the counseling profession. It has the potential to be a unique counseling service, yet it is integrally related to many existing counseling services. Leisure counseling will eventually achieve its own identity but the process leading to that identity will be a long and arduous one. As with any new venture, there is much to be said, written, and done. Good luck with your part of the venture.

Discussion Questions

1. What are functional differences between professional and paraprofessional counselors? What are the differences in the training/preparation experiences for professional and paraprofessional counselors? What are the implications of these differences for the provision of leisure counseling services?

2. What institutions, organizations or agencies in your local area would be receptive to the implementation of a leisure counseling program? How might a program be initiated in one of them?

3. What are the differences in the functions of leisure counselors in private practice as opposed to those in agency settings?

4. What are the major resources available in your area for your continuing professional development as a leisure counselor?

Study Activities

1. Develop a model curriculum for the professional preparation of a leisure counselor.

2. Develop a plan for a leisure counseling program which could be presented at a professional organization meeting or convention.

3. Write a "book review" on this book.

Bibliography

(including reference citations)

American Psychological Association. *Standards for educational and psychological tests.* (rev. ed.) Washington, DC: Author, 1974.

Annand, V.S. A review of evaluation in therapeutic recreation. *Therapeutic Recreation Journal,* 1977, *11* (2), 42-47.

Allen, L.R. Leisure and its relationship to work and career guidance. *Vocational Guidance Quarterly,* 1980, *28* (3), 257-262.

Association for Counselor Education and Supervision. *Standards for the preparation of counselors and other personnel specialists.* Washington, DC: Author, 1973.

Avedon, E.M. *Therapeutic recreation service: An applied behavioral science approach.* Englewood Cliffs, NJ: Prentice-Hall, 1974.

Barfield, R.E., & Morgan, J.N. Trends in satisfaction with retirement. *Gerontologist,* 1978, *18* (1), 19-23.

Barrett-Lennard, G.T. Dimensions of therapist responses as causal factors in therapeutic change. *Psychological Monographs,* 1962, *76,* 43.

Berger, B.M. The new stage man: Almost endless adolescence. In William J. Goode (Ed.), *The contemporary American family.* Chicago: Quadrangle Books, 1971.

Besag, F.P. Work, leisure and school. *Counseling and Values,* 1975, *20* (1), 25-28.

Best, F., & Stern, B. *Lifetime distribution of education, work, and leisure: Research speculations and policy implications of changing life patterns.* Washington, DC: Institute for Educational Leadership, George Washington University, 1976.

Biersner, R.J., Bunde, G.R., Doucette, R.E., & Culwell, C.W. Counselor Evaluation Inventory: Replication of factor structure on a military sample. *Measurement and Evaluation in Guidance,* 1981, *13* (4), 223-227.

Blocher, D. *Developmental counseling.* New York: Ronald Press, 1966.

Bolles, R.N. *The three boxes of life.* Berkeley, CA: Ten Speed Press, 1978.

Bosserman, P. Implications for youth. In M. Kaplan & P. Bosserman (Eds.), *Technology, human values, and leisure.* New York: Abington Press, 1971, 131-163.

Bosserman, P., & Gagan, R. Leisure behavior and voluntary action. In D.H. Smith, R.D. Reddy, & R. Baldwin (Eds.), *Voluntary action research.* Lexington, MA: Lexington Books, 1972, 109-126.

Brightbill, C.K. *The challenge of leisure.* Englewood Cliffs, NJ: Prentice-Hall, 1960.

Brightbill, C.K., & Mobley, T.A. *Educating for leisure-centered living.* (2nd ed.) New York: Wiley, 1977.

Bruner, J.S., Jolly, A., & Sylva, K. *Play: Its role in development and evolution.* New York: Basic Books, 1976.

Bull, N.C. One measure for defining a leisure activity. *Journal of Leisure Research,* 1971, *3,* 120-126.

Burch, W.R., Jr. The social circles of leisure: Competing explanations. *Journal of Leisure Research,* 1969, *1,* 125-148.

Burdge, R.J. Levels of occupational prestige and leisure activities. *Journal of Leisure Research,* 1969, *1* (3), 262-274.

Butler, A.L., Gotts, E.E., & Quisenberry, L.L. *Play as development.* Columbus, OH: Charles E. Merrill, 1978.

Carisse, C.B. Family and leisure: A set of contradictions. *Family Coordinator,* 1975, *24* (2), 191-197.

Cherry, C., & Woodburn, R. *Leisure: A resource for educators.* Toronto, Canada: Ministry of Culture and Recreation, 1978.

Clawson, M. How much leisure, now and in the future? In J.C. Charlesworth (Ed.), *Leisure in America: Blessing or curse?* Philadelphia, PA: American Academy of Political and Social Science, 1964.

Compton, D.M., & Goldstein, J.E. (Eds.) *Perspectives of leisure counseling.* Arlington, VA: National Recreation and Park Association, 1977.

Connolly, M.L. Leisure counseling: A values clarification and assertive training approach. In A. Epperson, P.A. Witt, & G. Hitzhusen (Eds.), *Leisure counseling: An aspect of leisure education.* Springfield, IL: Charles C. Thomas, 1977.

Crandall, R., & Slivken, K. Leisure attitudes and their measurement. In S.E. Iso-Ahola (Ed.), *Social psychological perspectives on leisure and recreation.* Springfield, IL: Charles C. Thomas, 1980.

Crandall, R., & Slivken, K. *The importance of measuring leisure attitudes.* Paper presented at the National Recreation and Park Association Convention, Miami, FL: October, 1978.

Day, H.I. A new look at work, play, and job satisfaction. *Recreation Review*, 1973, *3* (1), 4-11.

de Grazia, S. *Of time, work, and leisure.* New York: The Twentieth Century Fund, 1962.

Dickason, J.G. Approaches and techniques of recreation counseling. *Therapeutic Recreation Journal*, 1972, *6*, 74-78.

Dumazadier, J. *Toward a society of leisure.* London, England: Collier Macmillan, 1967.

Eason, J. Life style counseling for a reluctant leisure class. *Personnel and Guidance Journal*, 1972, *51* (2), 127-132.

Edwards, P.B. Finding the right leisure for every life style. *Journal of Health, Physical Education and Recreation,* 1974, *45* (11), 29-33.

Edwards, P.B. *Leisure counseling techniques: Individual and group counseling step-by-step.* (3rd ed.) Los Angeles: Constructive Leisure, 1980.

Edwards, P.B. The bridges of leisure counseling. In D.M. Compton & J.E. Goldstein (Eds.), *Perspective of leisure counseling.* Arlington, VA: National Recreation and Park Association, 1977.

Edwards, P.B., & Bloland, P.A. Leisure counseling and consultation. *Personnel and Guidance Journal*, 1980, *58* (6), 435-440.

Employment and training report of the president. Washington, DC: Superintendent of Documents, 1978.

Epperson, A. Educating recreators for leisure counseling. *Journal of Health, Physical Education and Recreation,* 1977, *48* (4), 39-40.

Epperson, A., Witt, P.A. & Hitzhusen, G. (Eds.) *Leisure counseling: An aspect of leisure education.* Springfield, IL: Charles C. Thomas, 1977.

Erikson, E.H. Play and actuality. In M.W. Piers (Ed.), *Play and development.* New York: W.W. Norton & Co., 1972.

Etzoni, A. Two playtime personalities. *Human Behavior*, 1978, *11*, 16-17.

Fain, G.S. Leisure counseling: Translating needs into action. *Therapeutic Recreation Journal*, 1973, *7* (2), 4-9.

Fink, R.S. Role of imaginative play in cognitive development. *Psychological Reports*, 1976, *39* (3, part 1), 895-906.

Gholson, R.E. Extracurricular activities: Different perceptions but strong support. *Phi Delta Kappan,* 1979, *61* (1), 67-68.

Godbey, G., & Parker, S. *Leisure studies and services: An overview.* Philadelphia: W.B. Saunders, 1976.

Goldman, L. A revolution in counseling research. *Journal of Counseling Psychology,* 1976, *23,* 543-552.

Goldman, L. *Using tests in counseling.* (2nd ed.) New York: Appleton-Century-Crofts, 1971.

Grossman, A. Meeting the need: A professional preparation for leisure counseling. *Leisure Information Newsletter,* 1980, *7* (1), 1ff.

Gunn, S.L. The relationship of leisure counseling to selected counseling theories. In D.M. Compton and J.E. Goldstein (Eds.), *Perspectives of leisure counseling.* Arlington, VA: National Recreation and Park Association, 1977.

Gunter, B.G., & Moore, H.A. Youth, leisure, and post-industrial society: Implications for the family. *Family Coordinator,* 1975, *24* (2), 199-207.

Haavio-Mannila, E. Satisfaction with family, work, leisure and life among men and women. *Human Relations,* 1971, *24* (6), 585-601.

Hartlage, L. Leisure counseling from personality profiles. *Journal of Physical Education and Recreation,* 1977, *48* (4), 43.

Hayes, G.A. Leisure education and recreation counseling. In D.M. Compton & J.E. Goldstein (Eds.), *Perspectives of leisure counseling.* Arlington, VA: National Recreation and Park Association, 1977.

Hitzhusen, G. Youth recreation counseling—A necessity in therapeutic recreation. In A. Epperson, P.A. Witt, & G. Hitzhusen (Eds.), *Leisure counseling: An aspect of leisure education.* Springfield, IL: Charles C. Thomas, 1977.

Howe, L.W., & Howe, M.M. *Personalizing education— Values clarification and beyond.* New York: Hart, 1975.

Hoyt, K.B. *Refining the career education concept, part II.* (H.E.W. Monograph on Career Education). Washington, DC: U.S. Government Printing Office, 1977.

Hubert, E.E. *The development of an inventory of leisure interests.* Unpublished doctoral dissertation, University of North Carolina at Chapel Hill, 1969.

Iso-Ahola, S.E. (Ed.) *Social psychological perspectives on leisure and recreation.* Springfield, IL: Charles C. Thomas, 1980a.

Iso-Ahola, S.E. *The social psychology of leisure and recreation.* Dubuque, IA: William C. Brown, 1980b.

Jarman, P.H., & Reid, D.H. The Importance of recreational activities on attendance in a leisure program for multihandicapped retarded persons. *Therapeutic Recreation Journal*, 1977, *11* (1), 28-32.

Jenkins, J., Felce, D., Lunt, B., & Powell, L. Increasing engagement in activity of residents in old people's homes by providing recreational materials. *Behaviour Research and Therapy*, 1977, *15* (5), 429-434.

Kahn, M., & Masud, R. On lying fallow: An aspect of leisure. *International Journal of Psychoanalytic Psychotherapy*, 1977, *6*, 397-402.

Kando, T.M. *Leisure and popular culture in transition.* St. Louis: C.V. Mosby, 1975.

Kaplan, M. *Leisure: Theory and policy.* New York: Wiley, 1975.

Keen, S. Chasing the blahs away: Boredom and how to beat it. *Psychology Today*, 1977, *10* (12), 77ff.

Kelly, J.R. Life styles and leisure choices. *Family Coordinator*, 1975, *24* (2), 185-190.

Kelly, J. Work and leisure: A simplified paradigm. *Journal of Leisure Research*, 1972, *4*, 50-62.

Kenniston, K. *Youth and dissent: The rise of a new opposition.* New York: Harcourt, Brace Johanovich, Inc. 1971.

Klieber, D. *Free time and sense of competence in college students.* Unpublished doctoral dissertation, University of Texas at Austin, 1972.

Kraus, R. *Recreation and leisure in a modern society.* New York: Appleton-Century-Crofts, 1971.

Kraus, R. *Recreation and the American schools.* New York: Macmillian, 1964.

Linden, J.D., Stone, S.C., & Shertzer, B. Development and evaluation of an inventory for rating counseling. *Personnel and Guidance Journal*, 1965, *44*, 267-276.

Loesch, L.C. *Leisure counseling (Searchlight Plus).* Ann Arbor, MI: ERIC Counseling and Personnel Services Clearinghouse, 1980a.

Loesch, L.C. Leisure counseling with youth. *Counseling Psychologist*, 1981, *9* (3), 55-67.

Loesch, L.C. Life flow leisure counseling for older persons. *Journal of Employment Counseling*, 1980b, *17* (1), 49-56.

Loesch, L.C. *The survey of leisure values* (Unpublished). Gainesville, FL: L*I*F*E Enterprises, 1980c.

Loesch, L.C., & Burt, M.A. Leisure counseling for the elderly: It's time for a change. *Counseling and Values,* 1980, *24* (4), 218-226.

London, M., Crandall, R., & Seals, G. The contribution of job and leisure satisfaction to quality of life. *Journal of Applied Psychology,* 1977, *62* (3), 328-334.

London, M., Crandall, R., & Fitzgibbons, D. The psychological structure of leisure: Activities, needs, people. *Journal of Leisure Research,* 1977, *9,* 252-263.

MacAvoy, L.H. Leisure components of the geriatric day care center program. *Therapeutic Recreation Journal,* 1977, *11* (2), 55-58.

Magulski, M., Faull, V.H., & Rutkowski, B. The Milwaukee leisure counseling model. *Journal of Physical Education and Recreation,* 1977, *48* (4), 49-50.

Mancini, J.A. Leisure satisfaction and psychologic well-being in old age: Effects of health and income. *Journal of the American Geriatrics Society,* 1978, *26* (12), 550-552.

Martin, P. (Ed.) *Leisure and mental health: A psychiatric viewpoint.* Baltimore, MD: Garamond/Pridemark Press, 1967.

McDaniels, C. (Ed.) *Leisure and career development at mid-life.* Blacksburg, VA: Virginia Polytechnic and State University, 1976.

McDowell, C.F. An analysis of leisure counseling orientations and models and their integrative possibilities. In D.M. Compton & J.E. Goldstein (eds.), *Perspectives of leisure counseling.* Arlington, VA: National Recreation and Park Association, 1977a.

McDowell, C.F. Emerging leisure counseling concepts and orientations. *Therapeutic Recreation Journal,* 1976a, *10* (2), 19-25.

McDowell, C.F. Integrating theory and practice in leisure counseling. *Journal of Health, Physical Education and Recreation,* 1977b, *48* (4), 51-54.

McDowell, C.F. *Leisure counseling: Selected lifestyle processes.* Eugene, OR: University of Oregon Center of Leisure Studies, 1976b.

McDowell, C.F. *The leisure well-being inventory.* Eugene, OR: Leisure Lifestyle Consultants, 1979.

McIntyre, F. *Motivator-hygiene comparison of work and leisure satisfaction.* Unpublished doctoral dissertation, Case-Western Reserve University, 1972.

McKechnie, G.E. *Manual for the Leisure Activities Blank.* Palo Alto, CA: Consulting Psychologists Press, 1975.

McKechnie, G.E. *The structure of leisure activities.* Berkeley, CA: Institute of Personality Assessment and Research, 1974.

Mehrens, W.A. Rigor and reality in counseling research. *Measurement and Evaluation in Guidance,* 1978, *11* (1), 8-13.

Mendel, W.M. Leisure: A problem for preventative psychiatry. *American Journal of Psychiatry,* 1971, *127* (9), 1688-1961.

Mercer, R., & Loesch, L.C. Audiotape ratings: Comments and guidelines. *Psychotherapy: Theory, Research and Practice,* 1978, *16* (1), 79-85.

Miller, N.P., & Robinson, D.M. *The leisure age, its challenge to recreation.* Belmont, CA: Wadsworth, 1963.

Mirenda, J.J., & Wilson, G.T. The Milwaukee leisure counseling model. *Counseling and Values,*, 1975, *20*, (1), 42-46.

Murphy, J.F. *Recreation and leisure service: A humanistic perspective.* Dubuque, IA: William C. Brown, 1975.

Myrick, R.D. *Consultation as a counselor intervention.* Ann Arbor, MI: ERIC Counseling and Personnel Services Information Center, 1977.

Myrick, R.D., & Moni, L.S. Teacher in-service workshops: A developmental consultation approach. *Elementary School Guidance and Counseling,* 1972, *7*, 156-161.

National 4-H Leisure Education Development Committee. *Leisure education: Guide for extension staff.* Chicago, IL: National 4-H Council, 1978.

Neulinger, J. Attitude dimensions of leisure. *Journal of Leisure Research,* 1969, *3* (1), 255-261.

Neulinger, J. Leisure counseling: A plea for complexity. *Journal of Health, Physical Education and Recreation,* 1977, *48*, 27-28.

Neulinger, J. *Leisure counseling: Process or content?* Paper presented at the Dane County Recreation Coordinating Council Conference on Leisure Counseling, Madison, Wisconsin, September, 1978.

Neulinger, J. The need for and implications of a psychological conceptualization of leisure. *Ontario Psychologist,* 1976, *8* (2), 18-20.

Neulinger, J. *The psychology of leisure.* Springfield, IL: Charles C. Thomas, 1974.

Ng, D., Smith, S., Stewart, T., & Wardle, L. (Eds.) *Canadian catalogue of leisure research completed in 1976 and 1977*. Toronto, Canada: Ontario Research Council on Leisure, 1978.

O'Morrow, G.S. Recreation counseling: A challenge to rehabilitation. *Rehabilitation Literature*, 1970, *31* (8), 226-233.

Ontario Research Council on Leisure. *Analysis methods and techniques for recreation research and leisure studies*. Toronto, Canada: Author, 1977.

Orthner, D.K. Familia Ludens: Reinforcing the leisure component in family life. *Family Coordinator*, 1975, *24*, 175-183.

Orthner, D.K. Leisure activity patterns and marital satisfaction over the marital career. *Journal of Marriage and the Family*, 1975.

Orthner, D.K. Leisure and conflict in families. *Leisure Information Newsletter*, 1980, *6* (4), 10-12.

Overs, R.P. A model for avocational counseling. *Journal of Health, Physical Education and Recreation*, 1970, *41* (2), 36-38.

Overs, R.P. Avocational counseling. *Counseling Psychologist*, 1977, *7* (2), 85-88.

Overs, R.P. Avocational counseling: Gateway to meaningful activity. *Counseling and Values*, 1975, *20* (1), 36-41.

Overs, R.P., Taylor, S., & Adkins, C. *Avocational counseling manual: A complete guide to leisure guidance*. Washington, DC: Hawkins and Associates, 1977.

Parker, S. *The future of work and leisure*. New York: Praeger, 1971.

Peppers, L.G. Patterns of leisure and adjustment to retirement. *Gerontologist*, 1976, *16* (5), 441-446.

Pfieffer, J.W., & Jones, J.E. (Eds.) *1980 Handbook for group facilitators*. San Diego, CA: University Associates, 1980.

Pieper, J. *Leisure, the basis of culture*. New York: New American Library, 1963.

Ragheb, M.G., & Beard, J.G. Leisure satisfaction: Concept, theory, and measurement. In S.E. Iso-Ahola (Ed.), *Social psychological perspectives on leisure and recreation*. Springfield, IL: Charles C. Thomas, 1980.

Rapoport, R., Rapoport, R.N., & Stretitz, Z. *Leisure and the family life cycle*. London, England: Routlege and Regan Paul, 1976.

Renwick, P.A., Lawler, E.E., & staff. What you really want from your job. *Psychology Today*, 1978, *11* (12), 55ff.

Rimmer, S.M. *The development of an instrument to assess leisure satisfaction among secondary school students.* Unpublished doctoral dissertation, University of Florida, 1979.

Rowe, W., Murphy, H.B., & De Scipkes, R.A. The relationship of counselor characteristics and counseling effectiveness. *Review of Educational Research*, 1975, *45*,, 231-246.

Severinsen, N.K. Should career education be founded in the Protestant Ethic? *Personnel and Guidance Journal*, 1979, *58* (2), 111-116.

Shank, J.W., & Kennedy, D.W. Recreation and leisure counseling: A review. *Rehabilitation Literature*, 1976, *37* (9), 258-262.

Sheehy, G. *Passages: Predictable crises of adult life.* New York: Bantam, 1977.

Shepard, J.H. A status recognition model of work-leisure relationships. *Journal of Leisure Research*, 1974, *6* (1), 58-63.

Sherrill, C., & Iwanski, R.A. Self concepts and leisure preferences of mentally retarded adult men. *Therapeutic Recreation Journal*, 1977, *11* (1), 23-27.

Simon, S.B., Howe, L.W., & Kirschenbaum, H. *Values clarification: A handbook of practical strategies for teachers and students.* New York: Hart, 1972.

Super, D.E. *Career education and the meaning of work* (H.E.W. Monograph on Career Education). Washington, DC: Superintendent of Documents, 1976.

Sutherland, W.C. A philosophy of leisure. *Annals of the American Academy of Political and Social Science*, 1957, *313*, 1-3.

Taylor, G.C. Work and leisure in the age of automation. *Humanitas*, 1967, *3*, 57-65.

Thorson, J.G. *Sociological and leisure correlates of life satisfaction among retired men and women.* Ann Arbor, MI: University Microfilms (No. 7731566), 1977.

Tinsley, H.E.A., Barrett, T.C., & Kass, R.A. Leisure activities and need satisfaction. *Journal of Leisure Research*, 1977, *9*, 110-120.

Tinsley, H.E.A., & Kass, R.A. Leisure activities and need satisfaction: A replication and extension. *Journal of Leisure Research*, 1978, *10*, 191-202.

Toffler, A. *Future shock.* New York: Bantam Books, 1970.

Travers, R.M.W., in collaboration with R. Harring, E. Start, L. Rynbrandt, & D. Fessler. *Children's interests.* Kalamazoo, MI: College of Education, Western Michigan University, 1978.

U.S. News & World Report. *How Americans pursue happiness.* 1977, *82* (20), 60-75.

Walshe, W.A. Leisure counseling instrumentation. In D.M. Compton & J.E. Goldstein (Eds.), *Perspectives of leisure counseling.* Arlington, VA: National Recreation and Park Association, 1977.

Wehman, P. Leisure skill programming for severely and profoundly handicapped persons: State of the art. *British Journal of Social and Clinical Psychology,* 1978, *17* (4), 343-355.

Wehman. P. Research on leisure time and the severely developmentally disabled. *Rehabilitation Literature,* 1977, *38* (4), 98-105.

Weiss, P. A philosophical definition of leisure. In J.C. Charlesworth (Ed.), *Leisure in America: Blessing or curse?* Philadelphia, PA: American Academy of Political and Social Science, 1964.

Wilensky, H.L. Work, careers, and social integration. *International Social Science Journal,* 1960, *12*, 543-560.

Wilson, G., & Mirenda, J. The Milwaukee leisure counseling model. *Counseling and Values,* 1976, *24* (3), 238-242.

Wilson, G.T., Mirenda, J.J., & Rutkowski, B.A. Milwaukee leisure counseling model. *Leisurability,* 1975, *2* (3), 11-17.

Winters, R.A. *Relationships between job satisfaction and leisure satisfaction.* Unpublished doctoral dissertation, State University of New York at Buffalo, 1973.

Winters, R.A., & Hansen, J.C. Toward an understanding of work-leisure relationships. *Vocational Guidance Quarterly,* 1976, *24* (3), 238-242.

Witt, P.A., & Bishop, D.W. Situational antecedents to leisure behavior. *Journal of Leisure Research,* 1970, *2*, 64-77.

Witt, J., Campbell, M., & Witt, P.A. *A manual of therapeutic group activities for leisure education.* (rev. ed.) Ottawa, Ontario, Canada: Leisurability Publications, 1975.

Wittmer, J., & Myrick, R.D. *Facilitative teaching: Theory and practice* (2nd ed.). Minneapolis, MN: Educational Media Corporation, 1980.

Woody, T. Leisure in light of history. *Annals of the American Academy of Political and Social Science,* 1957, *313*, 4-10.